The
New
World

The Making of the Past

The New World

by Warwick M. Bray
Earl H. Swanson
Ian S. Farrington

ELSEVIER · PHAIDON

Advisory Board for
The Making of the Past

John Boardman

Reader in Classical Archaeology, University of Oxford

Basil Gray

Former Keeper of Oriental Antiquities, British Museum

David Oates

Professor of Western Asiatic Archaeology,
Institute of Archaeology, University of London

Series Editor Courtlandt Canby
Managing Editor Giles Lewis
Editor for this Volume Courtlandt Canby
Picture Editors Andrew Lawson, Polly Friedhoff
Design Edward Gould
Index Sonia Argyle
Visual Aids Roger Gorringe, Dick Barnard

Frontispiece: Columbus landing in America: A woodcut of 1493

ISBN 0 7290 0017 6

Elsevier-Phaidon – an imprint of Phaidon Press Ltd,
Littlegate House, St Ebbe's Street, Oxford

Reprinted 1977

Filmset by Keyspools Limited, Golborne, Lancs

Origination: Art Color Offset

Printed in Belgium

Preface to the series

This book is a volume in The Making of the Past, a series describing in comprehensive detail the early history of the world as revealed by archaeology and related disciplines. Written by experts under the guidance of a distinguished panel of advisers, it is designed for the layman, young people, the student, the armchair traveler and the tourist. Its subject is a *new* history – the making of a *new* past, freshly uncovered and reconstructed by skilled specialists like the authors of these volumes. Since these writers are themselves leaders in a rapidly changing field, the series is completely authoritative and up-to-date; but it loses nothing of the excitement of earlier discoveries. Each volume covers a specific period and region of the world and combines a detailed survey of the modern archaeology and sites of the area with dramatic stories of the pioneer explorers, travelers and archaeologists who first penetrated it. Part of each book is devoted to a reconstruction in pictures of the newly revealed cultures and civilizations that make up the history of the area. As a whole, the series not only presents a fresh look at the most familiar of archaeological regions such as Egypt and Classical Greece, but also provides up-to-date information and photographs of such archaeologically little-known areas as the Islamic world, the Far East and Africa.

Contents

Introduction

The New World at the time of the European conquest was a mosaic of tribes, nations, languages and cultural patterns – not to mention the enormous variety of tool forms and art styles which are the basic materials of archaeological research.

The more advanced societies were concentrated in the middle latitudes from Mexico to Chile and Argentina, but within this general area two regions stand out above all others: Mesoamerica (the territory controlled by the Aztecs and Maya in the early 16th century) and the central Andean region (which corresponds roughly to the Inca Empire at its maximum extent).

As the Spanish conquistadors appreciated, the civilizations of Mexico and Peru were on a par with those of Europe. The invaders found great cities with palaces and stone-built temples raised on high pyramids. In the market places were sold new and strange foodstuffs (maize, potatoes, cocoa, turkeys, pineapples and tomatoes) as well as luxury goods like gold and silver trinkets, carved jades, richly woven textiles, and capes or headdresses made from rare tropical feathers. At the same time, the Spaniards realized that this was not mere barbarian glitter, but rather the product of a high level of social and political organization. They found no difficulty in translating native institutions into the terminology of 16th-century Europe. America, too, had its states and empires: Mexican and Peruvian rulers could reasonably be compared with European monarchs, and the Indian noblemen with their Spanish equivalents. In addition, these American states had all the mundane but essential elements of civilization: law courts, an established church, and an efficient civil service responsible for taxation, conscription, local government and the keeping of accounts. Behind the exotic costumes, the pagan gods and the strange customs was something a European could understand and respect.

Around the edges of civilized America were simpler tribal societies, such as the farming communities which occupied the southwestern United States, the eastern woodlands of North America and the tropical forests of the Amazon and Orinoco basins. With these can be classed the more advanced non-agricultural tribes: the Indians of the Pacific northwest, with their rich salmon fisheries, and the inhabitants of California, where abundant resources of fish and acorns supported large groups of people with an elaborate ceremonial life. On the fringes of the hemisphere – in the Arctic and in Patagonia, where harsh conditions permitted neither large populations nor complex forms of society – the older ways of life persisted, and the Europeans

encountered only bands of nomadic hunters, fishermen and collectors of wild plants.

This placement of societies along a scale, with hunting bands at the bottom and civilized states at the top, conceals a very important point – that even the simplest societies had long histories and were well adapted to the environments they happened to occupy. In the case of the Eskimo, for example, the roots of their culture can be traced back to about 2000 BC, which gives these people as long a pedigree as any in the New World. Their way of life, too, represents a finely balanced adjustment to Arctic conditions and, judged by the criterion of efficiency, it was as effective in its own way as the Maya adaptation to the Guatemalan rainforests or the Inca adaptation to the high Andes.

Human culture is not static, but is constantly undergoing changes and modification. The diversity of prehistoric American life was the end-product of thousands of years of experimentation, a process which began when man first crossed from Siberia more than 20,000 years ago. In the course of a slow spread from Alaska to Tierra del Fuego, bands of hunters and foragers colonized deserts, forests, sea coasts and mountain ranges, each of which offered its own challenge. In most parts of America hunting and the collection of wild plants gradually gave way to agriculture and settled village life. Some of these villages became towns and governmental or religious centers, until eventually – and in isolation from their contemporaries in the Old World – the native Americans developed their own forms of civilization.

The broken pottery, ruined temples, food remains and discarded tools which the archaeologist digs up are all that is left of vanished human communities as they existed at a particular moment of time. These artifacts represent fossilized human behavior. The fact that similar types of pottery decoration, spearheads, house plans or stone sculpture are found at several neighboring sites is not accidental; it indicates a concensus of opinion about what forms these things should take. In the same way, the evidence for religion, social organization, technology, diet, agriculture and town-planning proves the existence of standardized beliefs and customs, all of which give each community or "culture" its individual stamp.

The job of the archaeologist is to reconstruct these more general patterns of behavior and to see how they changed and evolved in the course of time. The theme of this book, therefore, is not only the growth of native American civilization, but also the study of human adaptation in all its variety.

Chronological Table

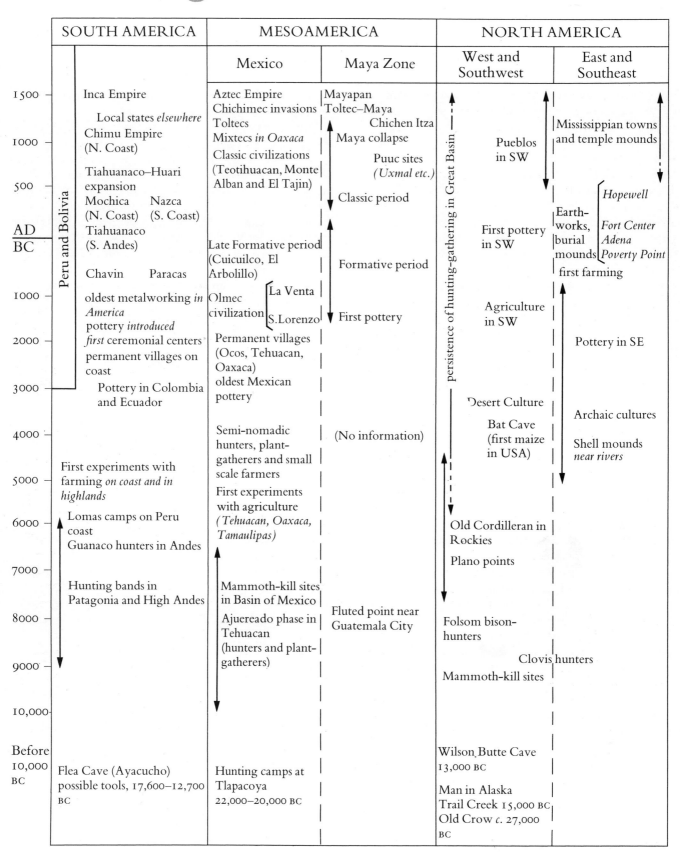

	SOUTH AMERICA	MESOAMERICA		NORTH AMERICA	
		Mexico	Maya Zone	West and Southwest	East and Southeast
1500	Inca Empire	Aztec Empire	Mayapan		
		Chichimec invasions	Toltec–Maya		Mississippian towns
	Local states *elsewhere*	Toltecs	Chichen Itza	Pueblos in SW	and temple mounds
1000	Chimu Empire (N. Coast)	Mixtecs *in Oaxaca*	Maya collapse		
		Classic civilizations	Puuc sites		
	Tiahuanaco–Huari expansion	(Teotihuacan, Monte Alban and El Tajin)	*(Uxmal etc.)*		*Hopewell*
500	Mochica Nazca		Classic period	First pottery in SW	Earthworks, burial mounds *Fort Center*
	(N. Coast) (S. Coast)				*Adena*
AD	Tiahuanaco (S. Andes)				*Poverty Point*
BC		Late Formative period (Cuicuilco, El Arbolillo)	Formative period		first farming
	Chavin Paracas				
1000	oldest metalworking *in America*	Olmec civilization { La Venta S.Lorenzo	First pottery	Agriculture in SW	
	pottery *introduced*				
2000	*first* ceremonial centers	Permanent villages (Ocos, Tehuacan, Oaxaca)			Pottery in SE
	permanent villages on coast	oldest Mexican pottery			
3000	Pottery in Colombia and Ecuador			Desert Culture	
4000		Semi-nomadic hunters, plant-gatherers and small scale farmers	(No information)	Bat Cave (first maize in USA)	Archaic cultures Shell mounds *near rivers*
5000	First experiments with farming *on coast and in highlands*	First experiments with agriculture *(Tehuacan, Oaxaca, Tamaulipas)*			
6000	Lomas camps on Peru coast			Old Cordilleran in Rockies	
	Guanaco hunters in Andes			Plano points	
7000					
	Hunting bands in Patagonia and High Andes	Mammoth-kill sites in Basin of Mexico			
8000		Ajuereado phase in Tehuacan (hunters and plant-gatherers)	Fluted point near Guatemala City	Folsom bison-hunters	
9000				Mammoth-kill sites	Clovis hunters
10,000					
Before 10,000 BC	Flea Cave (Ayacucho) possible tools, 17,600–12,700 BC	Hunting camps at Tlapacoya 22,000–20,000 BC		Wilson Butte Cave 13,000 BC Man in Alaska Trail Creek 15,000 BC Old Crow *c.* 27,000 BC	

Peru and Bolivia

persistence of hunting-gathering in Great Basin

1. Man in the New World

Previous page: Indian cliff dwelling in Canyon de Chelly, Arizona, built by the Anasazi people in pre-Columbian times. The canyon contains more than 400 ruins.

The Nenana River Valley near the Yukon, Alaska. After crossing the Bering Strait from Siberia, early man traversed such rugged country as this on his way up the Yukon Valley towards the interior of the continent.

North America. Man migrated from the Old World to the New World. Independent evolution within America is ruled out by the absence of the necessary primate ancestors, and the actual remains of early man in the New World indicate a type of homo sapiens, rather than any fossil species of man.

Controversy has arisen over the questions – when and how men made the crossing from Asia to America, and how many people comprised the initial migration. A land bridge at the Bering strait probably existed twice in recent prehistory – between 28,000 and about 26,000 years ago, and between 20,000 and 10,000–12,000 years ago. This would imply that it was at these times that migration took place. But it is also possible that the crossing was made on foot, over the ice in winter in pursuit of big game, or by boat during the summer months. Rafts or boats were used in the settlements of Australia 30,000 years ago.

As to the number of migrants, the genetic structure of American Indians would suggest the migration of only a few families. Most Indians have blood group O, and a few have A, while B is entirely absent. But in Asia all three groups occur. Blood group O is formed by two recessive genes which are hidden when one of them combines with a dominant gene for A or B. For a hemisphere to be populated by people with blood group O, random genetic drift is required – the accidental selection of a handful of people among whom the hereditary gene for O is most common, or perhaps unique. In a previously unoccupied land, all the descendants of the original population would be marked by nearly total dominance of the paired recessive genes for blood group O. This radical situation would be difficult to explain in terms of successive waves of migrants.

How can the population of the Americas be explained by the initial settlement of merely a few families? In a favorable environment the accidental selection of a gene or genes appropriate to it may result in directional selection. In other words, rapid increase in human population can occur where biological and cultural factors combine to provide an advantage for the initial population. As a result of their long settlement in the rigorous habitat of eastern Siberia, the early migrants to the New World were equipped for the environment they found in what is now Alaska, and were quite capable of expanding into diverse geographic regions as they had done in the Old World. We cannot be sure that a single gene provided a selective advantage, but the environment was certainly favorable for men accustomed to hunting, fishing and gathering of wild foods.

Natural selection works creatively to favor man's establishment as part of an ecosystem. Diversification of the physical characteristics of a rapidly expanding population would have been matched by diversification of cultural and linguistic characteristics as well. The size of a population is directly related to its adaptation to the environment. When a population reaches an equilibrium within its eco-system it stabilizes and improves its adaptation. By means of stabilizing selection a population is produced which is better adapted to the environment, and reproduction is increasingly successful. Major changes in technology and economic systems can enrich the environment artificially and also stimulate adaptation and consequently population growth within a single ecosystem. The initial migration of just a few families to the New World is thus a real possibility, when population increase is seen to depend so greatly on adjustment to the environment.

If there were two major migration waves across the Bering land bridge, it is possible that the Eskimos arrived on the second occasion, perhaps as late as 10,500 years ago. The Eskimos' genetic structure is different from that of the American Indians and is very similar to that of the people of northeast Asia. The Eskimos have all three blood groups – A, B and O – indicating that their migration to the New World was unconnected with the earlier migration which led to the first settlement of North and South America. Radiocarbon dates for Indian sites in Canada, Mexico and the Andes ranging from 27,000 to 19,000 years ago would fit with possible migration over the first Bering land bridge of 28,000 to 26,000 years ago. Sites with later dates can as well be explained by the expansion of the original popula-tion as by the arrival of fresh immigrants.

By 10,000 BC prehistoric hunters were to be found in all parts of the New World from Bering Strait to Tierra del Fuego. They adapted to regional variations in climate and vegetation and consequently their numbers grew. This increase in diversity and size of population coincided with the advent of a new climatic age, the long warming period after the last glaciation, which signaled the end of the Pleistocene geological epoch. Continental glaciation dis-appeared altogether by about 4000 BC, leaving only mountain glaciers as witness to past ice ages.

The change in climate and vegetation was followed by an important technological development. Early hunters began to make bifacial projectile points of remarkable beauty, whose lanceolate forms varied according to geo-graphic region. They utilized sophisticated flintworking techniques which entailed the use of subtle flaking rhythms. And these gave the toolmaker control of sym-metry, balance and a sharp straight cutting edge. Probably the points were used as spearheads, for they are frequently found with the remains of extinct animals.

The dramatic finds of points with extinct mammals give the impression that the first explorers of the New World depended mainly on big game for their food, but it is necessary to remember that very few elephant remains, for example, have been found with man-made tools. The earliest Americans also gathered wild plants and caught fish, so it is clear that the prehistoric food collectors had a

A typical Eskimo of today. The Eskimo differs markedly from the American Indian in his genetic structure.

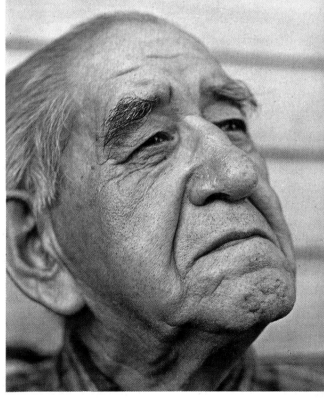

An Algonkian Indian from the eastern United States, showing a very typical Indian profile.

A Folsom spearpoint lies where it was found between the ribs of a form of bison extinct for 10,000 years.

balanced diet including plants, fish and large and small game.

The first period of settlement and development of man in the New World, which began 25,000 to 30,000 years ago, lasted until 6000 BC everywhere. After that, some food collectors began to farm, and their old hunting methods became of secondary importance. But for largely environmental reasons, many never took up farming or developed civilization. Up to the 20th century AD such people lived in high latitudes, or altitudes where the weather and terrain made farming difficult. Open grasslands were often too dry and tropical forests too wet for farming, though river valleys could be, and were, farmed even in hot desert regions.

There are areas, however, where farming would have been possible but the people, who had achieved a successful adaptation to the environment, chose to ignore it. In the hardwood forests of the eastern United States (outside the Southeast, or the major river valleys of the lower Great Lakes) life in the woodlands was so satisfactory that farming was always secondary to food collecting. Another area where farming might have been possible but was not taken up is the steppe flanking the northern Rocky Mountains. In historic times the northern and eastern Shoshone were horse-mounted bison hunters long before other Plains Indians took up the chase. In prehistory the ancestors of those horsemen also hunted bison and other game such as mountain sheep, elk, deer and antelope. For centuries their big game resources were enormous and they had migra-

tory fish and good plant foods at hand. Thus there was no obvious advantage to be gained from farming.

Natural resources were also abundant on the northwest coast. Sea mammals, ocean and migratory fish, deer and elk, plus the rich foods of the littoral offered as much or more than might have been gained by local farming. Whether those food collectors of southeast Alaska, British Columbia, Washington, Oregon and northern California knew about farming is uncertain, but by about 500 BC they had a strong economy and a varied social and religious life marked by high artistic achievements.

It is important to recognize that prehistoric hunting, fishing and gathering populations were often very large. This is a mark of evolutionary success we usually attribute to farming. Yet the highest average population densities north of Mexico were achieved by acorn-gatherers in California, even exceeding the average density (though not the maximum) among the farmers of the Southwest. Groups which succeeded so well were not likely to abandon old ways for tenuous new experiments.

The beginning of agriculture. The Amerindian food collectors of the early post-Pleistocene period cultivated a whole range of plants for food, dyes, medicines and textiles. They also domesticated four mammal and two bird species. But agriculture was not a universal trait throughout the Americas during prehistoric times.

It has been suggested that the reason why agriculture developed in the Tehuacan Valley of Mexico and not in the Great Basin (in the far west of North America), two areas with essentially similar non-agricultural gathering economies, was that in the former area wild grasses, such as maize or amaranth, were picked by hand whereas in the latter the grasses were beaten to release the seed. The harvesting practices of the Tehuacan Valley brought about a genetic change in the grasses to produce cobs which did not disperse their seeds, while in the Great Basin the beating of the grasses to release seeds merely speeded up the natural process of seed dispersal and produced no recognizable genetic change in the plant. Different species were domesticated in different areas and the same plant was often domesticated several times, each in a different place. For example, amaranth, cotton, chili pepper and some species of bean and squash were domesticated quite independently in Peru and Mexico.

For many years, botanists, geographers and archaeologists have sought to explain the origins of agriculture in the American tropics and have produced several theories. Archaeological fieldwork to test these has been concentrated in the semi-arid highlands of Mexico and Peru where ancient artifacts and plants are well preserved, and here evidence for the transition to seed crop cultivation has been found. Little or no testing, however, has been done on the highland margins of the tropical rain forest to evaluate the theory that root crop cultivation began in that area of northeastern Colombia.

Between 9000 and 7000 BC, i.e. after the last glaciation, man improved his hunting ability by developing pressure-flaked stone projectile points. At the same time he improved the technology of plant food-processing by using specialized grinding and retting tools. These prehistoric hunters and gatherers, like their modern counterparts, had a varied diet of wild plants, animals, birds, fish and shellfish. They led a migratory way of life within loosely defined home territories, moving periodically to exploit seasonal food resources within their lands. Analysis of modern collecting societies indicates that seasonal base camps, or "macroband" camps, would be established by a group of some six to eight related families in which there were no leaders or social stratification, other than on the basis of age. During the scarcer seasons the group would divide into smaller foraging units, or "microbands," generally composed of two to five people and probably comprising a single family.

Camps are found either in caves or in the open, where they were built of flimsy perishable material and can now only be located by the occupational debris left behind. Analysis of the subsistence and settlement data from the Tehuacan Valley, which dates to the 8th millennium BC,

Of · Florida .

Indian woman of Florida holding cobs of corn, a staple food of the Indians; by John White, the Elizabethan explorer. Detailed evidence for the early domestication of corn in the New World has been found in the Mexican highlands.

has demonstrated that the collectors of that time exploited six food resources – the maguey plant, cactus fruits such as the prickly pear, tree legumes like the mesquite, wild grasses, and deer and rabbits. This type of economy probably persisted from about 9000 BC until 7000 BC, and no plant or animal remains during this period show definite signs of domestication.

Agriculture began as an offshoot from this type of gathering economy. Genetic change to produce domesticated plants could have taken place in several ways during the seasonal round of this economic system. First, the wastage from seeds and roots gathered during a period of abundance and brought back to camp could have been dumped on the garbage tip which, being a man-made environment, would allow the plants to grow without natural competition, thus stimulating genetic change. Second, such changes could have been effected by food collectors tending plants by weeding around them. Third, there is the effect of different grass harvesting methods. Once genetic change had occurred, it must have been recognized by man and encouraged, usually by storing a selected part of the seed crop for planting.

The first plant to display any signs of change was the avocado, found in the Tehuacan Valley from around 7000 BC. It seems possible that this tree benefited from seed planting and tending by man. Over the next 1800 years man's attention to the wild grasses and legumes during his summer activities resulted in the domestication of two grasses, setaria and amaranth, and also species of squash and chili pepper. But these differences in seed and fruit size were not very significant in the economy of the Tehuacan gatherers. The traditional migratory way of life was still practiced, although amaranth, squash and chili seeds must have been sown in the dry barrancas (deep gulleys). After the summer rains, weeding must have taken place and harvesting would have been carried out as before, in the fall. Cultivated plants probably represented only 5 per cent of the diet as opposed to 54 per cent from hunting and 41 per cent from the collecting of wild plants.

Elsewhere in the highlands of Mesoamerica maize and the common bean were also domesticated. They were introduced into the Tehuacan Valley about 5000 BC. The yields of amaranth and setaria were not increased greatly by domestication, but the change in maize was quite dramatic, because its genetic structure could easily be altered by man. The cobs and seeds increased in size and did not shatter when harvested. Maize crossed quite readily with its wild relatives, tripsacum and teosinte, so that its environmental range and tolerability also increased. Eventually it became dependent upon man for its reproduction, and became a staple in the diet. Like most cereals, however, maize is rich in carbohydrates and proteins but lacks an important amino acid which, incidentally, is common in beans. The domestication of beans in combination with maize, therefore, was one of the major achievements of prehistoric man in the New World. It gave him a rich and staple diet, enabling him to develop agriculture and village life. By 1500 BC cultivated grasses had become dominant among the subsistence foods; hunting and gathering continued, but made only a small contribution to the diet.

Village life. Throughout the period of incipient cultivation in both Mexico and Peru, however, the population remained mobile, moving seasonally to exploit new resources. This was because no one part of their subsistence system could produce food for a whole year, or enough to be stored during the lean months. Eventually, however, the development of varieties of maize and beans with bigger yields enabled a surplus to be produced which could be stored at the base camp for the dry season. At this point sedentary village life became a reality.

In the highland-tropical forest margin a system of agriculture based on root crops – manioc and sweet potato – developed about 3000 BC. The earliest signs of manioc cultivation come from northern Venezuela, where griddles have been found in a level dating to 2700 BC. This indicates that the complex process of preparing the poisonous root of the bitter manioc had already been discovered, for griddles are used to bake manioc bread after the poison has been eliminated. Ethnographic parallels would indicate that the system of cultivation must have been "shifting," or "slash and burn." A plot was cleared from the forest, burned, and planted with a variety of crops, but chiefly manioc. After a few years it was abandoned because the yields declined as a result of loss of fertility and competition from jungle plants. With this system village life became established; but the village too was liable to be moved. Manioc provides only carbohydrates, and the proteins needed had to be obtained through hunting and fishing. Shifting seed cultivation, and hence village mobility, was also practiced in the tropical forests and savanas after 500 BC.

Village life arose not only in agricultural economies but also in other types which had a stable as well as staple food source. Then villages were located near to the resource. The salmon fishers of the northwest coast of British Columbia and Washington state were settled in villages by 1500 BC, but practiced no cultivation. They continued to live a non-agricultural, sedentary life until after European contact about 1600 AD. On the central coast of Peru villages were founded as early as 2800 BC by hunters and gatherers to exploit the protein-rich shellfish grounds immediately offshore. After 2500 BC the villages became larger as the population exploited the even more stable fish resources off the coast. Unlike the tribes of the northwest coast of North America, however, who never practised agriculture, the Peruvian fishermen adopted agriculture around 1500 BC because it offered better returns, and this eventually became their dominant activity.

In these permanent villages houses were built of materials which could not be easily dismantled and transported, such as stone, cane, wattle and daub, whale-bone, and mud bricks. The shape of the house varied from circular to rectangular and so did the size of the dwelling, ranging from tiny single-person rooms to larger family units. In the Oaxaca Valley of highland Mexico two villages have been excavated, dated to about 1300 BC, when agriculture became the dominant subsistence activity. Each contained 10 to 20 single-family, rectangular houses of wattle and daub facing onto an open plaza, and each household had its own pits for food storage. Four hundred years later each village had increased in size. On the Peruvian coast and in the Southwest of North America dwellings were often joined together in an irregular mass of stone, cane or adobe units. Each unit comprised a few rooms, i.e. suitable for one family, and each had its own storage facilities. This pattern applied equally to both the fisherfolk of about 2000 BC and the later agriculturalists along the Peruvian coast.

The establishment of settled communities gave ordinary folk the chance to develop such techniques as weaving, pottery-making and metal-working. Pottery, for example, is rarely found in hunting and gathering communities because it is too fragile and bulky for a people regularly on the move. Advanced technology is unnecessary when horns or gourds can be used as containers.

From tribe to empire. The type of social organization characteristic of these settled farmers was the tribe. Wherever they occur, tribal societies share a number of features. Villages are small, self-sufficient and roughly equal in size and importance. Social organization is simple. The community is normally divided into kinship groups or clans, and land ownership is often vested in the clan rather than the individual family. It is kinship rather than class which governs social relationships, and the life of each man is very similar to that of his neighbor. Craftsmen still participate in the agricultural life of the village and are not full-time specialists. Village leaders or headmen possess only weak authority and do not constitute a hereditary élite class. The presence of temples or shrines reflects the importance of religion, but there is not yet a full-time priesthood.

In many parts of North America and in the tropical forests of South America, tribal societies of this kind persisted until the European conquest, but in certain areas (usually those where efficient agriculture could support large populations) new and more complex forms of society began to emerge after about 1500 BC.

Some tribal communities developed into chiefdoms, characterized by the beginnings of class distinction and by an increasing separation between the rulers and the common people. Certain clans or families gained in power and status at the expense of others, leading eventually to the emergence of a hereditary élite. In present-day societies of this type, the chief often controls the best land, has a personal retinue of followers and assistants, and has the right to demand taxes and/or labor service from his people. His political influence is reinforced by the part he plays in ceremonial and religious activities, and in some cases he may become a priest-chief.

In Mexico the transition from farming village to chiefdom took place after about 1200 BC, when the inhabitants of San Jose Mogote, in the Valley of Oaxaca, began to build large platforms whose walls and floors were covered with polished lime plaster. Public works on an even larger scale were constructed after 1150 by the Olmecs of the Gulf Coast plain, and temple pyramids became common in the central Mexican highlands from 500 BC onwards. Some of these highland sites were true townships. Amalucan, in the Puebla Basin, covered some four square miles, with several pyramids and a canal system. In the Valley of Mexico the most important town was Cuicuilco, which embraced at least one square mile and had a unique temple platform of circular plan.

At the major sites there is evidence of craft specialization and long-distance trade in obsidian, jade, shell and other precious materials. Craftsmen worked primarily for the luxury market, producing goods for the emergent ruling class and for the gods. Differences in status were reflected

The "crying baby," an Olmec figurine. Settled communities, including those of the Olmec, began to emerge among the peoples of Mexico after 1200 BC.

"The lovers," Mexican figurines showing strong Olmec influence. The Olmecs were among the first Mexican people to develop a hierarchical society.

by differences in wealth. At La Venta, one of the principal Olmec sites, the richest sepulcher was a room-like structure made of imported basalt columns. On the floor of the tomb lay the remains of two infants covered with bright red pigment and surrounded by carved jade objects. The fact that such unusually rich burial was accorded to infants, who were too young to have earned status in the community by their own efforts, suggests that in Olmec society noble birth was more important than achievement, and a hereditary ruling class had come into being.

In Mesoamerica and the central Andes the more advanced chiefdoms were gradually transformed into states. States have populations measured in tens or even hundreds of thousands, with strong centralized government, specialized professions (administrators, priests, craftsmen, traders, lawyers and bureaucrats), and a hierarchy of social classes. The governing class gets more than its fair share of the produce of the community, may control the distribution of goods or land, and has few links with the common people. Class distinctions may be deliberately fostered by government policy through the granting of special insignia or privileges. This attitude is clearly seen in the law codes of Montezuma I, one of the earlier Aztec rulers:

"Only the king and the first minister may wear sandals within the palace. No great chieftain may enter the palace shod on pain of death. The great noblemen are the only ones allowed to wear sandals in the city and no one else, with the exception of men who have performed some great deed in war. But these sandals must be cheap and common; the gilded, painted ones are to be used only by noblemen. . . . The common people will not be allowed to wear cotton clothing on pain of death, but only garments of maguey cactus fiber." The central government administers the law, collects taxes, and conscripts the populace for work or war. The state religion is controlled by a full-time priesthood whose members are often drawn from the nobility.

In these terms, the words state and civilization mean much the same thing, although the more advanced chiefdoms may also qualify as civilizations. The Olmecs of Mexico and the people who created Chavin culture in Peru between 1000 and 300 BC already possessed an efficient farming technology, long-distance trade networks, large temples and public buildings, fine art, an official state religion, and social stratification with marked differences between rich and poor.

The emergence of civilization. The potential which was already recognizable during the last thousand years before Christ was fulfilled during the early centuries AD. In Mesoamerica, the Classic period (300 to 900 AD) saw the climax of Maya civilization in the forests of lowland

Guatemala, the rise and fall of the Teotihuacan state in the central highlands of Mexico, and the growth of vigorous and powerful regional civilizations centered on Monte Alban in the Valley of Oaxaca and El Tajin near the east coast. In South America, at about the same time, there were civilized states along the desert coast of Peru (Moche, Nazca, etc.), in the Titicaca Basin of Bolivia (Tiahuanaco), and in various parts of the Peruvian Andes.

The civilizations of native America have a superficial resemblance to each other which conceals a great deal of diversity. The similarities are in part conditioned by technology, for aboriginal America lacked many of the things which were taken for granted in the Old World. Iron and steel were unknown. Except in the Andes, copper and bronze tools were never in common use – though gold and silver were lavishly employed to make jewelry whose technical and aesthetic quality astounded 16th-century European goldsmiths. Architects were ignorant of the dome and the keystone arch. There was no knowledge of gunpowder, coinage, alphabetic writing, printing, distilled acids, glass or glazes. The principle of the wheel had been recognized in Mexico, but was nowhere employed for anything more serious than pull-along toys; there were no carts, windmills, potter's wheels, pulleys, or any of the machines which depend on wheels and gears. Outside Mesoamerica, where scribes used a system of hieroglyphic or picture writing, there were no books and no written documents. Thus the achievement of civilization is not dependent on advanced technology or particular environmental conditions. The key factor in the development of civilization is organization, the use of human intelligence and human labor in the service of the state. In the nature of their organization, the American cultures were very different from each other.

In the tropical forest the most productive form of agriculture is often shifting cultivation. Each family needs a large area of farmland, most of which lies fallow in any one year. Under a system of this type, a high density of population is hard to attain and there is a tendency for settlement to be dispersed, with each family living close to its fields. But a complex civilization requires some kind of central organization to administer religion, commerce and the everyday business of government. The Maya and the other lowland peoples solved this problem by a compromise. The great Maya sites of the Classic period were not true cities but religious and administrative centers, staffed by priests and officials and surrounded by the scattered dwellings of farmers who came into the center only to attend religious festivals, visit the market, or call at governmental offices.

Politically the Maya lowlands were organized in a hierarchical pattern. At the top were the few major capitals

Residential quadrangle at Uxmal, a late Classic Maya site. The buildings undoubtedly housed the priests and officials who served at this typical semi-religious, semi-administrative ceremonial center.

The Pyramid of the Niches at el Tajin (*left*), site of a Gulf coast culture of the Classic period (300 to 900 AD). The niches possibly housed figures of gods.

A priest or official, carved in shell. He served at Palenque, one of the principal Maya ceremonial centers.

Modern Maya Indian girl of Guatemala weaving with a loom of traditional design.

Jaina figurine of a Maya woman (Late Classic period) using a backstrap loom.

(Tikal, Palenque, Copan, Seibal, Calakmul and Motul de San Jose) which were larger than their neighbors, had finer buildings and a greater number of stelae (inscribed stone slabs). Around each major capital were five to eight equidistantly spaced secondary centers, and these in turn were surrounded by minor centers consisting of a few small temples without inscriptions, altars or ball courts.

In drier regions the same hierarchy of settlements existed, but the sites were true cities with closely-packed houses surrounding the core of public buildings. The relationship between urban life and arid conditions was not accidental.

In dry uplands the use of crop rotation, terracing, weeding and manuring can almost eliminate the fallow period. Two or three years of cultivation are followed by as little as one year of rest, and the farmland is not allowed to revert to forest. Under these conditions, shifting cultivation gave way to intensive agriculture, with permanent settlements and a higher productivity per unit of land. With the addition of irrigation to the list of techniques, crop yields were increased by 50 to 300 per cent over the dry-farming figure, allowing population densities to reach levels unimaginable in the tropical lowlands.

The development of intensive agriculture was slow and gradual. Farming systems varied a good deal, since they were adapted to diverse local environments. In the Americas, where the only farming tools were the digging stick, the hoe and (in the central Andes) the foot-plow, the first requirement for agriculture was a light soil which was easy to till, well-watered but also freely draining. The earliest agriculture in the Tehuacan Valley of Mexico (5000

to 3000 BC) was based on natural irrigation. But by the time of the first permanent villages, several new techniques were in operation in Mexico: using wells or canals, check dams to control natural flooding in narrow valleys, and terracing to increase the area of arable land.

The great agricultural works of Peru and Mexico were the product of societies which had reached the state level of organization and were able to call on a large communal labor force. Irrigation was the basis of life on the desert coast of Peru, and in this area one can still see the remains of canals, aqueducts and terraces dating from the 1st millennium AD. During the final centuries before the Conquest another technique was invented. Sunken fields were dug into the earth to lower the planting surface and bring it close to the level of the ground water. The crops grown in these plots were manured with fish and seabird guano.

State formation did not take place evenly. In both Mesoamerica and Peru the more powerful states were able to dominate their weaker neighbors and reduce them to subjection. By comparison with the ordinary sites they stand out as "superpowers." Archaeologically they are often linked with styles of pottery and art which quickly spread over large areas.

Archaeological evidence suggests that Tiahuanaco (Bolivia), Huari (Peru) and Teotihuacan (Mexico) may have been imperial powers during the 1st millennium AD, but only the most recent of such empires (Aztec Mexico and Inca Peru) are adequately documented from European accounts and the records of native historians. The historical data show that these two empires were organized in very different ways, reflecting different ideas of government.

Inca and Aztec. The Inca state was centralized and authoritarian in both its internal structure and its policy towards conquered peoples. The Inca himself, "Son of the Sun," was a divine ruler whose word was law. The common people were divided into ayllus, groups of related families living in the same place and owning their land collectively. The ayllus were grouped into provinces, each with its own capital, and the provinces were grouped into the four great "quarters" of the empire.

A rigid and uniform structure was imposed over most of the empire, with a direct chain of command leading from the ruler in Cuzco to the head of each individual family. The administration was organized like a pyramid. At the top were the provincial chiefs, below whom came the high officials who controlled the affairs of 10,000 households. They in turn were helped by subordinate officials responsible for 5,000 families, and below these were the ranks of lesser administrators who looked after units of 1,000, 500, 50 and 10 families.

A road system linked all parts of the empire, and a messenger service carried reports from the provinces and commands from the capital. The government kept a census of population, farmland and stocks of vital commodities. It was the government which also levied taxes and labor service, controlled commerce, and made sure that supplies were sent where they were needed.

At the same time an attempt was made to consolidate the empire in the Inca pattern. Quechua became the language of government, and local rulers were instructed in Inca ways and customs. Groups of loyal subjects were moved from their home provinces into newly-conquered territories, a process which hastened the breakdown of the old tribal and linguistic boundaries. The religion of Cuzco was imposed on subject peoples, but in return the local gods were given a place in the Inca pantheon. Every person had his allotted place in the system, and the needs of the state took precedence over the wishes of the individual. It was this centralized control which made a single unity of an

Above: Effigy pot of a Mochica warrior from the north coast of Peru. He holds a club or mace, and a small shield is strapped to his wrist. Martial scenes are typical of Mochica art, which attained to an astonishing realism in portraiture.

Right: Machu Picchu, Inca fortress city in the high Andes near Cuzco, exemplifies the matchless engineering of the Incas and the tight-knit organization that made it possible. It is the most perfectly preserved Inca city in Peru.

Turquoise mosaic snake with teeth of shell, made in Mexico for the Aztec market. This may well have been part of the loot, or presents, sent back to Europe by the Spaniards after the conquest.

empire which stretched for some 2,500 miles along the western edge of America from Ecuador to Chile.

Despite this high level of organization, the Inca empire was basically non-urban, and only a few of the existing Peruvian cities continued in occupation during the Inca period. Except perhaps for Cuzco, the Incas themselves did not attempt to build large towns, and the bulk of the empire's population lived in villages and small rural settlements.

Where the Peruvian system regulated every aspect of life, the Aztec system permitted a greater degree of personal freedom. Craftsmen worked for themselves and found customers wherever they could; every town had its market for the free exchange of goods; and long-distance trade was in the hands of a semi-autonomous class of merchants who were not under direct state control.

By the same token, the Mexican concept of empire allowed considerable freedom to subject peoples. The basic unit of Mexican politics was the city state, consisting of a single town and its rural hinterland. Many of these states were small. During the century before the Spanish conquest, the Valley of Mexico was divided between 50 or 60 city states, each of which had its own ruler and its own government, even though it paid taxes to the Aztecs and their allies. These little states owned between 40 and 80 square miles of territory and had approximately 12,000 to 50,000 inhabitants, many of whom lived outside the capital.

Like the city states of Classical Greece or Renaissance Italy, the Mexican towns were perpetually at odds with each other. Individual cities came together in voluntary confederations and the more powerful states dominated and exploited the weaker ones. The few great "superpowers" stood out above the others. The greatest of all was Tenochtitlan, the Aztec capital, which contained more than 150,000 people and, in alliance with the neighboring cities of Texcoco and Tlacopan, was able to extort tribute from 489 lesser city states scattered all over Mexico.

Strictly speaking, the "Aztec Empire" was not an empire at all. It was controlled by a confederation of three cities rather than a single power, and no attempt was made to impose political unity on the territory under Aztec control. Provided a subject state did not rebel, paid its taxes, and admitted the Aztec tribal god alongside the local deities, it was left alone. Its ruler remained in office as a client lord; language, dress, religion and customs were not changed; the political structure and local mode of government were not altered. The Aztecs did not try to impose their own way of life on the conquered peoples, and these in their turn felt no loyalty to the Aztec cause. It was only the threat of force which kept the subject provinces faithful to Tenochtitlan.

Neither the Aztec nor the Inca empire was able to stand up to the onslaught of a small force of determined Europeans. The technological superiority of the invaders was only one factor in the rapid collapse of American civilization. Others were the product of internal stresses rather than Spanish power. The centralized control of the Inca was a source of both strength and weakness: once the ruler was in Spanish hands the system did not encourage local initiative and resistance. By contrast, the Aztec empire was not centralized enough, and many of the subject states joined with the Spaniards in an attempt to throw off the Aztec yoke, not realizing that they were exchanging one master for another, more ruthless one.

The initial conquests were quickly followed by other expeditions which established the British and French in North America, the Portuguese in Brazil, and the Spaniards throughout the greater part of Central and South America. With the advent of European dominion and the colonial era, the New World became an outpost of the Old, and the Americas for the first time entered the mainstream of European history.

Spanish conqueror Hernan Cortes, with his Tlaxcalan Indian allies, at the battle of Aztamequa during his campaign against the Aztecs.

2. The Discovery of Ancient America

Mesoamerica. In Mexico, the first part of the American mainland to be invaded from the Old World, some of the best information about the final stages of native civilization came from those Europeans who played the largest part in destroying it. Conquistadors such as Hernan Cortes and Bernal Diaz have left eyewitness descriptions of the Aztec capital at Tenochtitlan before it was destroyed by siege in 1521, and after the soldiers came the bureaucrats and churchmen, some of them sympathetic and kindly men who tried to understand the Indians among whom they worked.

Two names stand out above all others. The Franciscan friar, Diego de Landa, wrote a lengthy manuscript about 16th-century Maya life in Yucatan. Archaeologists will never forgive Landa for burning irreplaceable hieroglyphic books, but his *Report on the Things of Yucatan* is still an essential reference book for Maya specialists. In Aztec territory another Franciscan, Bernardino de Sahagun, learned the Nahuatl language so that he could speak directly to informants who still remembered the old customs. Sahagun's methods, and his sympathetic objectivity, were those of a modern ethnographer, and his writings allow us to visualize the Aztecs as living people rather than mere subjects for scholastic enquiry.

Landa and Sahagun did not make collections of artifacts, but Spanish treasure lists give some idea of the vast quantities of gold and precious objects which were shipped to

Previous page: Stela and altar at Copan. A lithograph by the artist, Frederick Catherwood.

A Mexican feather shield. Since it has been in Europe for centuries, it may well have been one of the gifts presented to Cortes by the Aztec emperor, Montezuma.

Europe during the early years of the Conquest. A few items have survived, some of them made of fragile materials which are not usually preserved under archaeological conditions. They include wooden shields, masks and helmets encrusted with a mosaic of turquoise, black lignite and shell; shields decorated with designs executed in colored feathers; a headdress of green quetzal plumage; spear-throwers made of carved and gilded wood; three Maya hieroglyphic books, several Mixtec manuscripts, and a Spanish copy of Montezuma's tribute list which illustrates the commodities sent to the Aztec capital by all the subject provinces.

Some of these rare and beautiful objects can be matched with descriptions in the documentary sources. The expedition of Juan de Grijalva, which explored part of the Atlantic coast in 1518, exchanged beads, medallions, linen shirts and cheap European manufactures for native products which included "wooden masks, one inlaid with two straight bands of turquoise, one dog's head covered with little stones," and "seven flint sacrificial knives." These are the first European descriptions of Mexican mosaic work, and they correspond in general terms with objects preserved in a number of European collections.

Sixteenth-century Spaniards were not greatly concerned with the more ancient cultures of Mexico, but the Indians themselves were conscious of a long historical tradition and fully realized that they were the heirs of earlier peoples. Sahagun's informants told him about a semi-mythical golden age when a people called the Toltecs ruled central Mexico from the city of Tollan, or Tula, which they had founded in the 10th century AD. The description is quite detailed:

"They settled on the bank of a river close to the town of Xicotitlan, which now has the name of Tulla . . . and there are remains of many works which they carried out there, among them a thing which can be seen today (though still unfinished) which is called *coatlaquetzalli*. It consists of pillars in the shape of snakes, with the heads resting on the ground and the body and rattles in the air. . . . To this day people find Toltec things: pieces of pottery, clay cups and jars and bowls. And they excavate, from under the ground, jewels and precious stones, emeralds and fine turquoise."

These words show that the locality of Tula, and its links with the Toltecs, were known to 16th-century Aztec historians. But the information was ignored. In the 1870s Désiré Charnay, whom we shall meet again in the Maya zone, exposed some structures at the site, but it was not until the 1940s that the Toltecs were "rediscovered" when Mexican archaeologists, excavating at Tula, found serpent columns and pottery of the Toltec period, and were able to provide archaeological evidence for the Nahuatl legend.

Gentleman travelers in Mexico. In 1799 Alexander von Humboldt – Renaissance man par excellence – began a five-year journey through the Americas which was to result in 30 volumes on the geography, botany, zoology,

Catalogue cover of William Bullock's exhibition of Aztec antiquities in Piccadilly, London, featuring a cast of the Great Calendar, or Sun Stone at its center.

meteorology, geology and customs of the western hemisphere. Humboldt was one of the first Europeans to attempt a scientific study of pre-Spanish architecture. He collected legends, tried to distinguish between the architectural styles of different periods, and made drawings of the principal monuments. His study of the pyramid of Cholula, the largest man-made structure in Mexico, nicely illustrates the way in which the romantic and the scholarly were combined in one man. Having measured the pyramid and found it to be 180 feet high, with sides 1,500 feet long, he wrote of the colonial chapel which stands on the top:

"The symbolism of the new religion has not entirely dispelled the memory of the old. The people hasten to it in great crowds from all directions to celebrate the Feast of Mary on top of the pyramid. An unspoken terror, a pious shudder, overcomes the natives at the sight of this monstrous mass of brickwork, covered by eternally fresh grass and shrubbery."

Another early traveler was Captain Guillaume Dupaix, a retired officer of the Mexican dragoons commissioned by Charles IV of Spain to survey the antiquities of the region. Between 1805 and 1807 the Dupaix expedition made drawings of such important highland sites as Xochicalco and the Zapotec cities of Oaxaca, then moved on to the Maya zone where it paused to study the ruins of Palenque.

The reports of Humboldt and Dupaix were of interest to a few scholars, but did little to draw public attention to Mexican antiquities. The work of popularization was left to others, less academic but more entertaining. One such was the entrepreneur William Bullock. In 1812, at a cost of £16,000, he constructed an exhibition gallery (in the Egyptian style) in the heart of fashionable London, where his displays of curiosities met with great popular success. In 1823 Bullock spent six months in Mexico where he studied botany, bought a silver mine, examined the (then unpublished) drawings made by the Dupaix expedition,

visited Cholula, Teotihuacan and the major sites around Mexico city, collected antiquities, and made casts of some of the large Aztec sculptures discovered during building work in the Cathedral Square in the capital.

On his return, he put all his new finds on display in the Egyptian Hall. The exhibition contained (according to the catalogue) a "Panoramic View of the Present City, Specimens of the Natural History of New Spain, Maps and Pictures, Models of the Colossal and Enormous Idols, the Great Calendar and Sacrificial Stones, Pyramids and other Existing Remains – the whole forming a Rationally Instructive and Interesting Exhibition which is now open for Public Inspection." Part of Bullock's collection eventually found its way into the British Museum.

The wealthy gentleman traveler continued to play a significant role in Mexican archaeology as popularizer and collector. Sir Edward Tylor, himself one of the founders of the science of anthropology, gives a pen-portrait of one such dilettante, Henry Christy, member of a British hat-making and banking family:

"In the spring of 1856 I met with Mr. Christy accidentally in an omnibus in Havana. He had been in Cuba for some months leading an adventurous life, visiting sugar plantations, copper mines, and coffee estates, descending into caves, and botanizing in tropical jungles, cruising for a fortnight in an open boat among coral reefs, hunting turtles and manatis, and visiting all sorts of people from whom information was to be had, from foreign consuls and Lazarist missionaries down to retired slave dealers and assassins." The two men traveled through Mexico together, and Christy continued to purchase archaeological and ethnographical specimens after his return to Europe. When he died in 1865 and left his collection to the British

One of Frederick Catherwood's evocative lithographs of Maya ruins – a temple at Tulum.

Museum, 602 out of his 1,085 pieces were Mexican in origin and included three turquoise mosaic items which are among the Museum's greatest treasures.

One of the first, and greatest, of the professional archaeologists was Eduard Seler of the Berlin Ethnographical Museum. In 1887 he set out on a series of journeys which took him all over Mexico, collecting antiquities, studying linguistics, and striving all the time to understand the native American mind, using documentary sources and the picture manuscripts as well as the artifacts themselves. Seler's knowledge of the religion, ritual and arts of central America was unique, and his contributions in these fields still provide a basis for discussion.

The Maya explorers. Apart from a few accounts by colonial administrators, the Maya ruins had not attracted much attention until the final decades of the 18th century, when the new spirit of historical and scientific enquiry started to make itself felt in Spain. The home government began to interest itself in the antiquities of its overseas possessions and to urge local officials to collect information and, if possible, actual specimens of Maya antiquities.

Exploration and description were soon followed by excavation. By 1787, Captain Antonio del Rio was at Palenque, clearing ruins, breaking down partitions, rummaging in the foundations of rooms and courtyards, and preparing a report which eventually appeared in London in 1822. Its 17 engravings were by Frédéric Waldeck, self-styled Count de Waldeck, who carried out several explorations of Maya sites in his own right and published his own book on Palenque in 1864.

In the meantime other Maya ruins had begun to attract attention. Although it had been described in a letter as early as 1576, Copan had lain forgotten until the arrival of Juan Galindo in 1834 with a commission to study the ruins on behalf of the Guatemalan government. Galindo had visited Palenque in 1831 (where he noted the similarity between its Indian inhabitants and the figures carved on the ancient panels), but it was his work at Copan which was most significant for posterity. His reports, with maps, plans and rather mediocre drawings, were published in France, England and America, and brought yet another Maya site to public notice.

Scholarship and popular appeal were combined in the books of the American traveler, John Lloyd Stephens who, with the artist Frederick Catherwood, made two trips to the Maya zone between 1839 and 1842. Excited by the studies of Del Rio, Waldeck, Galindo and Dupaix, the two men resolved to visit all the known Maya sites. Their chance came in 1839 when Stephens managed to get himself appointed Special Confidential Agent of the United States in Central America.

By November of that year they were at Copan, clearing the jungle to expose the carved slabs. Everywhere they discovered more ruins, figures, walls, terraces and overgrown stairways half concealed by vines and creepers. While Stephens explored and cleared, Catherwood set up his drawing board and "camera lucida" (a device which allowed him to trace the image of a subject directly onto paper). On his second trip he experimented with an early daguerrotype camera. The work was demanding, the conventions of Maya art quite unlike those of the Old World civilizations, and the physical conditions unpleasant. Stephens has described Catherwood at work:

". . . standing with his feet in the mud and . . . drawing with his gloves on, to protect his hands from the moschetoes. As we feared, the designs were so intricate and complicated, the subjects so entirely new and unintelligible, that he had great difficulty in drawing. He had made several attempts, both with the camera lucida and without, but failed to satisfy himself or even me, who was less severe in criticism. The 'Idol' seemed to defy his art; two monkeys on a tree appeared to be laughing at him, and I felt discouraged and despondent."

There were other snags too. One of the villagers claimed – and was able to prove – that he was the owner of the land on which the ruins lay. Here was an unforeseen problem, but Stephens reacted with his usual decisiveness. Putting on his dress uniform coat, which made an incongruous contrast with his sodden Panama hat and muddy breeches, he offered to buy the ruins outright:

"The reader is perhaps curious to know how old cities sell in Central America. Like other articles of trade, they are regulated by the quantity in the market and the demand; but . . . at that time were dull of sale. I paid 50 dollars for Copan. There was never any difficulty about the price."

Adventures of this kind guaranteed that Stephens' books would be bestsellers, but the results were of prime importance for scholarship. On their two journeys the pair discovered more than 40 new sites and studied the major buildings at Uxmal, Chichen Itza and Tulum, as well as Copan and Palenque. Catherwood, a meticulous and sensitive draftsman, produced the first accurate drawings of Maya art and inscriptions, and set a standard which was to govern archaeological recording up to the present.

Catherwood's successors were Désiré Charnay and Alfred Percival Maudslay. Charnay had been entrusted by the French Ministry of Public Instruction with the study of ancient American civilizations, and from 1858 to 1882 he explored both highland Mexico and the Maya territory. Serious photography had not been Catherwood's main

Part of the Maya ruin of Kabah buried in the jungle. Stephens and Catherwood faced conditions such as these when they carried out the first accurate surveys of Maya ruins. Heat, mud, the "moschetoes" and the dense jungle growth make drawing difficult.

aim (and none of his daguerrotypes has been preserved), but Charnay traveled with a huge camera which took 45 × 36 centimeter plates. This was in the early days of photography when each plate had to be coated by hand in a tent or an improvised darkroom immediately before exposure. Charnay was also a pioneer, on his later trips, in the use of papier mâché for making molds of relief sculpture. He realized that the Maya monuments were recent by comparison with those of Egypt and the Old World civilizations, but was content to respect the Maya on their own terms. As he put it in his book, *The Ancient Cities of the New World*: "Why should the people who raised the American monuments be less deserving of our regard because they built them ten centuries sooner or ten centuries later?"

Maudslay first visited Copan in 1881 on what he called "merely a journey of curiosity," with "no intention whatever of making a study of American archaeology." In spite of this remark, his trip proved to be the first of seven which took him all over Maya territory and occupied him until 1894. His objective was to make photographs and casts, and he therefore returned to Copan at the head of a mule train carrying tools, photographic equipment, surveying materials, bales of tissue paper for molding, and four tons of plaster of Paris. By the time all this had reached the site, Maudslay estimated it had cost him some 20 times the price he had originally paid in England.

Working conditions had not changed much since the times of Stephens and Catherwood. At Quirigua, Guatemala, where he was making casts of the major sculptures, he wrote:

"Excavations became filled with water as soon as they were made, and no moulding could be done until a watertight roof had been made over the monument which was to be moulded. At one time the flood-water covered all but a few feet of ground on which our palm leaf shanty had been built; everything in camp had turned green with mould and mildew, snakes and scorpions became very troublesome, and mosquitos were a continual torment."

Maudslay's travels took him to all the principal sites, and he was the first to study Tikal and Yaxchilan. His labors resulted in an unparalleled series of casts, plans and photographs which, in his own words, "would enable scholars to carry on their work of examination and comparison, and to solve some of the many problems of Maya civilization, whilst comfortably seated in their studies at home." In this he was prophetic, for the inscriptions which he collected provided the basis for the first attempts to decipher Maya hieroglyphs.

But already, as Maudslay recognized, times were changing. Improved communications were making the Maya ruins more accessible from Europe and North America. The era of big expeditions and large-scale scientific excavation was dawning.

South America. Although the Incas of Peru were conquered rather later than the Mexican Aztecs, interest in the native peoples and ancient civilizations of South America had begun as early as the initial contact in 1492 between the Spaniards under Columbus and the aboriginal peoples of the West Indies. It is well known that it was Columbus' intention to sail westwards and open up a new route to the Orient, but instead of Japan and China he made landfalls

Maudslay encamped in the ruins of Chichen Itza in 1899. His seven trips to study Maya ruins in the late 19th century ushered in the day of archaeological photography and of exact planning and recording.

in the Bahamas, Cuba and Hispaniola. On the latter island the Spaniards observed the native chiefs wearing crowns, belts and other adornments of gold, and exploration inland revealed placer gold deposits.

The wealth of the islands was, however, exaggerated, and the deposits were soon worked out. But the Spaniards continued to hear of other "golden" kingdoms and over the next 20 years voyages were made to other islands. New colonies were founded and the coast of the mainland, Tierra Firme, was fully explored. The conquest of the Inca Empire began as part of this search for the golden land of "El Dorado," so named after a legendary chieftain, the "man of gold," who was covered with gold dust.

In 1513 a few Spaniards crossed the Isthmus of Panama and saw for the first time the Pacific Ocean. Francisco Pizarro and Diego de Almagro obtained the royal assent to explore and conquer the coasts to the south of the Isthmus. In 1526, after a long and profitless voyage along the jungle coasts of Colombia, they captured a large balsa wood sailing raft, laden with gold and silver ornaments and utensils, emeralds and other precious stones, and cotton and woollen clothing. It was a merchant vessel, probably trading with the tribes of Esmeraldas in northern Ecuador and exchanging Peruvian goods for the ceremonially important spondylus shell and tropical corals. This was the first evidence that there really was a land of gold to the south. In 1527 Pizarro made a reconnaissance southwards along the Peruvian coast and landed at Tumbes, an Inca city, which the chronicler Molina described as "a well-ordered town." From Tumbes Pizarro sailed as far south as Santa, calling at other points along the north coast.

The conquest. Amazed by what he had seen, Pizarro was determined to go ahead and conquer Peru. After three years he launched his expedition, and in the spring of 1531 Tumbes was taken. With this foothold on the mainland, Pizarro and his 170 men set out to meet the Inca Emperor himself. After marching southwards along the coast and then into the mountains they found him encamped with his army outside Cajamarca. A few of the soldiers recorded their impressions of ancient Peruvian society and provided the first descriptions by Europeans of the towns, agriculture and public works of the Inca Empire. Francisco de Jerez, for example, has left a fairly accurate account of the town plan of Inca Cajamarca:

"In the middle of the town there is a great square surrounded by walls and houses. . . . The plaza is larger than any in Spain and entered by two gates which lead to the streets. The houses are more than 200 paces in length, and the roofs are covered with thatch . . . their walls are of very well-cut stone. . . . In front of the plaza is a fortress [*the pyramid-like usnu*] made of hand hewn stone; a staircase leads from the plaza to the fort. . . . Above the town there is another fort . . . surrounded by three spiral walls."

But the main object of the meeting with the Inca Atahuallpa was to claim Peru for Philip of Spain and to demand gold. The Emperor was eventually captured and his army routed. From captivity, Atahuallpa tried to appeal to the Spanish lust for treasure by offering to fill a large room with gold and two rooms with silver. He ordered two temples (the Sun Temple in Cuzco and the Oracle Temple in Pachacamac) to be stripped of their treasures, which were then melted down by the Spaniards. The Emperor was eventually murdered, and the colonial era began.

In the first decade after the Conquest, European domination of Peru was disastrous for the native culture. The people were decimated through disease and forced labor in the mines, a depopulation which was described by Cieza de Leon when he journeyed down the coast in 1547. Cieza's chronicle is one of the main sources for the Central Andes. He traveled through the Andes from Colombia to Bolivia and took special care to describe the customs of the natives and the landscapes through which he passed. He spent four years journeying through Peru and Bolivia, the last two as the official "Cronista de Indias." Some of his site descriptions show how devastating the initial conquest had been. For example, of Paramonga, the great Chimu fortress, he wrote: "It is now all in ruins, and has been undermined in many spots by those searching for buried gold and silver." Cieza de Leon also recorded Inca legends and wrote an Inca history. He noted the Inca modes of organization and social institutions and his works are still used today as a valuable historical source.

Scholars and robbers. In the latter half of the 16th century the government, intent on gaining as much information as possible on the population, economy and social organization of the natives, sent government inspectors into various provinces in the Andes to record such information, while the attempt to eliminate idolatry provoked interest in the native religion. Thus a number of important historical documents have come down to us; but it must be remembered that many of these were written over 40 years after the Conquest.

Wanton destruction of pyramids, tombs and cemeteries in ancient Peru in the search for treasure continued throughout the colonial period and has never ceased up to the present day. For example, Miguel Feyjoo wrote a book in 1763 in which he mentioned that a certain Gutierrez of Toledo gave to the Spanish king, as the "royal fifth," over 5,000 castellanos of gold which he had taken from a huaca in the city of Chan Chan in 1576. The nearby pyramid, the massive Huaca del Sol, was also ransacked. The looters diverted the River Moche into the mound in order to expose the "treasure" in the center, thus destroying about two-thirds of the main platform.

The 18th century has provided the earliest systematic recording of archaeological finds. Father Louis de Femillé, a French priest, excavated in southern Peru at Ilo and Arica and also took back to France many artifacts from the whole coast. And a Peruvian scholar, Baltasar Jaime Martiñez Compañon, who was Bishop of Trujillo in northern Peru from 1779 until 1791, also began to study

Francisco Piazrro, Spanish conquistador who toppled the Inca empire with a handful of troops in 1531.

Peru's past. He traveled widely throughout his diocese spending a large part of his spare time sketching and making plans and maps of the natural and social phenomena which interested him. He assembled a collection of nine volumes of watercolors and line sketches, one for each of his main interests, and sent them to King Charles III. Volume IX is the one which is of antiquarian interest. It comprises several maps and sketches of sites, such as Chan Chan and Huaca del Sol in the Moche Valley, as well as drawings of graves and artifacts.

Martiñez Compañon also excavated graves and made drawings of the contents of seven tombs. He arranged the burials in descending order of status, from king to commoner, which he inferred from the quality of clothing and offerings. He noted precisely the colors and patterns of the shrouds and the grave goods that were to accompany the corpse to the next life. The bishop also drew many individual artifacts, such as textiles, belts, staffs, pots and wooden and metal objects in great detail. In all, he made a considerable, and still useful, contribution to Peruvian archaeology.

The first half of the 19th century saw an upsurge of interest in the ancient civilizations of the Andes. Following the successful revolutions against the Spanish Crown in Peru and Bolivia in the 1820s, these Central Andean Republics became more accessible to European anti-

A watercolor by Martiñez Compañon of the mummy of a Chimu king, well preserved in the dry climate. He wears a feathered headdress and clasps a ceremonial digging stick.

Six Chimu burials, sketched by Bishop Compañon and arranged in order of social status. The aristocrats (*below, left*) wear spondylus shell headdresses indicating high status, and ceremonial robes; weaving equipment was buried with the woman at the center. The three commoners (*above*) are buried with Chimu pottery.

quarians, travelers and explorers, whose presence and writings also stimulated indigenous research. The first major work of this type was by a Peruvian, Francisco Barreda, who in 1827 wrote a treatise on graves and temples. One of the best known expeditions was that of Mariano Rivero and Jacob von Tschudi who spent a couple of years in the Cuzco and Titicaca areas and along the coast. They described such sites as Chan Chan, Pachacamac and Cuzco and illustrated their book with woodcuts and plans.

From about 1845 onwards, academic interest focused on two closely related subjects. The first was the rediscovery, translation and publication of many of the early Spanish accounts of the Conquest of Peru and the nature of the Inca Empire. Much important work on these lines was done by the American historian, William H. Prescott, and a British sailor, Sir Clement Markham. Both of them read the early chronicles and produced best-selling accounts of the Incas and the Conquest, and Markham published accurate translations of the documents themselves.

The other line of inquiry was that of the antiquarian traveler, who not only described his travels and encounters in popular books, but used the nascent techniques of archaeology in his work. Ephraim George Squier is perhaps the best known of these men. He had already carried out outstanding archaeological surveys and reconnaissance in the United States and Mexico before he arrived in Peru in 1864.

His first major work was a survey and excavation of Pachacamac. He knew from written sources that the chief temple was of pre-Inca date and that in Inca times the place had been so much revered that the Inca built a shrine and an *acllahuasi* nearby. He was able to distinguish these imperial buildings by their pottery and architecture. He also knew from his previous work that ancient Peruvians frequently buried their dead near the temples, and that these sites were a good source of artifacts. He understood the principles of stratigraphy, and excavated a number of graves. He surmised the status in society of the dead person by the quality of the shrouds and offerings, and meticulously described the excavation of "A Plain Man's Tomb" in an article written in 1869. He decided that the flexed body of the adult male was that of a fisherman, from the fish net and copper hooks which were placed with him prior to enshrouding. The adult woman was wrapped up with spindles, whorls and thread inside her mummy bundle. The bodies of three children were also found in this tomb. That of the eldest girl was crouched on a workbox full of miniature spinning tools. The body of the young baby was found with a sea shell, full of stones and sealed with pitch to form a rattle. Squier photographed and drew each artifact.

He also worked in Chan Chan, Tiahuanaco, Cuzco and other sites, making many illustrations, both plans and views, of tombs and grave goods. As a result of his wide-ranging surveys and excavations in the Andes, Squier became the first scholar to attempt to arrange the different cultures into a sequence.

His work was a great stimulus to further research in the country. The Germans Wilhelm Reiss and Moritz Stübel carried out grave excavation and analysis at Ancon, while Adolph Bandelier and Max Uhle traveled across Peru, visiting and excavating sites and building up composite pictures of the ancient civilizations.

Bandelier was sent to Peru in 1892 as part of his job at the American Museum of Natural History in New York. His major work was done in the Titicaca basin where he recognized a difference in burial practices between the *chullpa* people and the Incas. He associated the pottery he had found in the city of Tiahuanaco with that of the chullpa graves, thus delimiting the Tiahuanaco culture. Uhle worked mainly along the Peruvian coast and in certain highland valleys, such as Tiahuanaco. His tomb excavations and his study of sculptures and architecture enabled him to distinguish several cultures and to place them in sequence. He recognized that the Tiahuanaco style was much more widespread than Bandelier had suggested, and detected its influence on the pottery style of the coast. He postulated the following sequence: an early period characterized by regional cultures, such as proto-Chimu, Mochica and Nazca; then the spread of Tiahuanaco, followed by the revival of local cultures, e.g. Chimu; and finally, Inca. Basically this is still the sequence accepted for the latter phases.

The earlier cultures were only recognized much later, in the 20th century. One of these, Chavin, was discovered by Julio Tello in 1919. Tello, a Peruvian, had been greatly influenced by Bandelier and Uhle and was trained in archaeology at Harvard. His research on Chavin and his revised sequence constituted the first major work by a Peruvian since Barreda. His association with the great anthropologist Kroeber, who worked on the Uhle pottery collections in the 1920s, clearly established the currently accepted chronology.

Machu Picchu. Many explorers particularly wanted to find Vilcabamba, the last independent Inca city, which was known to be situated in the mountain jungle area to the northeast of Cuzco. Sixteenth-century chroniclers had described Inca Vilcabamba and its main shrines, and by using these descriptions explorers over the last 150 years have attempted to locate the site.

The first was a Frenchman, Sartiges, who in 1834 found an Inca ruin at Choqquequirau near the Apurimac river. When he had cleared the surrounding jungle, he con-cluded that this was Vilcabamba, the last refuge of the Inca Tupac Amaru in 1572, an opinion shared by several other explorers. In 1909 an American explorer, Hiram Bingham, made the difficult journey to Choqquequirau and was so impressed that he planned to return two years later with a larger team to explore the site and the surrounding region. Meanwhile, he met a Peruvian historian who was working on early documents and claimed that there was another Inca city, Vitcos, near the village of Puquira and an ancient shrine, yurac-rumi – "a great white rock over fresh water."

This was the lead Bingham needed. He trekked down the Urubamba into the jungle. One day, his party stopped to eat with two Indian peasants and Bingham found that they were still farming ancient terraces. His guides led him up the steep hillside and he records:

"Suddenly I found myself confronted with the walls of ruined houses built of the finest quality Inca stone work. It was hard to see them for they were partly covered with trees and moss, the growth of centuries, but in the dense shadow hiding in bamboo thickets and tangled vines, appeared here and there walls of white ashlars carefully cut and exquisitely fitted together."

He found a cave which had been used for burials, and a round building he thought was a Sun Temple. He had discovered, quite by chance, one of the world's most spectacular ruins, Machu Picchu, an Inca city perched on a ridge-top high above the Urubamba gorge. His expedition roughly cleared the site and mapped parts of the city.

They then turned deeper into the jungle and Bingham found the great white rock of yurac-rumi and the site of Vitcos. He also located ruins at a place known as Espiritu Pampa, only 3,000 feet above sea level and thus the lowest Inca site in the jungle. Believing that Machu Picchu was most likely to be the site of Vilcabamba, Bingham returned in 1912 with an excavation team. The whole site was carefully cleared and mapped, and excavation began. Bingham's most important finds were the burial caves below the town where decaying mummies were found, together with funerary offerings such as pots, beads, spindle whorls and bronze ornaments. Digging within the city proved to be unproductive except in an area of high status dwellings where hundreds of potsherds were found. Bingham's theory that Machu Picchu was Vilcabamba was supported by the discovery in some graves of glass beads of colonial Spanish origin.

However, in 1964 another American explorer, Gene Savoy, using the same documents as Bingham, was soon convinced that Machu Picchu was not the legendary Vilcabamba because it did not tally with the descriptions left by the Spaniards – and Vilcabamba appeared to be in a remoter area. Savoy followed the supposed route of the Spanish invaders in 1572, and at Espiritu Pampa he found an extensive city, much larger than Bingham had recorded, covered with trees and vines. He made plans of this large Inca ruin and proved conclusively that it was post-

Primitive methods of 19th century archaeology: digging up mummy bundles in the desert near Ancon, Peru, from a book by Reiss and Stübel. Note the discarded pots and bones in the foreground.

Thomas Jefferson, third President of the United States (*below*), was one of the first to excavate an Indian mound on rational principles.

Conquest by the discovery of Spanish-style roof tiles. In 1966 Savoy also discovered many cities, forts and terraces in the jungle area of the ancient kingdom of Chachapoyas and the Pajaten. His contribution to Peruvian archaeology has been enormous.

North America. In the late 18th and 19th centuries several new ideas were in circulation, of great importance for the study of man's past. One of these was the principle of superposition, applied in the description of the proper relation between different layers of earth, which permitted geologists and archaeologists to establish the sequence of events represented in the earth. A second useful concept was that of uniformitarianism, by which deposits are explained as the result of uniform processes occurring at more or less uniform rates. This idea opened up great vistas of time for the formation of rocks and the fossils they contained. The third idea was that of evolution, which for the first time permitted the present to be linked with the past by a process of gradual change, governed by natural selection.

These ideas, as formally expressed, were probably unknown to the first explorers of archaeological sites in North America. But they were in the air, and most of the early travelers were well-informed men, with disciplined, yet curious and inquiring minds.

One of the earliest of Americans to look into the Indian past, also renowned as a political figure, was Thomas Jefferson, the third President of the United States. His interest in exploration and discovery prompted him to send Meriwether Lewis and William Clark to the far west, and in 1784 he opened by hand excavation a prehistoric mound in the Virginia Piedmont. It remains a notable feat because he observed and correctly deduced the sequence of prehistoric events from the superimposed layers of earth his workmen uncovered. For a comparable standard of excavation, one must look down the years past much lesser work to the beginnings of modern archaeology.

Jefferson noted the distribution of mounds on low ground near prehistoric villages, and the physical differences in appearance between two construction materials. Through the use of old accounts of Indian visits to the mounds he attributed their construction to historic Indians. Jefferson dug his trench so that an observer might walk in to examine the walls of his excavation where he could note that layers of earth succeeded layers of bone, that all the bones did not go together in a single layer and that burials were successively less weathered towards the top. This indicated that the mound was built up gradually over a period of years. Observations of the human skeletons were concisely recorded: their orientation, the condition and age of teeth, the presence of children and adults. Such observations allowed Jefferson to answer some of the questions that many early Americans asked about Indian origins and behavior. His excavations made it clear, for example, that burial mounds were not for fallen warriors, but for a whole community. Jefferson's thinking also anticipated the convergence of archaeology, ethnology, history and linguistics which has marked the training of American archaeologists for nearly a century.

Mississippi mounds. Squier, whom we have already met in Peru, and Edwin H. Davis carried out the first systematic reconnaissance in the eastern United States in the 19th century. The two men surveyed the mounds of the Mississippi valley, differentiating the various types, securing topographic data by instrument survey, and initiating the first archaeology publications of the new Smithsonian Institution in Washington. The appearance of the mounds led Squier to surmise a possible connection between the eastern States and Mexico, as well as the Old World. In 1851 he published a book on the distribution of serpent earthworks and related features. He pointed out that these were not enclosures or burial mounds, but were ceremonial structures. He commented in particular on large serpent mounds over 1,000 feet in length in Ohio, Iowa and Minnesota. His comparisons were cautiously made, and he argued that the similarities of such features to some in the Near East were probably the product of similar thought processes and response to the necessities of life, rather than of any actual contact with the Old World.

Frederick Putnam, like other early students of American prehistory, started with a non-archaeological background, yet he established academic training for archaeologists. Although his interests were many, he had a marked capacity for fine observation and sound field work. In 1885 Putnam excavated at the Serpent Mound, along Brush Creek, Ohio, first discovered by Squier and Davis. With the economy of a fine strategist, he cut trenches to expose sections of the serpent, the "egg" at the mouth of the serpent, and open ground. These sections showed a common depth of modern soil, establishing that all the features thus examined were of the same relative age. He showed that there was no contemporary soil layer below the earthworks which implied that the mound-builders removed the top-soil before starting work. Putnam's sections thus established that the Mound had been built as a single human event and not in a series of episodes. The original features were at least several centuries old, and the Mound exemplified careful prehistoric planning and construction with durable materials. Even though the Serpent Mound was clearly a product of considerable skill, Putnam was able to prove that most earthworks were built by Indians rather than by some mysterious lost race.

His examination of the Serpent Mound convinced Putnam it should be saved for posterity. Money was raised in Boston to buy 60 acres of land, which later became a state park. This large tract gave the mound a setting which reflected its importance. The money raised for purchase and preservation included an allocation for archaeological excavations, which was in keeping with Putnam's sense of the importance of establishing several forms of public trust with private money.

John Wesley Powell. In the Southwest there were several explorers whose exploits stand out in bold relief. One of the most important was John Wesley Powell, scientist-adventurer. Powell explored the Green and Colorado River canyons by boat in 1869, a hazardous undertaking even in modern rubber boats with good maps and aerial photographs. He recorded archaeological sites and interpreted the geological history of the Grand Canyon with remarkable skill. He was also a modern ethnographer in several respects, explaining both his own methods and the attitudes of his Indian informants to being interviewed. He recorded the sequence and duration of

The great Serpent Mound in Ohio, first excavated by Frederick Putnam in 1885 and later saved by him for posterity. The mound was built by the Hopewell people about 200 AD.

events he observed, and was usually careful to take account of his own shortcomings.

Powell also recorded observations which have interested later archaeologists. In his travels, for instance, he recorded that Paiute Indians dug a pit in the ground, into which they put glassy rock. Powell realized that flint-like material was being heated to make it easier to work, but it was almost a century later when Don Crabtree rediscovered this technique.

Among his other accomplishments, Powell classified American Indian languages into 52 groups. These have now been reduced to five, but the groups within the modern classification are still spoken of as Powell units. The accomplishment is not unrelated to prehistory. The American archaeologist is literally digging Indian prehistory from beneath the feet of living Indians, and Powell's units express old historical relationships of great importance for North American prehistory.

Powell also played an important part in the establishment of the United States Geological Survey and the Bureau of American Ethnology. The B.A.E. had much to do with the development of modern American anthropology through its support and publication of research in archaeology, ethnology, linguistics and physical anthropology. It has now been given an administrative face-lift and the new title of Office of Anthropological Research.

Mesa Verde. One of America's great photographers, William Henry Jackson, was among the first to visit and photograph the cliff dwellings at Mesa Verde in Colorado. Jackson was a member of the Hayden Geological Survey, an experienced traveler and observer and one of those rare photographers whose pictures capture the character of the countryside through which they pass. Public interest was aroused by Jackson's photographs, which were complemented by clay models of some of the Mesa Verde ruins. But before the Mesa Verde National Park became a reality, rancher Richard Wetherill had begun to explore the site. Wetherill discovered the great showpieces, Balcony House and Cliff Palace, and guided scholars such as T. Mitchell Prudden and Nordenskiöld, whose works relied heavily on Wetherill's firsthand knowledge. Although Richard Wetherill was an amateur by present standards of training, he was a keen observer and thinker. Wetherill appears to have discovered the Basketmaker culture, which represents a pre-Pueblo stage of culture in the Four Corners region where Utah, Colorado, Arizona and New Mexico come together. Dr. T. Mitchell Prudden also contributed to our understanding of the development of Pueblo culture and pointed out that prehistoric Basketmakers were warriors as well as farmers.

Adolph Bandelier. Bandelier was the archaeological counterpart of the naturalist John Muir. Both traveled light, fast and far, living according to the traditions prevailing in the country they were studying. Each man left written accounts of his work. Bandelier's contribution to the history of the Southwest is especially important, although, as we have seen, he also worked in Mexico and Peru. He used a direct historical approach, proceeding from the known condition of the Indian in his own and colonial Spanish times to the landscape and its prehistoric ruins. The observations he made of Keres-speaking Pueblo Indians are a good example of Bandelier's work. Keres

The Wetherill brothers, 1890s. Richard Wetherill (center), discovered Mesa Verde.

One of Mesa Verde's ruined pueblos, sheltered under caves. This Anasazi community is in Colorado.

Indians occupied the lower Jemez and Frijoles tributaries of the Rio Grande. The Frijoles canyon then had a striking appearance, as caves alternated with prehistoric doorways cut into its vertical northern wall of volcanic tuff. Bandelier examined the number and size of the ruins, estimating a probable prehistoric population of between 1,500 and 2,500 people. Frijoles had fertile soil and formerly numbers of big game. Communal hunts and Apache raids were credited with the eventual loss of game, but it seems likely now that historic European stock-raising also had some effect, on the mountain sheep in particular.

Bandelier was careful about his historical judgments, separating Indian from Spanish features. He measured nearly every cave, saw that nodules as well as flakes of obsidian were present, and commented that Frijoles pottery types were similar to those at two nearby ruins. Bandelier also measured the diameters of kivas (Indian

An east coast Indian, ceremonially painted for the hunt. John White, Elizabethan explorer and artist, was one of the first Europeans to record the North American Indian with brush and pencil.

ceremonial structures) and noted details of masonry and benches.

Archaeological observations were complemented by folktales, and from these Bandelier observed that Cochiti Indian legends seemed to originate at Frijoles canyon, thus linking the canyon with the first Pueblo Indians at Cochiti, San Felipe and Santo Domingo. Communal Indian hunts appeared to fit the topography of the Mesa del Rito, and native net fishing seemed to be connected with the narrowness of the river canyon between Cochiti and San Ildefonso pueblos. Bandelier's work at Frijoles is memorable for its breadth of knowledge and vision, which resulted in a lively account of Keres Indian land and life. Fittingly, Frijoles canyon and its ruins is today the center piece of Bandelier National Monument.

Adolph Bandelier was at home in so many natural settings that it is difficult to convey the freshness of his writing. He entered the Gila River Valley of southern Arizona by descending the southern slope of the Gila Range on May 9, 1883. His account of the bare rocks, denuded landscape and haze-hidden peaks well conveys the mood of that thorny land of cactus and mesquite. A few well-chosen words describe the deep canyon of the Gila, with a descent of 3,000 feet in 20 miles in one direction and in 12 miles in another, and he was entranced by the beauty of the native flowers. As he descended to the desert, Bandelier recorded the presence of ruins on Ash Creek. Despite the 100-degree midday temperatures, Bandelier was quick to recognize that the soil could be fertile when irrigated. This and the mild winters made it a suitable land for prehistoric farmers, if not for hunters.

Another problem about prehistoric irrigation ditches caught his attention. He recorded one ditch 350 meters long by an average of two meters wide with raised ridges, about eight miles east of Fort Thomas. What was curious was that the ditch sloped down to the Gila River rather than away, and it had no obvious source. Bandelier deduced that this and other ditches collected runoff from rainwater which in deserts accumulates rapidly in flash floods.

The conclusions which Bandelier reached anticipate present thinking. Prehistoric ruins varied from small and simple to large and complex, but they were all variations on a theme which could be traced back to Mexico. He observed that northern pueblos combined residence with defense, but that on the hot desert defensive places were built separately. He also noted that as one proceeds southward houses increase in size and doors and windows get larger with the warmer climate. The surface finish of exposed walls in the moister climate of Mexico is finer than the rough adobe of the Southwest. Pottery symbols were also similar across the Southwest, but Bandelier was cautious enough to say that common architecture did not imply a common origin for the people.

We might not agree with some of his deductions now, but Bandelier made exploration an important component in the development of modern American archaeology.

Don Crabtree: Master Flintworker

Don Crabtree (*right*) has had little formal education. But he does have a native genius for shaping glassy rocks into replicas of the kind of stone implements used by prehistoric peoples. As a boy he began experimenting with tool-making as a hobby; later it became a lifelong interest and has recently gained him an international reputation in prehistoric archaeology. He runs a program of experimental flintworking at the Idaho State University Museum and often travels to other universities or even to Europe to give lectures and demonstrations on problems of point typology.

Why is Don Crabtree's work so highly valued among prehistoric archaeologists? Archaeology is dedicated to the reconstruction and understanding of the life patterns of ancient peoples through the study of their remains. Since prehistoric remains are scanty at best, there is a growing tendency among prehistoric archaeologists to find out exactly how things were done in those ancient times by actually trying to do them today – building huts with the tools known to have been used by ancient man to discover the problems they faced; sowing and reaping primitive cereals to throw light on early agricultural methods; reproducing stone tools to find out just how the ancient flintworkers faced and solved their problems. Don Crabtree's combination of experimental genius and manual skill makes his work invaluable to the archaeologist who wants to know just how the ancient tools were made.

The first migrants from Siberia carried tool-making traditions from the Old World into the New. These included the reduction of a core or block of raw material to make an implement in a series of steps involving the manufacture of blanks and preforms as part of the process. A blank is ordinarily a core reduced in bulk by pressure flaking but whose final tool shape is not yet discernible. The preform is any one of a series of steps, after producing the blank, in which the final shape of the tool can be discerned. Most ancient points in western North America were made by reducing a core.

A simpler technique is to modify a flake detached from the core. The flake then becomes a blank to be worked into a finished implement – and the process requires less time. Many of the Archaic tools produced in the New World were manufactured by this method. Flaked stone tools in general are made from glassy rocks which are elastic and will fracture in a cone, leaving a shell-like scar on the rock where a flake has been detached. Flakes are removed by striking a direct blow (direct percussion) or by striking a punch placed on the stone (indirect percussion) or by applying leverage with a pointed antler or bone against an edge (pressure flaking). Detaching a flake involves controlling the fracture by use of a platform – a point or surface against which force is applied. The finest North American flaked stone tools were produced by pressure flaking, and almost all were heat-treated first to make flaking easier.

Don Crabtree at home (*right*) carrying out direct percussion flintworking. A flintworker has to sit on a low stool or stump so that his knees are high enough to enable him to use his lap as a type of "work bench." While working he must always use protective padding, usually of leather. In this picture Crabtree is beginning the initial reduction of a cobble, using a hammerstone. The cobble is supported on his thigh. Note the array of flintworking tools scattered close together on the ground, ready for use.

Crabtree's deductive powers have led him to convert experience into the development of new techniques in all areas of working and flaking glassy rock. He does not simply set out to make a copy of a finished blade found at an archaeological site, but studies the discarded flakes found at the site, left over from the tool-making process, and with these before him he tries to discover and reproduce the actual process used in the making of the blade. He will often, for instance, develop a new technique to meet a new challenge, matching his work against the archaeological specimen he is studying.

Previous page: Don Crabtree displaying a large percussion biface. Magnificently-worked implements such as this one were used both for trade and for prestige-ownership by the Indians of western North America. To make a replica like this requires a high degree of flintworking ability.

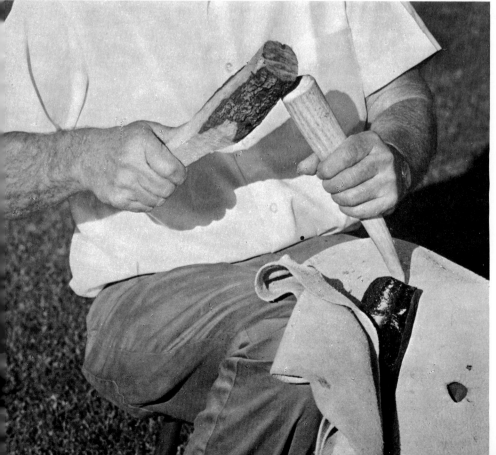

Left: Don Crabtree at work, using an indirect percussion technique. This enables the worker to control, quite precisely, the direction of applied force and the point at which the flake is to be detached. The punch is made of elk antler and the baton of wood. The material he is working is obsidian, a black volcanic glass.

Crabtree's skills are such that he deserves his fame. In 1962 he opened the first conference of Western archaeologists on problems of point typology with a display of his flintworking skills. This brought him national attention from the many distinguished archaeologists present at that occasion and he began to receive invitations from other universities. This led to a 1964 conference at Les Eyzies, France where he and another skilled modern flintworker, François Bordes of the University of Bordeaux, replicated prehistoric stone tools from both the Old World and the New.

Direct percussion techniques

The photograph (*right*) shows Crabtree using a hammerstone to start the manufacture of a biface. The stone being worked is supported by his padded left thigh, while he strikes the hammerstone against the edge of the tool he is making using a downward and inward rolling type of motion. The right arm holding the hammerstone may or may not be supported on his right leg, this type of support being optional among flintworkers. The hammerstone itself is made of a silicified, sandy limestone, a stone which has a particular yielding characteristic that enables the worker to produce good flakes without undue shattering. Crabtree's left hand holding the piece of stone has the function not only of supporting the stone while being worked but it is also used to turn the piece in numerous directions to allow removal of the desired flakes.

Of paramount importance to the flintworker is the proper preparation of the striking edge of the stone being worked. The picture (*right*) shows one technique often used – that of grinding the stone edge with a hard, coarse-grained material. The purpose of this grinding is to remove weak edges and overhangs on the object being worked so that when a blow is delivered by the hammerstone the flintworker can be assured of complete flake removal without crushing. Other typical methods of edge preparation include either the removal of small flakes, using a hammerstone to isolate the platform, or the careful beveling of the edge to obtain the proper platform angle for flake removal.

Right: A hammerstone is used on the edge of the artifact, in this case an obsidian blade, by direct percussion, using a downward and inward, rolling type of motion. The artifact is supported freely by the left hand, with the first and second fingers feeling the underside for ridges and imperfections. The left forearm of the hand holding the artifact may or may not be supported on the left leg. For this kind of work the hammerstone must be of a yielding type and have a rather rough surface.

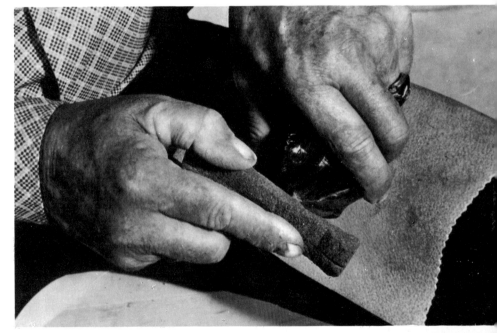

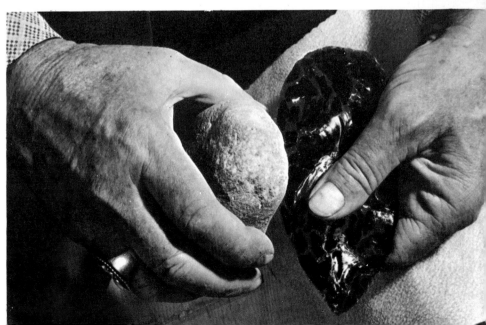

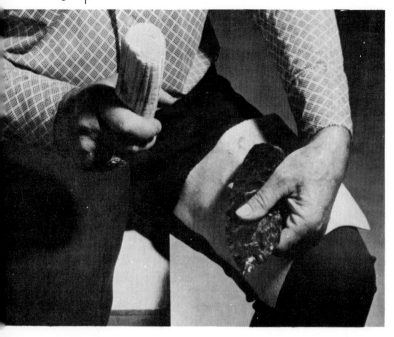

The rounded end of an antler is used by direct percussion to remove flakes from the underside of the artifact. The item is free-hand supported and the fingers of the left hand are used to feel for ridges and imperfections on the underside of the artifact. The hand holding the biface being worked may or may not, at the flintworker's discretion, rest on the left leg.

The side of a moose antler base is being used here for flaking, using a motion similar to that of the hammerstone. The flakes are being removed from the underside of the artifact. Since antlers from different animals differ in hardness and weight, several varieties are used in flaking, thus allowing the flintworker a useful flexibility in his techniques.

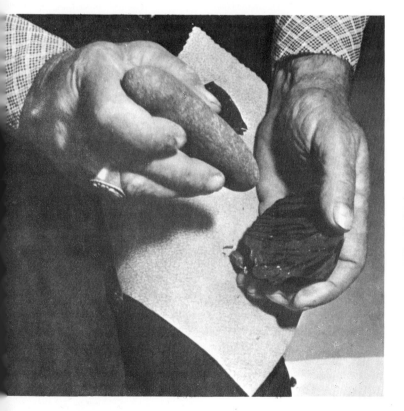

Here Crabtree is using a hard stone hammer to produce small blades from a conical core. The use of a hard hammer requires a modified technique. The flakes are removed well in from the margin of the core and have large accentuated bulbs of force. These flakes may be used as blanks for arrowhead-making.

A double burin (cutting tool) is here being made by using direct percussion on an anvil stone called a "backing." The picture shows the flake in position on the anvil stone during the grooving part of the production. This particular type of burin is manufactured, using the backing technique, by producing a V-shaped groove in the distal end of a blade. This produces two tang-type projections on the bottom of the blade, which can be used as platforms for the removal of further spalls, or chips off the burin. Crabtree's long experience has made him an expert in such delicate tasks.

Indirect percussion techniques

Don Crabtree (*right*) holds blades which have been removed by using the punch technique. Also shown is the core from which the blades were removed as it sat in his lap. The antler punch is held at approximately the correct position and angle for removing another blade. This technique enables the flintworker to produce uniform blades from a prepared core, as shown here. A continuous series of blades of regular size, shape and thickness are produced when the flintworker precisely controls the direction of applied force and the point at which the flake is detached.

The photograph (*below*) shows the technique used by Don Crabtree to produce fluted Early Man points. This technique of supporting a preform in a wooden vise and removing the channel flake by indirect percussion was devised by Crabtree as a means of replicating some Early Man point types. The vise not only supports the stone being worked, but also is used to remove the channel flake without fear of breaking the proposed artifact. The sides of the preform are held firmly in the vise and the tip is supported solidly on a wooden base with the weight of the flintknapper on the vise. Note that a small nipple is produced at the point where the flintworker seats the punch. This is to insure an adequately strong and well-aligned platform for flake removal.

Pressure techniques

Below: Crabtree pressure flakes a point using the Fells Cave technique. The artifact is supported by the thumb and first finger and the forward thrust is in alignment with the thumb. The flaking direction is towards the worker. A wooden pressure flaking tool is usually used and is made of a fine-grained hardwood. This photograph, however, shows a variation in the technique, since an antler is being used.

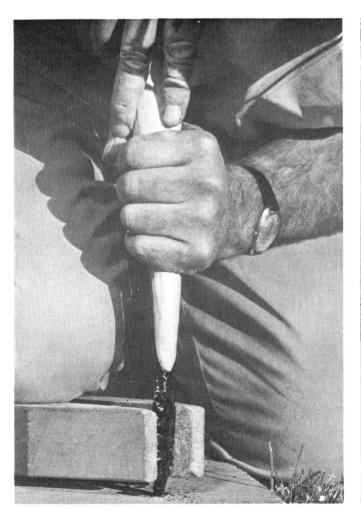

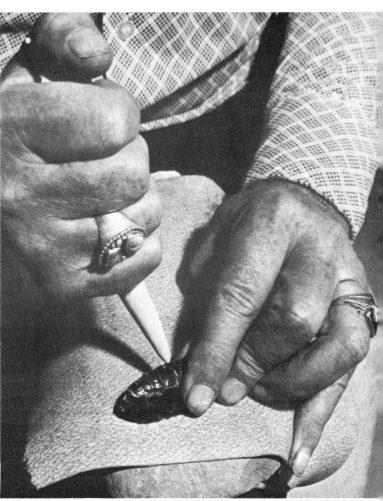

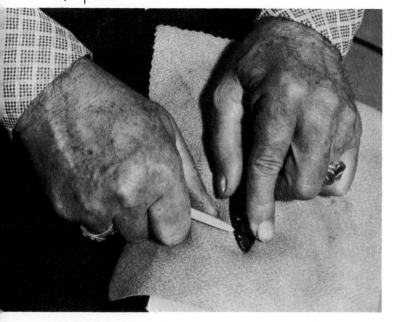

Don Crabtree is here shown using a pressure flaking technique which was actually observed by early ethnographers, explorers and trappers in North America. The artifact is supported on the left thigh. The pressure from the fabricator, held in the right hand, is applied downward. The flake scars on the artifact produced by this technique are usually short and have a feather termination.

Here Crabtree manufactures a point, using a palm technique once common in western North America and very similar to the Eskimo's palm-holding. The object is held in the palm of the left hand, protected by a pad, and is flaked by a tool of antler or bone. Since the flake scars can be directed at different angles (note the angle shown here), a bi-directional point can be produced with considerable ease.

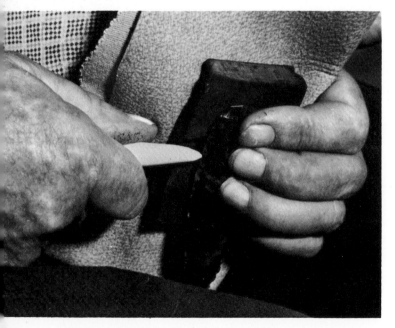

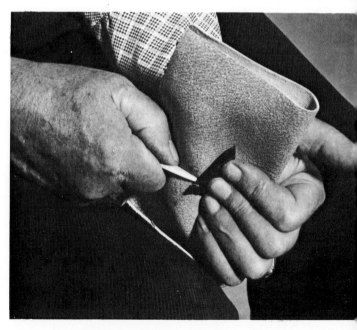

A large point is being pressure flaked here, using a hard support which produces expanding collateral flake scars. In this technique the rigid support required is held on the palm of the hand. The Scotts Bluff type of points were characteristically made this way. The point being made is held vertically, which gives better alignment, and the flakes feather at the middle, which removes the dorsal ridge. Flake scars are very deep at the edge. This technique, with the flakes terminating at the middle of the point, leaves a sub-diamond transverse section typical of Early Man.

Don Crabtree is shown here using a forceful technique to make a notch in a projectile point. He is supporting the point on the palm of his hand, which is placed on the inside of his right thigh, near the knee. Much material can be removed by using this technique, which is very much like the common palm technique in its application of force. Crabtree's most commonly used method is the palm technique, although he has experimented with many different types of pressure flaking, including a variation of an Australian technique and another which was common in western coastal Mexico.

Right: Crabtree holds a notched point and notching tool, after using another method of notching, which is a simple free-hand rolling technique. The flakes are removed from one side, the point is turned over and a flake is then removed from the opposite side. The thumb of the left hand is placed on the side of the artifact at the desired point of notching.

Below: Crabtree uses a finger support to pressure flake the tip of a point with great care. The point is supported on padded fingers. Pressure is applied by pushing down on the edge of the point which is stabilized by the right hand. Using this technique, very fine articulations are produced on artifact margins.

Right: A close-up view of Don Crabtree carefully placing the tip of a large pressure flaker on the edge of a polyhedral core. Crabtree's numerous attempts at replicating Mesoamerican prismatic blades has resulted in the development of a complex technique of core preparation, core support and application of pressure. Very regular prismatic blades are consistently removed from a well-prepared core supported in a wooden vise. The vise not only holds the core but increases its relative mass, thus enabling the flintworker to concentrate on the complex application of downward and outward flaking pressures. The pressure tool is a long crutch which is rested against the flintworker's chest. Note that the tip of this pressure flaking tool is made from copper wire. Years of experience at flintworking have shown Crabtree that copper wire is of nearly the same hardness and consistency as materials used by aboriginal people. This enables accurate replication of techniques and artifacts but eliminates the involved task of continued resharpening of aboriginal-type pressure flaking tips.

Replicated items made by Crabtree

The photograph shows Crabtree holding an Old World tranchet blow cleaver, typical of the rather crude implements produced by Paleolithic (Old Stone Age) man in Europe. The cleaver was made by using direct percussion. The final flake, carefully removed from the end of the tool, was precisely positioned so that when it fell away it created a strong, sharp, single cutting edge across the end of the biface. During his career as an archaeological flintworker Don Crabtree has been able to reconstruct many different tool-making techniques used throughout the world – and as a byproduct, many different and accurate replications of the artifacts themselves, including Mesoamerican polyhedral cores, Paleolithic artifacts as here, Clovis and Folsom points from the early North American big game hunters, and Cumberland points from the eastern part of North America.

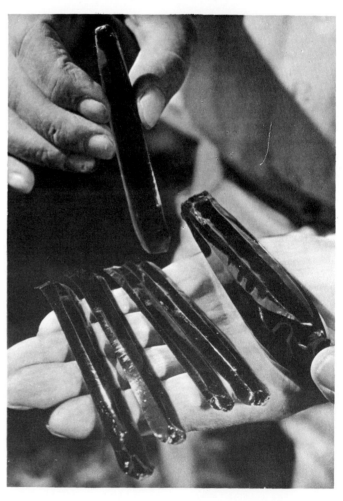

Crabtree holds in his hand one of his replications of the famous North American Folsom point. Folsom replication involves a highly complex and complicated set of techniques and procedures, including numerous stages of flintworking from the initial preforming through the final manufacture. This photograph shows the basal end of a beautifully-replicated Folsom point. Note the large parallel-sided channel flake, typical of the type, the careful marginal retouch around the outside edge of the point and the delicately retouched concave base, thin and sharp. To ensure accurate replication of such a point, all these features must be manufactured in proper sequence. The Folsom is typical of Early Man in North America.

The photograph shows Don Crabtree holding a polyhedral core of obsidian and the associated prismatic blades or flakes that came from it. These blades are replications of those produced in Mesoamerica in prehistoric times. The blades are made by using a pressure flaking technique on a highly prepared and regular core. Note the astonishing uniformity of the blades in shape, length, width, flake scar and platform size. The edges produced on such blades are actually sharper than a modern steel razor blade, and although no one wants to make or use such blades for modern purposes, their unexpected efficiency does throw new light on the supposed crudity of prehistoric implements.

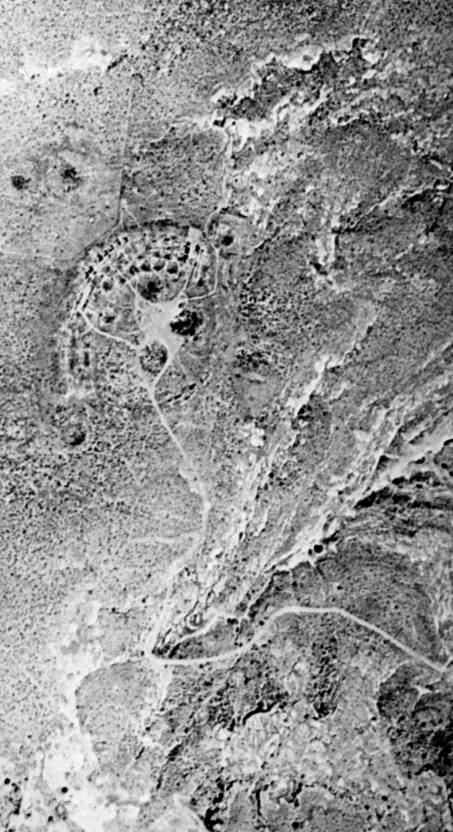

3. The Development of Modern Archaeology

The main concern of the 18th and 19th century travelers was to describe the more conspicuous monuments and to collect curiosities or works of art.

The first stage in writing history is to put events (or successive cultures and civilizations) into their right order. Jefferson's excavations in the 1780s were a pioneering attempt in this direction, but the layers of earth in his Virginia mound were of fairly recent date. It was not until the 1860s that the antiquity of man in America was demonstrated. By this time the enthusiasm generated by the discovery of fossil man in western Europe had been transmitted to the New World, where there were hopes of similar finds. The French "Commission Scientifique" to Mexico included expert geologists and palaeontologists, and within a few years they had discovered tools of chipped stone in three separate localities. All the tools were in undisturbed geological deposits and were found alongside the bones of extinct animals.

Studies of this kind demonstrate that, long before the end of the 19th century, the principles of both geological and man-made stratigraphy were understood by archaeologists, though these early leads were rarely followed up. Stratigraphic studies by themselves, however, provided only relative dating. In the 19th century, before the de-velopment of modern science, historical dates in calendar years could be provided only by Maya inscriptions. Diego de Landa's manuscript, rediscovered in 1863, made it possible to identify the signs for different colors and the cardinal directions. Then, between 1880 and 1887, Ernst Förstemann recognized the symbol for zero, worked out the basis of Maya arithmetic, and deciphered the calculations dealing with the revolution of the planet Venus. Förstemann's original work was done on a Maya book preserved since the 16th century in a Dresden library, but the twin streams of field archaeology and library research came together when Förstemann applied his skill to the inscriptions newly recorded by Maudslay at Copan. Förstemann soon managed to understand the nature of the calendrical system used by the Maya, and by 1905 Joseph Goodman (an American newspaper proprietor) had worked out a formula for converting Maya figures into Christian dates.

Previous page: An aerial photograph of a ruin in Chaco Canyon, New Mexico. "Remote sensing" from the air, including the use of false color photography to bring out ground details, is one of the latest tools of archaeological investigation.

Below: Panel of hieroglyphs from the Maya center of Palenque.

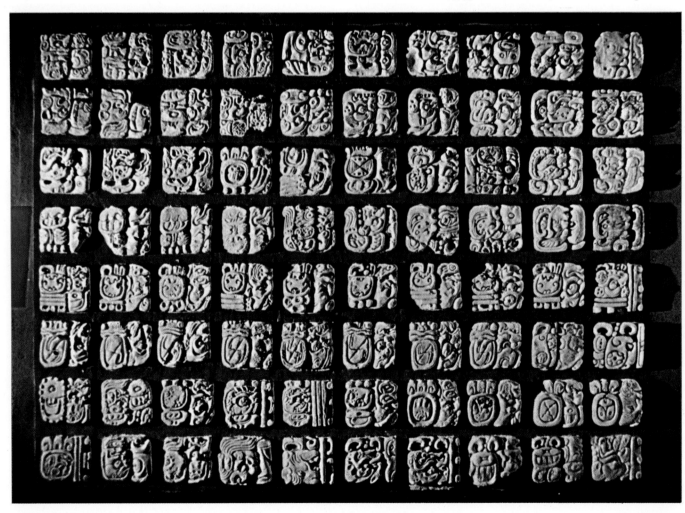

Although still beset with problems of interpretation, this was the first real breakthrough in the dating of Meso-american civilization. Having established the sequence of events in the Maya zone, the local dating was extended to other areas by the recognition of similarities in pottery and sculpture, by the finding of datable Maya export items in excavations outside Maya territory, or by foreign pieces traded into the Maya zone.

Archaeology in the 20th century. The development of modern American archaeology really began after the turn of the century. What separates this period from that of the early travelers is a professional concern with the solution of problems. The period of pioneering lasted until World War II, and most of the new ideas were developed or applied by North American archaeologists who worked in the Southwest or in Mesoamerica.

These developments are interesting for another reason. The early professionals were trained in departments of anthropology, so that some early (and good) archaeology was done by ethnologists working part of the time with Indian informants. From the informants they collected kinship terms and folktales, while from the earth they collected pottery and millingstones.

Although the principle of superposition embodied in stratigraphy was known, the Americanists had a special problem. The antiquities under study were in sediments that often showed no change from top to bottom. How could one find out if there were historical changes in the times represented by a uniform deposit? N. C. Nelson, working in the Southwest for the American Museum of Natural History, hit on a solution. He divided the deposit into uniformly spaced but arbitrarily defined layers. By examining the pottery and specimens by their relative levels he could show whether culture changes had occurred during whatever period of geological time was represented in that layer of earth. The technique was in use during the years of World War I, and its subsequent widespread application led to the recognition of important changes in the customs of prehistoric Southwesterners.

In the decade after World War I there were a number of important developments. Archaeologists knew that they needed to identify people and cultures, but that the nature of society – language, kinship, political systems – could not easily be determined by archaeological means. This is a problem which still plagues archaeologists, who need a system for processing, classifying and analyzing excavated material.

In 1924 Alfred Vincent Kidder, of the R. S. Peabody Foundation, Andover, Massachusetts, wrote *An Introduction to the Study of Southwestern Archaeology*. Kidder's work remains of value for several reasons. First, he thought that regional archaeology could make an important contribution to a general understanding of man's past. Second, he was able to define the Basketmaker and Pueblo cultures by reference to a variety of traits. Third, he defined key

Two renowned archaeologists, Alfred V. Kidder (*left*) who laid the foundations for Southwestern archaeology, and Emil W. Haury, who developed Kidder's methods at Snaketown, Arizona.

archaeological questions and explained the fundamentals of dating the past. His own excavations at Pecos Pueblo, New Mexico, were models of good stratigraphic excavation. He demonstrated the means by which relative time is measured, and was acutely aware of the need to compute dates in terms of calendar years, pointing to tree-ring dating and crossdating with the Maya calendar as the two most promising techniques. Kidder also realized, it is worth noting, that tree rings could indicate regional prehistoric climates as well as dates for particular events.

One of the most striking insights in the *Introduction* is the definition of a basic culture as the foundation for later agricultural achievements in arid western America. The culture was not given the formal name of Desert Culture until 1953, but Kidder's deductions about its significance have to be admired because they concern a much debated idea, fundamental in American archaeology. He surmised that maize domestication must have occurred in the Mexican highlands, and that it must have taken place by about 3000 BC. From this, Kidder estimated that maize farming must have reached the Southwest by 2000 to 1500 BC. New data obtained by using scientific techniques unknown to Kidder have not contradicted his theories, but have merely placed these events further back in time.

In 1927, when Kidder was still excavating at Pecos Pueblo at the eastern foot of the Rocky Mountains in New Mexico, he called a conference of archaeologists to work out a classification of prehistoric Pueblo culture. They divided the span of the culture into two stages – Basketmaker and Pueblo – seven sub-periods overall, which were assigned names and numbers. The Pecos classification is still used today, though modifications have been made.

Tree rings and radiocarbon. While the development of geological and archaeological time-scales had helped to assign a relative chronology to finds, there remained the major problem of absolute dating. An astronomer, Andrew Ellicott Douglass, provided one solution. He was studying sunspot cycles and needed to know if an apparent 11-year fluctuation extended back into the past. He began to examine tree rings to see if they changed in character, and this led him to develop the science of tree-ring dating. He started with living trees several centuries old, developing a graph to represent changes in ring width relative to rings on either side of the one examined. Patterns emerged which were especially visible in the yellow pine, Douglas fir and juniper. The technique of tree-ring dating rests on differences in the width of one ring relative to others in a tree. In a dry land precipitation is critical, so that a wide ring is added in a good year, a narrow ring in a bad year. Douglass found that some series of rings formed a distinct pattern, or signature, and that these patterns of tree rings from different trees could be correlated. By 1924 Douglass was using 200 to 300-year-old pines in the Southwest, and millennia-old sequoia in California. Today, bristlecone pines take the record back 4,000 years.

After rings in living trees, Douglass investigated old beams in 17th century churches and late prehistoric ruins. Eventually a master calendar was devised, extending back to the time of Christ so that, for example, an archaeologist excavating a pueblo ruin could send a piece of wood to Douglass and receive a date for the cutting from the post or beam. Because the bark was often missing, the date had to be expressed with a margin of error, i.e. plus or minus 25–50 years; but at least the archaeologist could obtain an approximately "absolute" date. The Laboratory of Tree Ring Research at the University of Arizona is now the world center for this research.

A postscript to tree-ring dating is its increasing use to check the accuracy of radiocarbon dates. Radiocarbon dating, first developed by the American, Willard Libby, in the 1950s, is the most widely used absolute dating method in archaeology today. It depends on the measurement of carbon 14, a radioactive isotope of carbon present in all organic substances, e.g. bone, wood, plant remains. Carbon 14 disintegrates at a known rate, once an organic substance has ceased to absorb carbon, i.e. when a living creature or plant dies. Recently, most of the older dates have proved to be inaccurate due to fluctuations in the amount of carbon present in the world's carbon reservoir. By computing the difference between the tree-ring and the radiocarbon dates of the same wood samples (particularly those from the long-living bristlecone pines of California) a correction curve can be produced. This can be applied to radiocarbon dates to translate them into historical, calendrical dates.

Ecology. We tend to think of the study of human ecology as a new science, but it was applied to New World archaeology in lectures given by Clark Wissler, of the American Museum of Natural History, as early as 1923. His lectures concerned the significance of geographic distributions, but he also applied his ideas to ethnographic and archaeological data. He observed that the distribution of mounds and other earthworks in the eastern United States suggested that the Ohio River Valley was an early

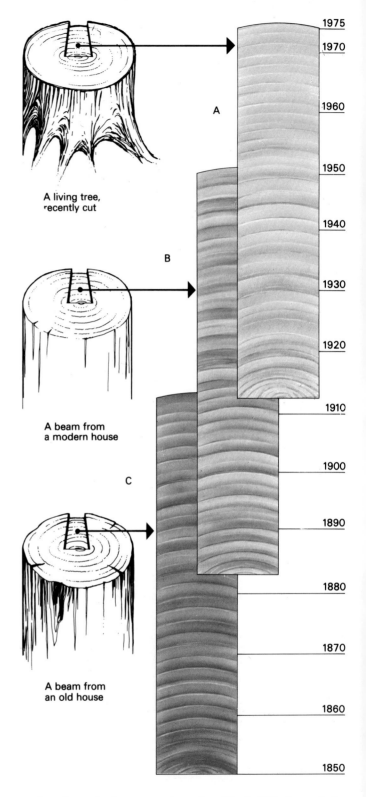

A living tree, recently cut

A beam from a modern house

A beam from an old house

center of cultural development in North American prehistory. He also demonstrated a similarity of characteristics that pointed to Mexico as the likely origin of civilization in North America. As he observed changes in race, language and culture he reasoned that changing physical environments must have been their cause.

Field studies of prehistoric environments, led by Ernst Antevs and Kirk Bryan, were intensive in the 1930s. A major stimulus was the discovery that ancient Americans had hunted extinct forms of bison on the high plains near Folsom, New Mexico, but studies were also made of climatic changes and their influence on prehistoric peoples. Antevs and Bryan constructed a series of geological sections representing the last 12,000 years, and began to put together a picture of changing temperatures and precipitation. They identified a three-fold set of sediments which represented three climatic cycles in the Southwest. Antevs was interested in temperature changes denoted by the depositional cycles, while Bryan was looking at water and its relation to pre-Columbian farming in the Southwest.

The most important, and perhaps still the best, single study was made by John Hack, one of Kirk Bryan's students, in the Hopi country of northeastern Arizona. Hack was able to show that temperature and rainfall were critically affected by altitude, so that only a restricted zone was suitable for farming. Above that zone temperatures were too low, and below it rainfall was insufficient for agriculture. In that zone alone the Hopi could use floodplains, sand dunes and alluvial fans for agriculture, and had developed simple but effective techniques for irrigation and flood control. Hack postulated a set of major environ-

The long-lived bristlecone pine, an ancient tree whose rings can now take the tree-ring dating sequence back as far as 4000 years ago with remarkable accuracy.

Left: In the tree-ring method of dating, chronologies are constructed by matching the rings of a living tree with the rings from wood cut in the past, as shown in the diagram. Specimens from ruins extend the chronology still further back into prehistoric times.

Right: The radiocarbon dating laboratory of the British Museum, London. Discovery of the radiocarbon dating method brought about a revolution in archaeology.

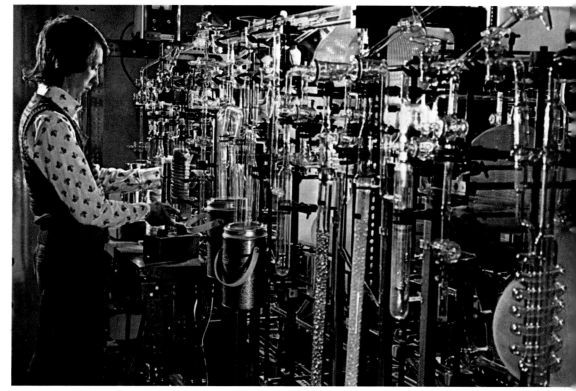

mental changes which corresponded to those defined by Antevs and Bryan, and he also demonstrated that erosion reduced the size of the field system, while deposition, coupled with a favorable climate, could create new fields and extend old ones.

In the eastern United States W. C. McKern, of the Milwaukee Public Museum, proposed a system for classifying archaeological remains, often referred to as the McKern or Midwestern taxonomy. The McKern system differed from the Pecos and later Southwestern systems by leaving out time as a factor for consideration. McKern and his colleagues used the same criteria for identifying types of culture regardless of when and where they were found. The Archaic Pattern, for instance, is marked by hunting, fishing, gathering, absence of pottery, regional adaptation to the natural setting, and distinctive tools and ornaments. We now know that this life-style had developed in the Southeast by 8000 BC and had disappeared there by 2000 BC. On the other hand, it began later and lasted longer in the Northeast. Thus a culture can be similar in two different areas at two different but overlapping times.

Archaeological surveying. The Southwesterners developed the archaeological survey, a system of investigation at once cheap, efficient and effective for pioneering work. The idea was to survey large areas, locate archaeological sites and collect surface finds. The distribution of discoveries was plotted on a base map and from this cultures could be correlated with culture limits, cultural sequences and natural phenomena. When Leslie Spier made his Zuñi survey, he collected artifacts by walking back and forth at random over each site. He also excavated one site and compared potsherds from the surface with those in the top soil. The distribution of types was similar and the differences could be shown to be a matter of chance. Spier was thus able to demonstrate changes in settlement patterns and he noted similarities with prehistoric events in New Mexico 200 miles to the east.

During the 1920s and 1930s reconnaissance systems were greatly elaborated by research institutions such as Gila Pueblo in Arizona and the Museum of New Mexico, where H. P. Mera used surveys to determine prehistoric population movements in the Rio Grande River Valley. Vast areas were examined and numerous sites recorded. E. B. Sayles of Gila Pueblo surveyed Texas and Chihuahua, using a checkerboard pattern in Texas to solve his sampling problem. At Gila Pueblo an interesting visual technique was developed for showing the distribution of pottery types and the archaeological cultures they represented. On large mounted maps thumbtacks with large heads were used to mark known archaeological sites. On each flat head were painted colors representing the frequencies of distinct pottery types – red paint on buff background, red-on-brown, black-on-white, etc. One could see at a glance the distribution of the pottery and thus the prehistoric cultures in the Southwest. This technique could

also be used to facilitate map-making for publication.

Such close scrutiny of an area was often followed by limited test excavations which frequently confirmed in stratigraphic sequence what could only be inferred from surface collections. Some survey areas might be selected for the study of a culture sequence, others for a single phase of development. It may be no accident that Gila Pueblo archaeologists conducted the excavations which defined two new cultures in the 1930s. These were the Hohokam of the Arizona desert and the Mogollon of the Arizona and New Mexico mountain regions.

When the Roosevelt administration created the Tennessee Valley Authority to construct hydroelectric dams in the area, archaeologists recognized the threat to antiquities. The T.V.A. was neither the first nor the only threat posed by Federal projects, such as Grand Coulee dam on the Columbia River, where, in the 1920s, Herbert Krieger of the National Museum carried out rescue excavations behind Cascade Locks on the lower Columbia. He was followed by other archaeologists on the Columbia and in the Tennessee Valley, where a very large survey and excavation program was carried out. These early rescue excavations were forerunners of modern salvage or emergency archaeology being carried out on the sites of proposed reservoirs, Federal highways and land development projects.

Archaeology in South America. Up to about 1960 archaeology in much of the New World remained primarily concerned with descriptions of the more spectacular parts of major sites – architecture, stelae and other iconography, graves, gold and silver work and the finer ceramics – in an attempt to establish the rudiments of a relative chronology. The advances in environmental archaeology made in the first half of the 20th century in the Southwest of the United States and elsewhere had little or no impact south of the Rio Grande. In Peru, for example, all the work of Max Uhle, A. L. Kroeber, Wendell C. Bennett and Julio Tello followed the traditional descriptive pattern. They traveled widely in Peru and recorded and excavated many large and important sites, such as the Huaca del Sol near Trujillo, Pachacamac, Tiahuanaco and Chavin de Huantar. From their own material they devised relative time sequences for the major sites in the whole country on the basis of ceramic styles, and derived, from their limited data, theories about the origins and nature of ancient Peruvian society.

In 1946 Gordon Willey, together with Bennett, William Strong, Clifford Evans, Donald Collier and Junius Bird, mounted a three-month intensive surface survey and excavation program in the tiny Viru Valley on the northern coast. Its object was to describe all the prehistoric sites, arrange them in a chronological sequence and check this against the schemes of Kroeber and Bennett; also to reconstruct the cultural patterns of each period by analyzing site types and relative locations. This approach,

Detail from a Hohokam pot of the early Christian era, excavated at Snaketown, Arizona. The Hohokam culture was first defined in the 1930s as a result of a detailed reconnaissance survey of the Southwest.

derived from Southwestern archaeology and ethnography, was designed to look at man and the way he lived rather than simply at what he built or made.

But Andean prehistory continued to be studied along traditional lines. It was not until the late 1950s and early 1960s when Edward Lanning, Frédéric Engel, Thomas Patterson and Michael Moseley arrived on the Peruvian coast, that Willey's work began to bear fruit. Their intention was to study man and his environment and they concentrated on the period of transition from hunting and gathering to agriculture. Their chief interest was where and how people lived and what they ate. After 1960 a more interpretative approach to archaeology became the norm, not only in Peru but in New World archaeology as a whole.

Prehistoric diet. The archaeologist has always been interested in human diet, but in the early years of archaeology it was very difficult to recover microscopic remains.

Consequently, food was only recorded if it was found inside graves as funerary offerings or illustrated in art, or in pottery shape or models. The earliest academic reports of prehistoric plant remains in the Americas were made by a Frenchman, Saffray, in 1876. He described a mummy bundle from Peru and identified the plants from which the sandals, bags and dyes were made, as well as the narcotic leaves of the coca plant.

But it was not until 1931 that a botanist, Melvin R. Gilmore, published a pioneering report on the plant remains from excavations in 1922 and 1923 in the Ozarks. His meticulous analysis identified 68 species of plant in archaeological levels associated with human activity, and of these he concluded that half had been used for food and some of these had even been cultivated. Gilmore founded the first ethnobotanical laboratory in the United States, at the University of Michigan, specifically to study man's utilization of plant life throughout his history.

During the interwar period, too, several papers were

published about the origins and spread of agriculture, such as those by the Russian botanist, Vavilov, and the American geographer, Carl Sauer. Vavilov traveled widely throughout the world collecting cultivated plants from gardens and fields in order to determine where the greatest number of varieties of a particular crop plant, such as wheat or maize, occurred. This, according to him, would indicate its center of origin. Sauer employed a similar approach but included a discussion of plants used by primitive gatherers and farmers in an attempt to explain the process of domestication. Both decided that the Mexican Highlands area was the original center for the cultivation of corn, beans and squash and that the Central Andes had produced the potato and other lesser crops.

In the 1930s Paul Mangelsdorf and R. Reeves studied the ancestors of Indian corn or maize, the staple crop of prehispanic America, and wrote an interesting paper suggesting that it was first cultivated in the southern highlands of Mexico. None of these scholars had any archaeological evidence to support his arguments, having based them on ethnographic data and the distribution of modern primitive plants. Then the vegetable remains from the dry Bat Cave in New Mexico, which had been excavated by Herbert Dick in 1948, were analyzed by Mangelsdorf and C. Earle Smith. All levels contained corn cobs and other pieces of the maize plant, and there appeared to be a distinct evolution in cob size between the lowest and higher levels of the stratified site. Those at the bottom had a radiocarbon date of 3600 BC. These earliest forms of maize were both popcorns and podcorns (the seeds were enclosed by the chaff). Mangelsdorf returned to his laboratory and began a series of experiments in which he crossed primitive races of pop and podcorn until he produced a corn similar to those he had examined from Bat Cave. The archaeologists now had a better idea of what to look for.

In 1949 and 1954 Richard S. MacNeish excavated a series of dry caves in the state of Tamaulipas, northern Mexico, in an attempt to discover early races of maize and perhaps even its ancestors. He was unsuccessful but, with advice from Mangelsdorf, he moved the center of his activities far to the south, to the tropical highlands of Guatemala, Honduras and southern Mexico in search of dry caves where preservation would be good and an environment suitable for maize cultivation could be found.

His first season yielded no traces of very ancient maize. Then he decided to excavate several caves in the semi-arid Tehuacan Valley of Puebla state in central Mexico. Initial findings encouraged him to make a detailed investigation of the whole valley with the help of many trained botanists and archaeologists, including Mangelsdorf, Smith,

Cutler and Whitaker (who were interested in the early history of squash) and Kaplan, who was concerned with beans. It became clear that maize was not the only plant to have been cultivated by the Indians of Mexico in early times. Only later did it become the great staple of the New World because of its adaptability to the many differing environments of Mexico – hot, wet forests and hot, dry mountain plateaus.

In levels dating to about 5000 BC tiny cobs of corn were found. The oldest cobs belonged to a very primitive form of corn whose seeds were able to disperse naturally, whereas in modern cultivated corn they remain attached to the cob, and hence the seed has to be planted by man for the plant to reproduce. Cobs from levels dating to a few centuries later had similar characteristics, but they were much larger. The earliest corn was small, only a few centimeters long, but deliberate selection had been made for bigger and better varieties, for specific colors and tastes and for particular environments. The MacNeish excavations were able to trace the evolution of all the traditional maize variants in Mexico. The maize plant responded so well to interference and tending by man that by 1500 BC it had become the staple diet of much of the area. Thus the combined skills of the archaeologist and the botanist have answered one of the major questions concerning the transition to agriculture in the New World.

Recovery techniques. In order to analyze such complex questions as the nature of prehistoric diet, archaeology had

to find methods of recovering plant and animal food remains from occupation areas, such as caves, houses and rubbish dumps. On a stratified site, all the soil from each level has to be processed to recover very small particles, because it is very rare that plant and animal remains are found in large pieces. Initially the soil is passed through a series of sieves to recover anything greater than a quarter of an inch in size. There is now a fairly sophisticated way to separate and categorize even finer material. The technique is called flotation, and is based on the principle that differ-

Left: Terraced hillsides, a canalized river and gentle terracing of the valley floor itself are features of this sophisticated Inca water conservation system near Pisac, Peru. Irrigation, agricultural and settlement patterns, food supplies and human diets are the preoccupations of modern environmental archaeologists.

Above: Coxcatlan cave in the Tehuacan Valley, Mexican highlands. Excavations in this and neighboring caves have produced detailed evidence for a long sequence of agricultural development in the New World, from the earliest domestication of the main staple crops by man to about 1500 BC.

Corn cobs from the caves of the Tehuacan Valley Project under Richard S. MacNeish illustrate the domestication of this staple. The cobs range from the small "wild" corn (dated 5000–3500 BC) through two primitive cultured varieties to the last two (dated 800–1500 AD).

ent substances, such as stone, clay, bone, shell and plants, settle in water at different rates. Stone and clay sink faster than bone, and plant remains sink very slowly. The only equipment needed is a large basin, a water source and a sieve and strainer to scoop off each individual item. By repeatedly soaking a sample of soil and scooping off the surface remains, one can separate the plant from the bone and insect remains. Stuart Struever first used flotation in his work in the Illinois and Mississippi valleys to gather detailed information about diet in an area of relatively poor preservation.

In occupation areas where preservation is good and all remains have been dried naturally, it is also possible to establish what people ate by studying fossil human excreta, or coprolites. As early as 1910 sunflower seeds, water melon seeds and hickory nut shells were recognized in excrement from Salts Cave in Kentucky, merely by extracting relatively undigested pieces. In 1955 Eric Callen and T. Cameron analyzed coprolites from Junius Bird's Huaca Prieta excavation of 1946 and recovered soft plant and animal tissues by a technique previously used in the medical examination for tapeworm. The excreta were soaked in an aqueous solution of sodium triphosphate for three days, which softened them and allowed the sediment of digested tissue to be siphoned off and studied. The results showed that the inhabitants of the Huaca Prieta midden had a mixed plant and seafood diet, comprising mainly mussels, clams, crabs and fish, as Bird had suggested from his analysis of the midden itself. But shellfish predominated, and fish formed only a minor part of the diet, along with a few cultivated plants such as beans, squash and peppers, and roots gathered locally. This technique, used extensively since 1960, has provided a major breakthrough in establishing the exact proportions of plants, animals and fish actually consumed by prehistoric man.

Pollen analysis has provided valuable information about prehistoric climates, vegetation and man's impact on his environment. It entails the separation of pollen from the soil and its analysis under a microscope. There have been few studies from Latin America, but the most significant one identified grass pollens, including maize, in the Oaxaca Valley of Mexico, about 2,000 years before the first excavated specimens of the plant from Tehuacan. The frequency of maize is seen to increase at the expense of other grasses, giving some indication of man's interest and involvement with the plant from a very early time. Soil samples have also been widely analyzed throughout the New World to establish the climatic conditions – wet or dry, hot or cold – at the time when a particular level in an excavation was formed. But the study of diet can only partly explain how man lived in prehistoric times. The archaeologist must also study the implications of where man settled.

Settlement archaeology. The first major attempt to answer settlement questions was made by Gordon Willey

The flotation process employs a tank in which the light materials in soil samples, such as carbon and seeds, float to the top and are skimmed off for analysis.

Right: Settlement patterns in the Viru Valley on the Peruvian coast. This pioneer study of Mochica settlements (200 to 900 AD) by Gordon Willey became a model for later projects.

in 1946. He followed up an idea of Julian Steward, the anthropologist, who had realized that the distribution and settlement pattern of the Great Basin's Indians was a significant indication of their organization and could be tested archaeologically. Willey was a member of the Viru Valley Project and began to test Steward's theory in that desert valley along the northern coast of Peru. The team located over 315 ancient settlements and then visited them all to collect datable material, such as sherds, and to describe in detail their apparent architecture and layout. Willey then took all of this information and divided the sites into four categories: living areas, community or ceremonial centers, forts and cemeteries. He then plotted the distribution of settlements for each chronological period. Significantly, settlements seemed to occur around the community buildings, such as pyramids and forts, and lines were drawn around discrete groups to describe an area which was probably dependent upon the central community core of (generally) religious buildings.

One resulting map is typical of Willey's work. It describes the community settlement pattern for the Huancaco or Mochica Period (200 to 900 AD). During this time the valley appears to have been divided into seven districts, each having as its focus a pyramid or group of pyramids or a fort, although the latter are not forts in the military sense, merely platforms or pyramids on hilltops in the middle or on the sides of the valley. Around the core of each district were lesser, possibly dependent, temples and the houses and cemeteries of the folk who maintained the center. The largest site, and possibly the valley capital, was the pyramid-platform complex known as Huancaco on the southern edge of the valley. This first work of Willey's set the trend for many subsequent projects on settlement in the New World.

In the 1950s Willey turned his attention to the tropical forest region of the Maya zone where, despite a few small-scale house mound surveys in the 1930s, the emphasis had been on the ceremonial centers. With William Bullard, he organized a Viru-type expedition in the Belize Valley of (formerly) British Honduras. They located, dated and mapped house mounds and pyramid complexes and from this calculated population figures, but were unable to establish definite community patterns because of the density of settlement. Later, in the Peten, Bullard was able to distinguish the territories controlled by ceremonial centers of various ranks. This tended to confirm archaeological evidence of class distinctions – poorer quality pots in the

houses compared with the ceremonial areas, and a graded system of small states.

Not only rural settlements but also the cities have been subjected to detailed settlement analysis. Both Teotihuacan and Chan Chan have been mapped in very great detail, excavated, and surface finds collected to give some indication of the nature of the occupation in each unit. For both of these cities, work has also concentrated on establishing how they functioned and what were their relations with the surrounding rural areas.

Such surveys of settlement do not tell the complete story. More interpretative work has appeared in the last few years which, by borrowing analytical techniques from ecologists and geographers, has taken into consideration the diet and the exploitation of resources. These studies are mainly concerned with explanations. The Tehuacan Valley project gathered not only archaeological data but environmental information too, and this has been subjected to a community pattern study by MacNeish and an ecological study by Flannery in order to determine the social and ecological processes operating during the transition to and development of agriculture. The settlement evidence shows an initial (c. 5000 BC) series of temporary camps, both small and large, demonstrably associated with the pattern produced by a band of nomadic hunters and

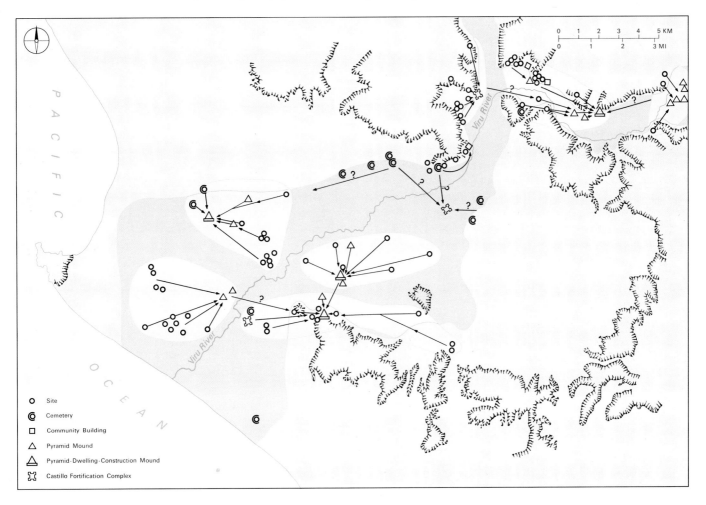

O Site
ⓒ Cemetery
▢ Community Building
△ Pyramid Mound
◮ Pyramid-Dwelling-Construction Mound
✛ Castillo Fortification Complex

gatherers, collecting seeds and berries in season. The pattern changes by 3000 BC, when there are more permanent settlements located in areas where agriculture could take place. Flannery's study shows what the Tehuacan folk ate and demonstrates that wild grass exploitation became important up to the point of cultivation, because these plants were the most receptive to interference by man, growing in profusion in cleared areas and capable of producing larger seeds as a result of man's selection.

The association between environment, diet and settlement has been clearly demonstrated at Otuma in Peru, where the shores of an old bay are flanked by over 30 middens containing shells and domestic refuse, each dating to about 1500 BC. On the floor of the abandoned inlet are the shell beds which were being exploited when, a little after 1500 BC, there was local uplift of the land surface. This dried out the bay and made it a salt desert. The collectors had to abandon their settlements and never returned.

Documentary evidence. In order to study Aztec Mexico, Inca Peru and some areas of Colombia, historical sources have been used. The Spaniards left documents, written immediately after the Conquest, which describe local populations, social and political organization, religion and economy. These accounts can be used by the archaeologists in two ways. They may enable him to investigate in more detail a local population by providing an explanatory background, or help him in explaining archaeological patterns found in the field. In 1962 John Murra of Cornell University organized a project to study the area around the Inca provincial capital of Huanuco Viejo, for which a detailed house-to-house census made on behalf of the Spanish Crown in 1562 was available. It gave details of two local tribes and of their chief, who paid tribute both in goods and in labor service to the Inca at Huanuco Viejo, but it did not tell how the ordinary folk lived. The archaeological survey of the city showed that it was entirely planned and built under Inca control. In the villages, on the other hand, differences in house form between the two tribes could be detected and the chief's dwelling was easy to pick out because it contained better quality, imported pottery. There was also a third tribe, the Wamali, which was not subject to the 1562 census, but which formed an integral part of the tribal setup of the area. Wamali houses were a different shape from those of the other two, being circular and multi-story, and consequently their settlements could easily be located. In this case, archaeology was used to supplement information already available from documents.

These settlement studies represent a shift of interest away from the individual site and towards the total landscape, both natural and man-made. They also mark a change in the scale of operations.

Air photography. The first big advance in archaeological exploration came with air photography, which allowed large-scale survey of arid or grassland regions where features were not hidden by forest. The open conditions of the Peruvian desert coast and the arid highlands of Mexico were ideal for this type of work. Air photographs, followed up by exploration on the ground, were used for mapping the cities of Chan Chan and Teotihuacan, and also provided the basis for the settlement studies in the Viru Valley and the Basin of Mexico. Experiments in the Tehuacan Valley have proved that different types of vegetation can be distinguished on air photographs taken with false-color infrared film, so that it is now possible to make rapid and accurate maps of the ecological environment to which man has to adapt his way of life.

Air photography can also reveal features which cannot be recognized on the ground. At Amalucan in central Mexico, for example, photography showed up a previously unknown system of canals dating from about 500 BC, marked by slight changes in the height of the vegetation and the color of the soil. Even more spectacular are the vast

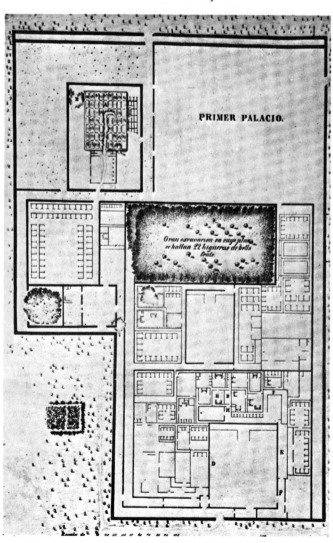

PRIMER PALACIO.

Plan of a royal compound in Chan Chan, the Chimu capital, by Rivero and Tschudi (about 1840) serves as useful documentary evidence today. An orchard covers part of the ruin.

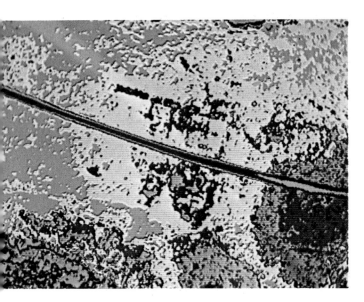

A false color aerial photograph of a prehistoric field (center) at Chaco Canyon. This 8-color representation of discrete density levels helped to define the field prior to excavation.

areas of ancient fields, in the shape of long, low, ridge-shaped mounds, which are currently being discovered in grassland and swamp areas all over America. Within the last few years they have been found in the Maya lowlands, the high Andean basins of Bogotá (Colombia) and Titicaca (on the Peru–Bolivia frontier), in the Venezuelan savannas, and in the flood plains of the major rivers of northern Colombia and coastal Ecuador. The scale of these engineering works proves the existence of organized societies as

well as a high level of farming technology, and is causing archaeologists to revise their ideas about native life in what once seemed marginal regions.

Locational analysis. This kind of large-scale exploration allows the study of problems which used to be reserved for geographers and ecologists. Archaeologists are now looking to these subjects for theoretical concepts which might help to interpret settlement data. In some cases it has been found that centers of population were located close to good farmland, abundant water supplies or important raw materials; in other cases the key factors turned out to be political or economic.

The lowland Maya sites of the period 600 to 900 AD fell into the second category. Bullard's explorations in the Peten had already suggested the existence of a state organization based on a three-tier administrative hierarchy. At the top were a few large ceremonial-governmental sites which controlled a greater number of smaller ones, and these in turn served a great many scattered hamlets and single houses. The techniques of locational analysis developed by geographers gave mathematical shape to this theory. Sites of the first rank proved neither to be randomly spaced nor located with an eye to particular resources. Instead they were distributed evenly over the landscape and were roughly the same distance apart.

It had long been known that, other things being equal, a hexagonal lattice is the most economic pattern for the division of an area between a number of cities which are in political and economic competition with each other, but

An aerial photograph of Pueblo Pintado, one of the many ruins in Chaco Canyon, New Mexico.

not until large-scale surveys had been carried out could this theoretical model be tested against archaeological data. The result was very close to what had been predicted: a honey-comb pattern of hexagonal areas, each of which represented the sphere of influence (and perhaps the national territory) of a single important Maya site.

Archaeology and modern science. Archaeology is no longer a self-contained subject. One of the main trends in recent years has been the borrowing of techniques, instruments and ideas developed in other fields of study.

Some of these borrowings (e.g. radiocarbon and tree-ring dating) are concerned mainly with chronological problems; others, such as pollen analysis, are used primarily to reconstruct the changing environment of the past. Another group of devices has been employed for prospecting and for locating buried features on archaeological sites. Their main function is to save time, money and effort by showing the excavator where he should dig.

The prospecting instrument which has had the greatest success in the New World is the magnetometer, a portable

Above and right: Excavating the mud wall of an Inca/Chimu irrigation canal in the Moche Valley of Peru to find its gradient and capacity. Careful studies of irrigation systems can lead to an understanding of how the ancient Peruvians managed to maintain their civilization in a hostile desert environment.

device capable of detecting small changes in the earth's magnetic field above pits, ditches, wall foundations or buried objects. In 1968 a magnetometer survey was carried out at the Olmec site of San Lorenzo Tenochtitlan on the Gulf Coast plain of Mexico. Test pits were dug at points where the instrument showed magnetic anomalies, and buried sculptures were discovered below the surface. On sites like San Lorenzo, which are too big for complete excavation, haphazard trenching is an inefficient way of locating buried remains. Without scientific methods of prospecting, much information will inevitably be missed.

Instruments devised for chemists and physicists are increasingly used in analytical work, revealing subtle differences which cannot be recognized by the eye alone. Studies of this kind have helped to show how things are

At the other end of the size range, geological analysis has been used to pin-point the source of the stone used for architecture and sculpture at the Olmec site of La Venta, in the Mexican state of Tabasco. Basalt was imported from the Tuxtla mountains, lava from the volcano of La Union 65 miles away, and thousands of tons of serpentine were brought from quarries more than 100 miles from La Venta.

Similar analytical studies are at present being carried out on jade, on the iron ores used to make polished mirrors during the 1st millennium BC, and above all on obsidian, the natural volcanic glass which was the favorite material for chipped stone tools. Sources of good obsidian are few, and in Mesoamerica they occur mainly in the volcanic mountains of central Mexico and highland Guatemala. Although not always distinguishable by eye, obsidian from each source is chemically unique. As an essential raw material for knives, scrapers and lances, obsidian was widely traded from earliest times. More than 3,000 samples from Mexico and Central America have been analyzed by neutron activation or X-ray fluorescence, many of them from known sources but others from quarries which have still to be discovered. By plotting the individual findspots on a map, each period separately, archaeologists have obtained information about the changing popularity of the various types of obsidian and about the ways in which trade patterns changed in response to political and economic factors.

In this type of study the individual piece of evidence has little value in itself. The significant information does not begin to emerge until all the data are considered together, allowing the archaeologist to recognize patterns in space or time. In searching for these patterns he must sometimes ask quantitative, or statistical questions. What proportion of the obsidian tools at a particular site comes from each source? Do villages closest to the sources have more obsidian than those further away? If so, how much more? Are the samples representative or are they biased in some way? What is the probability that the results are due to chance rather than to economic factors or to human choice?

These are not new problems. All that is new is the way of phrasing the questions so that the answers come in numerical form. The advent of the computer, with its ability to handle masses of numerical data at high speed, makes it possible to look for more complex patterns and to work at a finer level of discrimination than ever before.

The existence of these new and more rigorous techniques has broadened the scope of research. Influenced by anthropology and the social sciences, more and more archaeologists have become interested in the investigation of social relationships, in the hope of gaining a better understanding of the nature of human behavior and the processes of cultural and historical change. The study of present-day peoples is used to generate theories about the vanished societies of the past and to identify the most significant problems. Then, once the key problem has been selected, the questions are put into forms which can be

made (for instance the composition of metal alloys, or the firing temperature of pottery), and also to provide information about the source of the materials.

Microscopic examination of pottery used in about 2000 BC at Tutishcainyo on the river Ucayali, in the tropical forest of eastern Peru, showed that the clay of certain vessels contained crystals which could have originated only in a region where recent volcanoes have been exposed to rapid erosion. The most likely source is somewhere in the Ecuadorian Andes, and these pots must therefore be imports. By 1500 BC five per cent of all the pottery used by the community was of foreign type – evidence of long-distance trade between very different ecological regions. At the same time, examination of Tutishcainyo pottery produced evidence of what the local people were eating. Ten per cent of the fragments contained bits of crushed shell from edible freshwater molluscs, and others had inclusions of fish bones and fish scales. Since shell and bone decay very quickly in rainforest conditions, the pottery gives the only evidence for some of the most important foodstuffs.

A modern Indian pueblo in the Southwest of the United States. Comparison of such living pueblos with ancient ones helps the "new archaeology" to elucidate the living patterns of vanished peoples.

tested in the field, showing the excavator what kinds of detail to look for and allowing him to modify his excavation strategy as the answers come in.

This type of project first became common in the 1960s. The main trends of the "new archaeology" can be clearly seen in James Hill's study of Broken K Pueblo, a 13th-century Indian village in Arizona. The ruin consisted of 95 single-story rooms, 46 of which were excavated. Each room was described in terms of a list of features – floor area, height of doorway, style of architecture, and the presence or absence of food bins, firepits and ventilation.

By applying statistical methods to these data, Hill was able to distinguish various types of room. Most of them belonged to one of two categories: large rooms with fireplaces, ventilation devices and food bins, or small rooms which lacked all of these. Comparison with the villages of modern Zuñi and Hopi Indians, the descendants of the prehistoric Pueblo population, suggested that the large rooms were for domestic activities and the small ones for storage. Every household would have at least one room of each type, and large and small rooms should occur in roughly equal proportions. This proved to be the case at Broken K. In addition, analogy with the modern Pueblo Indian village indicated that four rather unusual structures might be kivas,

where ceremonial and ritual activities took place.

To test this interpretation, Hill listed the objects found in each kind of room in present-day pueblos and then analyzed the finds from the excavation to see whether they conformed to the same pattern. Allowing for the gaps in the archaeological record, the fit was good. The large rooms contained the debris of everyday life (objects of stone, bone and antler, waste material from tool manufacture, and types of pottery used for cooking, storing water and serving food) and the earth within the food bins contained pollen of edible plants. The small rooms contained mainly fragments of storage jars and very large quantities of pollen from food plants. The kivas yielded a high percentage of pollen grains from plants used in modern Hopi and Zuñi medicine ceremonies. The excavator's predictions were verified.

The Broken K study illustrates the way in which a sociological problem can be investigated archaeologically by bringing a variety of techniques to bear on the central question. This example also makes it clear that modern technology in no way reduces the importance of the archaeologist. Machines cannot think for themselves; good archaeology, now as always, depends on the skill of the investigator in knowing what questions to ask.

Chaco Canyon: Archaeology from the Air

Chaco Canyon National Monument is a showpiece of North American archaeology. Lying 100 miles northwest of Albuquerque, New Mexico, it is about 12 miles long and a mile wide and today carries no running water. But in the 10th to 12th centuries AD it was well-watered and may have supported a population of 10,000 people or more who engaged in floodwater farming and built a series of spectacular masonry pueblos, or communal dwellings, some with as many as 800 rooms apiece. Pueblo Bonito (*below*), a multi-storied apartment house ruin with great curving walls, dominates the canyon, but there are many other lesser ruins to attract the interest of the archaeologist as well as the traveler. Chaco Canyon, when inhabited by the prehistoric Anasazi Indian people, was one of the great social and ceremonial centers of the American Southwest. Archaeologists have long wondered why the canyon was abandoned at the height of its history. Some have argued that a change of climate to arid conditions similar to those at present may have led to its abandonment in the 13th and 14th centuries. Others suggest that internal social collapse or changing patterns of winter and summer precipitation, leading to floods and erosion, may have been responsible. In any case, a rather sophisticated social system seems to be implied by the towns, villages and roadways recently discovered in this part of the Southwest. The roadway system has been studied by the Chaco Center, a National Park Service, using the most sophisticated methods of aerial photography, as the following pictures attest.

Left: The great curving wall, four stories high, of the ruins of Pueblo Bonito, principal ruin of Chaco Canyon. It is estimated that a population of as much as 1200 persons may have lived in this huge "apartment house," which once had as many as five stories. The complex was gradually built up from a smaller pueblo. Tree-ring dating indicates that Pueblo Bonito was occupied between 850 and 1130 AD.

Below: A general view of Chaco Canyon as it is today, taken from the air with color infrared film to bring out details, especially culturally disturbed areas. Among the ruins, Pueblo Bonito and Pueblo del Arroyo may just be discerned. A number of enigmatic disturbed areas appear in white against the red and pink of the vegetation on the canyon floor.

Below: Pueblo del Arroyo from the air. Located near Pueblo Bonito, it lies on the north bank of the dry Chaco River, and is tree-ring dated 1065 to 1100 AD. Some 800 people may have lived in the pueblo.

Below, right: Kin Ya-a, a four-story kiva over 30 miles south of the canyon, may have served as a fire platform for night signalling. A prehistoric roadway runs by it towards the south.

A handsome white-ware jug with decorations in carbon paint, excavated at Chaco Canyon. Archaeological investigation of the canyon has been almost continuous and increasingly sophisticated, culminating in the present remote sensing experiments from the air by the Chaco Center.

Below: A stairway cut into the rock at Chaco Canyon. There are many such stairways cut into the walls of the steep cliffs of the canyon. But the existence of an elaborate system of roadways was difficult to note on the ground and had to await the advent of aerial photography to be fully revealed.

The prehistoric petroglyph shown here, located near Penasco Blanco, is believed to be an Anasazi representation of a supernova which occurred in 1066 AD and is also documented in the form of rock paintings in Arizona, California and China.

Below: Certain segments of roadway were clearly discernible on the ground, such as this example near Pueblo Alto in Chaco Canyon, which is approximately nine meters wide and is bordered by low masonry walls. But the extent of the roadway system was not realized.

Left: A prehistoric roadway runs across the lower part of this picture, exposed with color infrared film to bring out the traces of the road. Such an emulsion accentuates vigorous vegetation (red or pink in color) and thus aids in the identification of the roadway segment, which can be traced by a line of vegetation cutting through the trash area associated with a small ruin.

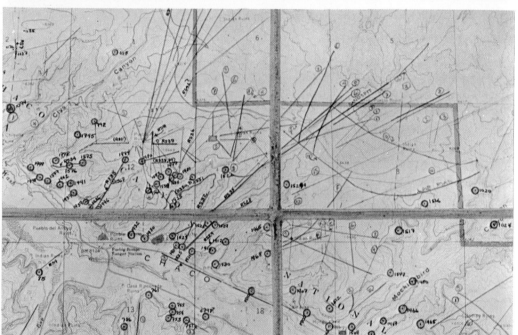

Left: Part of the final 1973 map, made in the field, of the extensive Chaco roadway system. The map illustrates the complex nature of the transport patterning. The existence of stairways and ramps had long been known, and they had suggested the possibility of a roadway system. With the mapping of the area, however, many features which had previously not been understood took on new meaning in terms of the network.

Left: To complete the study of the Chaco Canyon road system, the services of a satellite were obtained in 1974. This annotated ERTS space photograph complements the ground mapping in illustrating the extent of the transport network, which connects 13 major ruins in Chaco Canyon itself with a number of outlying ruins and areas where there were important resources. It was noted in particular that the roadways, even in 1974, seem to have been directed towards the more heavily vegetated and wetter areas of the region.

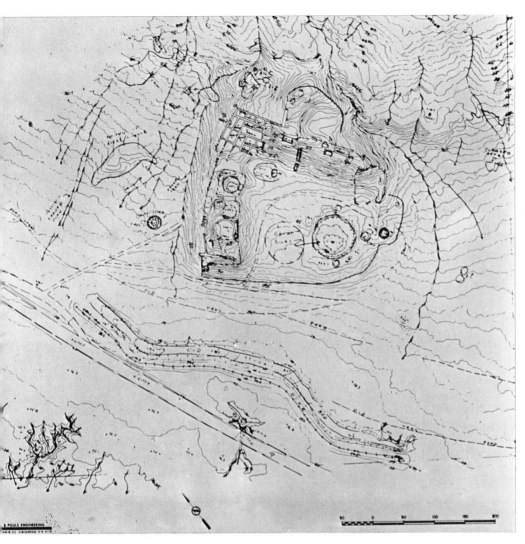

Left: Map of the pueblo of Una Vida, made from the air. Chaco Center experiments have shown that photogrammetric mapping, ie: using stereo aerial photographs, can produce more accurate maps more quickly, and at least as economically, as traditional ground methods. Una Vida ruin has been assigned to the Pueblo III period at Chaco Canyon.

Below: Photogrammetric mapping and a computer as well have been brought into play to construct this plan of Kin Bineola pueblo. The photogrammetric map has been digitized: the x, y and z coordinates of selected points (some of which are shown as "x's" on this map) have been recorded on computer cards. This information can then easily be recovered or plotted by the computer to produce floor plans, wall profiles and three-dimensional reconstructions.

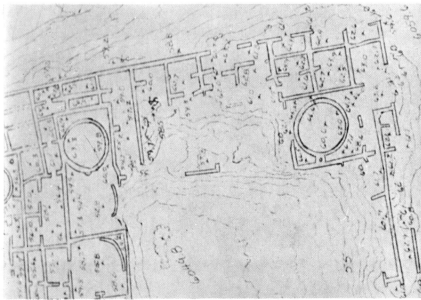

Left: A contrast-enhanced view of Penasco Blanco, a large ruin (about 700 rooms). In Chaco Center's electronic densitometry system, aerial photographs are processed by what is essentially a closed-circuit video system, thus obtaining definition by imagery manipulation.

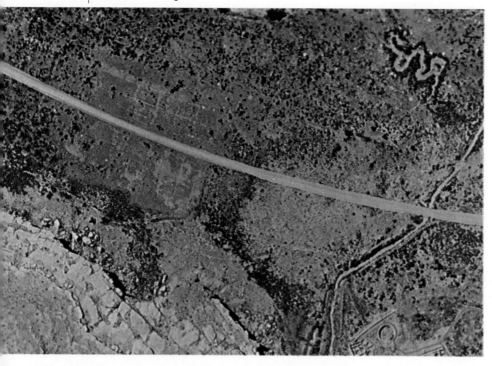

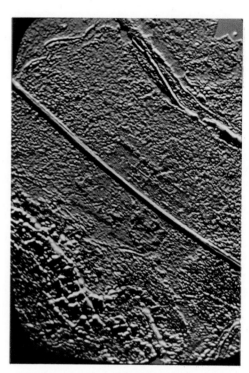

A prehistoric field which has been studied from the air by the Chaco Center's Remote Sensing project. The photograph illustrates another capability of the Center's electronic manipulative equipment – the representation of a continuous-range photograph in the form of artificially-colored density levels. The prehistoric field, near Chetro Ketl ruin at Chaco Canyon, is seen at the lower right, straddling the modern road.

An aerial photograph of the same prehistoric field near Chetro Ketl, this time edge-enhanced, that is, electronically manipulated to emphasize contrasts in the photograph.

A false color view of Chaco Canyon – a video picture of a portion of a space photograph. False color levels help to define vegetation and other ecological features at Chaco. Mesa tops are yellow and red; the canyon black or blue.

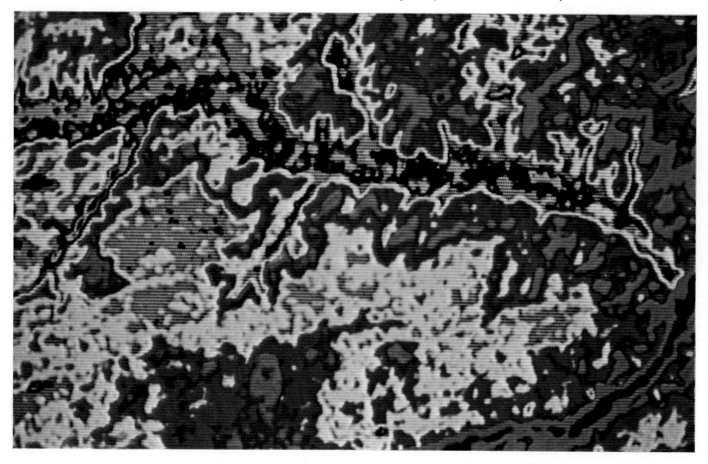

Theire sitting at meate.

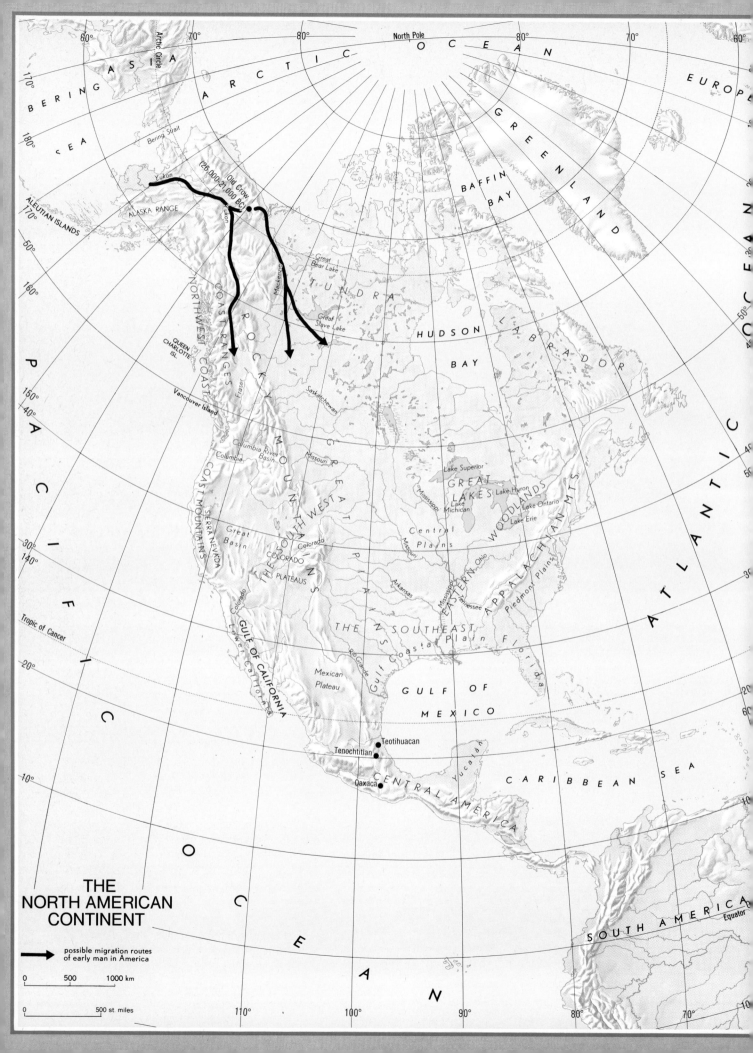

THE
NORTH AMERICAN
CONTINENT

→ possible migration routes
of early man in America

0   500   1000 km

0   500 st. miles

Page 65: Indians at a meal, by John White, the Elizabethan artist. These primitive tribesmen of the east coast of North America were the first Indians to be encountered by the English explorers.

[Map No. 1:] *Left*: The North American Continent.

Early hunters and food collectors. The first hunters, fishers and gatherers in North America found a land quite suitable for settlement. The climate was milder than it had been or would be in the future. Water flowed through the Bering Strait, probably as much as 15 feet below the present level. We may perhaps imagine a family examining the crossing from the Asian mainland and considering how to make it. A summer trip meant a boat or raft from the mainland to one of the Diomede islands. A winter crossing meant snow shoes and a long walk.

The initial settlement probably occurred about 28,000 BC, according to radiocarbon dates obtained from elephant bones at the newly-discovered site of Old Crow on the Yukon river. When the first explorers set foot in North

Matanuska glacier in southern Alaska. Early man, migrating across the Bering Strait from Siberia, may have settled in this valley before moving on down into the North American continent. Here he must have stayed for some time until he was ready to move on.

America they found plants and animals like those in Siberia. Tundra covered the hinterlands of the Yukon River valley, with willows, birch and alder growing along the banks. Frozen ground was widespread, even though the migration took place between episodes of glacial advance in Cook Inlet and the western Alaskan ranges. Mountain glaciers formed only in Alaska and the countryside was open. In the summer along the Yukon these hunting folk found and killed elephants and camels, but left behind only the bones of these butchered animals and some bone tools. Many kinds of mammals could be found here as the herb tundra expanded during the brief interglacial interval.

Within the next few thousand years the climate changed. The sea level was dropping rapidly, glaciers were advancing in mountain valleys and a continental ice sheet was spreading southward of the continental divide in Canada. The first families had already multiplied in response to the untapped resources of the far north. The valleys of the Yukon basin, perhaps the Matanuska valley near Cook Inlet, may have been among their first homes. Within a century the immigrants had probably multiplied and spread southward into similar tundra and steppe habitats. The migration continued swiftly until men were to be found from Alaska to the Andes and beyond.

Some early sites have few or even no stone tools, but the first people definitely had sophisticated tools for hunting, fishing and gathering. Their toolmaking techniques had originated in Asia and may have been known to man for two million years. In that time men had spread throughout most parts of the world, moving from the tropics to subtropical regions, then to temperate areas of Europe and Asia. By perhaps 100,000 years ago, during the later Pleistocene, human beings were occupying near-glacial environments. Semi-subterranean dwellings, the hunting of elephants and other large mammals, and cutting and scraping tools of stone were certainly known. Among other tools were those known as blades – the fine knives and points of the Upper Paleolithic hunters.

Blades are long, parallel-edged flakes, at least twice as long as they are wide, with one or two ridges on one face. They are produced by special techniques so that the blade is ready for use when detached from a stone core. Properly made, a blade is exceedingly sharp, and when pointed, may be used as a spearhead. If the base is trimmed the blade can be hafted. It can also be blunted on one edge to make a backed tool similar to a modern, single-edged hunting knife. Steeply angled end-scrapers, blades and burins (engraving tools) would have constituted a basic hunting kit.

Bifacially-flaked stone tools, or handaxes, were known to the first men who came from Asia but so far do not appear in the sites known to be older than 20,000 BC. Tools of this kind were in use 500,000 years ago in Europe and western Asia and were still used in very late times in parts of the New World. Tool forms changed but some basic techniques did not. It seems certain that bone, wood and fibers were also used to make tools and build houses, but these have not been found in North America. This may be due to insufficient excavation or the problems of preserving organic material.

The earliest hunters may have spread east of the Rocky Mountains into the upper Saskatchewan River valley. At the same time they could also have made their way south through the mountain plateaus to the Fraser River Valley. On this route there were grasslands and parklands with game and fish already familiar to Siberians and their North American descendants. Once in the plateaus between the Rockies and the coastal ranges, men could have spread far south without experiencing a significant change of climate or vegetation. It is possible that the first migrants followed the coast, but no evidence exists for this now. The difficult

coastal route offered steep mountains, narrow beaches, dense vegetation and deep waters. Since the coast appears formidable even now, men may also have found it so 25,000 years ago. Once south of the main mountain glacier systems and the increasing continental ice, however, men could have spread west to the southern Californian coast where the grassland would have been more abundant than now. Burials dated to more than 20,000 years ago indicate early if not initial occupation of the southern Californian coastlands.

The climate changed in the 5,000 years after men entered Alaska for the first time. The advance of the continental ice sheet east of the Rocky Mountains set in motion a series of other environmental changes which affected the prehistoric peoples. Between 20,000 and 18,000 years ago the ice was at its maximum, reaching south of the Great Lakes. In Montana the ice sheet joined up with mountain glaciers. Between the western cordilleras mountain glaciers massed to form a huge sheet where the first hunters had passed through Canada. On the coasts the ice reached to the sea. The sea level dropped 400 feet or more so that the Columbia River joined the Pacific 200 miles west of its present mouth. The Bering Strait became a continental bridge 800 miles wide, across which plants and animals could migrate. Men may also have crossed it, unaware that they were passing from one world to another. It is thought unlikely by most archaeologists that men in Alaska were in touch with people south of the ice masses, but it is not impossible.

In the Great Basin, lakes Bonneville and Lahontan rose and occupied vast areas of land. Little cool desert remained for hunters as pine forests grew on the basal plains, spreading down from western mountains in response to colder conditions. The open grassland which supported steppe animals was much reduced by forest expansion on the prairies and in the eastern woodlands. Spruce forests spread from New England to the Rockies and as far south as Kansas. In New England tundra was widespread while the oak forests of the East were much reduced.

During this most continental of all glacial episodes prehistoric food collectors increased in numbers, a fact possibly reflected in a greater number of known archaeological sites yielding radiocarbon dates for animal remains of between 18,000 and 10,000 BC. These include Trail Creek, Alaska at about 15,000 BC; Wilson Butte Cave, Idaho (13,000 BC), and Laguna Woman, California (12,000 BC).

These sites appear to be where the first food collectors settled. This suggests that the later finds are the camps of direct descendants, living where their forefathers lived. The population increase during the preceding 10,000 years may have been small, due to the reduction of grazing land 15,000 years ago. But a second migration is not necessary to account for the apparent increase in population. And, indeed, ice may have blocked the way south out of Alaska, despite the fact that the Bering Strait land connection between Asia and America was at its widest at this time.

The hunters of 15,000 years ago hunted camel, sloth and

elephant. Their tools included burins, blades and various flakes. One of the most characteristic implements of the period is known as the Lerma point. These points are blocks of glassy rock shaped by percussion flaking on both faces of the block or flake. Lerma points look crude by comparison with later points. The toolmaker apparently concentrated on the tip because this is long and steeply tapered. The steepness of the edges near the tip leaves them blunt, and the base has the suggestion of a stem or tang. These Lerma points, whole or fragmentary, are found from Alaska to Mexico and one fragment at Wilson Butte Cave is dated 12,500 BC by association with small mammal bones from which a radiocarbon date of this order was obtained. So far the artifact complex is limited in number and variety. Whether these early hunters spread east of the Great Plains is not known. No barrier prevented men moving eastward, but the people in the West may have lacked the incentive to move if their numbers maintained a state of equilibrium with the natural resources of the area.

Clovis and Folsom hunters. About 12,500 years ago a new climatic era began as continental ice retreated under the impact of a warm, dry episode. Spruce forests migrated north in the wake of the ice, pines spread west from the Appalachians, oak forests moved north from the Gulf and grasslands spread east from the plains. In the West, Lake Bonneville had overflowed north, lowering its level and reducing its size. On the Columbia Plateau the last of the ice dams collapsed, sending floods down the Columbia and across the channeled scablands. All over the West pine

forests retreated upwards and sagebrush grassland expanded rapidly.

The change from an ice age to an interglacial or post-glacial episode reduced the cover for forest and parkland game. Grassland grazers and browsers, however, found their habitat expanding. The human population also increased, and this coincided with the beginnings of a radical new stone technology. It resulted in a hunting pattern called the Llano complex, characterized by the use of Clovis points. A Clovis point is a triangular lanceolate spear point made by one of several techniques. The western points were made by reducing a large handaxe-like biface by a careful series of manufacturing steps. The biface was the blank out of which a finished tool was made. Direct percussion flaking removed large flakes, thinning the block of stone (flint, obsidian, quartz, etc.), making it symmetrical and determining the eventual character of the cutting edge. As the point took shape it reached a stage where an observer could see what the finished product would be like.

At this stage the object is known as a preform, a more or less arbitrary designation of one of a series of stages reached in the manufacturing process. The final flaking may have been by indirect percussion with a punch set along the edge. There are some Clovis points which were probably completed by pressure flaking – with an antler fabricator held in the flintworker's hand. The final step on most Clovis points was to thin the base by driving off one or more flakes up one or both faces from the base. One of the most interesting aspects of Clovis points is their wide range in length. The longest known is $7\frac{1}{2}$ inches, although

Stone points of the early hunters: *Left*: Points from Sandia Cave, New Mexico, perhaps 12,000 BC, a rare type characterized by a single notch at the base. *Center*: A Clovis point (9500 to 9000 BC) from the Simon site, Idaho, about seven inches long. *Right*: A Folsom point from Colorado (9000–7000 BC) the finest achievement of the early toolmakers.

specimens only slightly more than one inch long are also known.

Llano hunters stalked big game along streams, taking elephant, bison, horse and tapir, and these localities were often revisited. Spears were driven into the animals from several angles, indicating either the frantic efforts of one or two hunters, or a larger group of men making a co-ordinated attack. Remains of butchered elephants from this period of the Llano complex (9500–9000 BC) occur both west and east of the Rockies in ancient and modern desert grasslands. Blades, burins, scrapers and flakes were derived from earlier New World forms.

The early Clovis hunters are sometimes thought to have been responsible for the extinction of some species of game, including the elephant. But this is questionable. Rather few elephant remains, for example, occur on kill sites compared with the many remains of contemporary elephants that were not killed by man, and there were too few elephants to have supported the rapidly increasing numbers of Clovis folk. But Clovis people may have been the first whitetail deer hunters of eastern North America. Deer and mountain sheep did not, like the elephant, become extinct, although killed in hundreds 11,500 years ago in the northern Rocky Mountains.

In the West, Clovis points evolved into Folsom points, the climax product of the toolmaker. These points varied in size and finish but at their best were truly remarkable. Fine parallel oblique pressure flaking produced a preform of small lanceolate shape with a waist near the base. Most of the length of both faces was thinned by one long flake removed from a specially prepared base by pressure or indirect percussion. The making of a Folsom point required such planning that it represents a unique regional skill, practiced for 500 years or so on both sides of the Rocky Mountains. These points were being used in western grasslands while Clovis points were still in use east of the Mississippi River. The fluting technique was applied to eastern points which otherwise look like Clovis points.

Folsom hunters killed bison in or around old water-holes. These bison became extinct, but not as a result of hunting. They simply evolved into the modern forms which were roaming the grasslands by the million when Europeans first went west. Folsom food collectors are better known than their Clovis predecessors. A wider variety of tools and ornaments, paint palettes and camps survive, suggesting a successful life of early food collecting in North America.

Folsom points are occasionally so small that their practical use is uncertain. In place of burins of older type these people often used perforators with needle points produced by fine flaking. Some perforators may have been used to put triangular holes along the edge of a skin, allowing an early seamstress to use a lock stitch. Like Clovis hunters before them, the Folsom people collected wild plants. Their meat diet may have been less varied because they were more restricted in their choice of animals.

Folsom flintworkers were followed by makers of many varieties of lanceolate points, some stemmed, some basally thinned, but most made by variations of two pressure-flaking techniques. One technique produced wide collateral scars feathering at their margins to give a smooth lenticular cross-section. The other technique left narrow, parallel oblique flake scars which extended over the mid-line on each face. This implies that the flintworker controlled the elastic behavior of the flake so well that he could bend a detaching flake over the midline of the object. This process was also employed in Folsom points. Both techniques have been found on a single implement and were used with surpassing skill to make projectile points of remarkable beauty.

All makers of early points, from Clovis and Folsom to the Plano points – as the lanceolate specimens are called – knew how to modify glassy rock by heat treatment. The toolmaker reduced a block of flint, obsidian (volcanic glass) or other glassy rock to the size of a blank or preform. He then dug a pit in the earth, lined it with rocks, built a fire and prepared a bed of coals. Into the pit he put his preforms. The pit was then covered over and left for a day or two. This allowed gradual cooling of the preforms which were then removed. The heating of the raw stone changed its internal characteristics, often its color and sometimes its visible texture. The normal result was to make flaking easier, an important factor where pressure flaking was used. Since fine pressure flaking was the outstanding accomplishment of early North American food collectors it

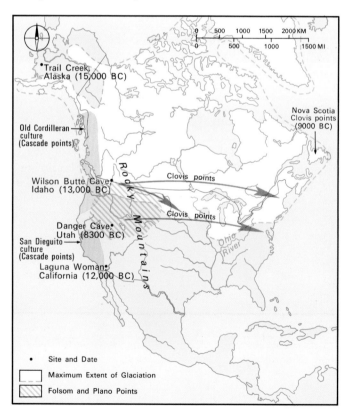

[Map 2:] Early Man in North America (18,000–6000 BC).

Danger Cave, Utah. Twenty layers of human habitation refuse in this remarkable site, starting at 8300 BC, have documented the transition from hunting to foraging for food such as nuts and seeds, and even the earliest use of woven baskets.

is not surprising that heat treatment was common. This technique was probably brought from Asia but was used increasingly in North America with the development of the fine lanceolate points of the period between 10,500 and 5000 BC.

Clovis point-making, and perhaps Clovis people, spread north of the Ohio River valley. The hunters found parkland and prairie south of the Great Lakes and followed it eastward to the Atlantic shore. Of the now extinct mammals they found only mastodons, but probably did not hunt them. They may have killed deer and a few barren-ground caribou which had survived in the region. Fish may also have been an important element in their diet.

South of the Ohio early food collectors began to manufacture small triangular points known as Dalton projectile points. These were soon modified by notching from the side or the corners at the junction of the sides with the base. Made on flakes rather than by reduction of a core through blank and preform stages, they show much less use of heat treatment than do the Plano points. Dalton and related forms were basally thinned, but no distinctive fluting of Folsom type was employed. Perhaps the most distinctive feature of these early triangular forms is their association with hardwood forests. Camps were made in uplands, on ridges overlooking valleys and at high points with com-

manding views. Since it was a time of apparently cool, moist conditions these locations may reflect easy travel routes which avoided the dense undergrowth in south-eastern river valleys. Or they may merely reflect the state of our knowledge.

In the cool, humid environment of the Pacific coast men hunted mule deer and elk, fished for salmon and collected freshwater mussels and berries. They made points called Cascade points and used a cobble edge for flaking and for skin working. They occupied inland areas as far as oceanic climate and vegetation extended. In the Northwest their culture is called the Old Cordilleran culture, and in southern California the San Dieguito. Towards the Rockies they overlapped in territory with makers of Plano points, the original bison hunters, who reached west into the Columbia Plateau and the Great Basin.

Little is known of the hunting methods of the Old Cordilleran people, but Plains bison hunters are known to have driven their prey into arroyos (dry stream beds) or stalked them by water courses. Small circular houses ten feet or so in diameter may have been used in the western grasslands and wind breaks were possibly placed in front of rockshelters, but so far no other evidence of construction is available for Dalton folk or Old Cordilleran communities.

The period of the early food collectors, marked by rapid

population growth and diversification of activity, neared its end about 8,500–8,000 years ago. Then solar radiation began to increase and temperatures rose, although the climate remained moist. This produced a last great expansion of the grasslands with a corresponding increase in the bison population. The influence of the makers of small triangular points was spreading.

Early cultures. By 6000 BC there was a continent-wide change in prehistoric cultures. The change coincides with a marked rise in temperature all over North America. Continental ice disappeared from the Arctic slope of Canada and mountain glaciers shrank for the first time in 5,000 years. Vegetation zones moved northward everywhere, and up the mountain slopes of the western ranges. Bison herds dwindled and the last mastodons and camels died out. In the desert grasslands of the Great Basin grass increased as the lakes shrank, while prairies expanded eastward at the expense of the hardwood forests, reaching well eastward along the southern edge of the Great Lakes. On the West Coast oak woods advanced northward as evergreen forests retreated. To any three generations of men, the changes of a century must have been remarkable. Many such generations experienced the denudation of once hospitable terrain, because the episode lasted about 1,400 years (5200–3800 BC, computed from numerous radiocarbon dates) in most places and even longer in lowlying and southern localities.

By 3800 BC temperatures began to drop again and precipitation increased, a change especially noticeable at high altitudes. In some places the environment remained more or less as it had been since 5200 BC. However, there was a marked increase in precipitation about 2200 BC with resurgent mountain glaciation, and game began to increase in the old grassland areas. Between 1500 and 1000 BC another drought affected western grasslands, but this was followed by a return to moderately moist conditions. In most places

the modern climate and vegetation patterns date from about 1000 BC so that, when the first Europeans arrived, prehistoric food collectors had been adapting to these conditions for 2,500 years.

In some regions people and habitat together had already developed their essential characteristics by about 6000 BC. In the dry West, sagebrush-grassland covered more than 200 million acres while in the East the forest bogs known today were forming 4,000 years ago. These climate and vegetation changes established the several biomes, or plant-animal associations in which prehistoric food collectors lived so successfully until the advent of the Europeans.

In the East the oak/deer biome reached from the Gulf Coastal Plain northward above the Great Lakes, and in this northern fringe maple, pine and woodland caribou were common. The spruce/moose association, a relatively poor human habitat, extended from Labrador to British Columbia. Across the Arctic regions herb tundra stretched, and here the large barren-ground caribou flourished. West of the Mississippi were central grasslands, with tall grass prairie up to the 100th meridian, where prairie and desert grassland interfingered. Bison were important in both, but antelope were restricted to the short grass of the west. Down the western Cordilleras from Canada to Mexico vast ponderosa pine and Douglas fir forests extended. In the north these reached to the Pacific Coast but in California they gave way to oak. The conifer forests were home to mule deer and elk and along all the western ranges mountain sheep abounded.

Successful occupation of new areas meant a population increase until a state of equilibrium was reached. The opening up of the Arctic encouraged the northward migration of forest and man. By 4000 BC the maritime provinces of Canada were settled by hunters, fishers and gatherers, perhaps 4,000 years after the diversification of food collection began in the southern forests of the Gulf states and the

A copper harpoon, a very early use of metal, from the Laurentian culture which flourished in the western Great Lakes region after 4000 BC.

A socketed ax from the Laurentian culture. Like the harpoon, the ax was fashioned from native copper and shaped by hammering, hot or cold. The copper seems to have been mined from sites near Lake Superior.

Carolina piedmont. We find cultures fitted to these variations in both time and habitat.

In eastern North America the earliest adaptation occurred in what is now the southeastern United States. Native camps and villages were shifted from upland stations to the main river valleys. There people gathered varieties of freshwater shellfish, creating huge middens as by-products of their livelihood. They hunted whitetail deer and collected berries. Although they were locally self-sufficient, they appear to have traded steatite bowls from the Appalachians to the Gulf Coasts.

The period after 6000 BC was marked by a remarkably precise fit of culture to nature. The success of earlier collectors was reflected in population growth. In turn these populations occupied adjacent habitats, diversifying to meet new needs and opportunities. The common character of the eastern woodland cultures (called collectively the Archaic culture) is shown by the fact that mid-continent people shared 60 per cent or more of their culture content with those nearer the eastern seaboard.

The Archaic culture can be subdivided into an earlier, southern culture called Indian Knoll and a later, northern culture known as Laurentian. In the South (the Indian Knoll area) the culture is traceable, with variants, in the Carolina piedmont, on the Florida coast, in the lower Mississippi valley and the uplands of the Tennessee and Ohio River valleys. Even within the area between the Appalachians and the Mississippi there were eastern and western forms by 4000 BC. Large rock shelters as well as village houses were used as dwelling places. Houses had clay floors with hearths and upright posts to support a roof of perishable fibers. The inventory of artifacts includes very early side-notched points dating from perhaps 1000–8000 BC, basin-shaped milling stones, atlatl weights (spear throwers), awls and baskets. Deer bones from southern archaeological sites represent as much as 90 per cent or more of the mammal bone refuse in the Indian Knoll culture area. A total of 55,000 artifacts testifies to the adaptive success of the later food collectors in the oak/deer biome.

In the Northeast, adaptation to the northern forests was achieved by 4000 BC. This Laurentian culture made use of bone for ornaments, harpoons and other tools. In these cold regions the people easily adapted to different habitats, such as the Canadian Shield, the spruce/moose biome, and the fisheries on the Great Lakes. Along the Labrador coast the Laurentian people came face to face with the early Eskimo people of the tundra, and their respective cultural boundaries moved in accord with the shifting zones of vegetation.

A surprising feature of the Archaic culture in the western Great Lakes area about 3000 BC is the appearance of copper tools or weapons. Naturally-occurring metallic copper was mined on a large scale at a number of sites around the shores of Lake Superior, and was worked by hammering in a cold or hot state. Copper axes and ornaments soon appeared in burials throughout the area and south of the Great Lakes. Kame burials (the burial of many individuals

[Map 3:] Later food collectors, after 6000 BC.

in kames, or mounds of stratified glacial deposit) were characteristic, while to the east flexed burial was practiced and the dead sprinkled with red ocher.

The culture pattern throughout the Great Lakes area appears to have been Laurentian, distinguishable by its working tools such as adzes and gouges. These northern food collectors used knives and points of slate as well as many copper tools (made along the shores of Lake Superior) – gouges, semi-lunar knives and points with bayonet-like stems – which suggests that the manufacture of these implements by the people of the Laurentian culture constituted a local industry whose products were traded throughout eastern North America. The Laurentian culture included elements of more southern type but it also demonstrated its adaptive ability in the northern forests.

West of the forest border on the Great Plains there were still people hunting bison with lanceolate points. These people were beginning to use notched and stemmed triangular projectile points, apparently for the same hunting purpose. The old lanceolate forms continued at least until 4000 BC on the prairies and perhaps longer north of the Great Lakes.

On the plains the tools and customs of earlier food collectors lasted into the early centuries of maximum temperature rise, but there was a gap in occupation between 4000 and 3000 BC. The gap is larger in some but smaller in other areas. One supposes that earlier collectors retreated eastward out of the prairies and westward from the short-grass country into mountain camps. By 3000 BC there emerged on the prairies and the southern plains a culture pattern derived from the older eastern Archaic type. Most points were notched or stemmed; bison, deer and small mammals were hunted and plants collected. In the area between eastern Texas and the Edwards Plateau the Balcones culture emerged, while a variant of the Archaic culture developed on the central plains; a typical example is to be found at Logan Creek, Nebraska. North along the forest border the culture pattern is certainly derived from the eastern woodlands.

Bison drives were based on drive lines converging towards a canyon. The lines were made of rocks and brush and led either to a steep slope formed by an alluvial fan or to a sheer drop over which the animals plunged. Butchering took place at the spot where the animals fell. These sites were especially common and are best known on the northwestern plains, but others have now been found west of the continental divide. On the high plains the return of the bison after 1500 BC led to the use of the drive and the pound for killing or capturing these huge animals. These techniques were commonly used by 500 BC and in a few places lasted into the late 19th century AD.

In the desert grasslands of the West, notched and stemmed points were first used about 6000 BC, but did not altogether replace lanceolate forms until 1500 BC. The old forms lasted longer at high altitudes and latitudes in and along the Rocky Mountains. This may reflect the continuing presence of big game in sheltered regions, hence the persistence of old hunting traditions. In the northern Rockies people moved up to higher altitudes between 5200 and 3800 BC, but continued to hunt big game. Their culture is called the Bitterroot culture. During later, moister episodes they spread out of the high valleys on to open plains, their numbers increasing with the returning bison.

In the high grasslands of the northern Rocky Mountains later food collectors built villages in forested valleys, such as the Salmon River, and hunted bison, elk, deer, antelope and mountain sheep. By comparison with their relatives in the western Great Basin, they were well off. Their villages include bigger houses and more of them, reflecting the superior habitat. In addition to big game, these relatives of the Bitterroot people caught salmon and steelhead (a type of trout) with harpoons, a technique still in use in the Salmon River valley. Skin working was practiced and bows backed with sinew and made of laminated mountain sheep horns were used, probably before the birth of Christ. Pottery was occasionally made. The earliest pottery was in use in a few areas, possibly several centuries before Christ, but the next pottery tradition began as late as 1500 AD. This round-bottom pottery was followed by protohistoric flat-bottom, or flower-pot ware. Almost all the pottery was made and used on or along the flanks of the Snake River plain in the Idaho.

In the desert regions below 5,000 feet and south of the 42nd parallel, populations dispersed and declined with the

big game. The survivors turned to hunting small mammals and to collecting seeds. The adaptation to these conditions gave rise to the Desert culture, one of whose regional expressions is the Lovelock culture of Nevada. These desert people apparently lived in family groups of about five, frequently moving from one area of limited resources to another. They made extensive use of plant fibers for making mats, twine and baskets.

Environmental differences led to variations in the Desert culture. In the Great Basin, hunters, fishers and gatherers were involved in a relentless food quest. Some areas were more productive than others. Around lakes, springs and marshes people congregated to hunt water game and catch fish. These people achieved a high degree of adaptation. Small camps practiced specialized activities such as spear-fishing or the collection of mussels or pine nuts. Characteristic goods were made of grass, reeds and rabbit skins, and the dew-claws of deer were made into rattles for dancing. In the mountains bighorn sheep were stalked by men wearing leather helmets with mountain sheep horns. A successful antelope drive could support several families for days.

The Desert culture variant in the Southwest, called the Cochise culture, is found in the high grasslands and mountain valleys. Implements attributed to the earliest phase of the Cochise culture have been found in association with elephant remains. Milling stones evolved from small flat slabs, for nether stones, to deep basin forms in the latest pre-pottery period. Cochise adaptation to grasslands included hunting activity, attested by side-notched points which appear after 4000 BC. The adaptive ability of the Cochise people was important, because they were to become the first North American farmers and the first Southwesterners to make pottery, serving as the earliest link between the civilized people in the south and the food collectors and village farmers in the north.

In southern California the later food collectors followed stream valleys to the coast, collecting shellfish and processing plant foods with the help of milling stones. The southern California variant of the Desert culture, the La Jolla culture, bears a close resemblance to the post-5000 BC Basin cultures except that adjustment to coastal waters was important in southern California. During the period of high temperatures some coastal bays became silted up, due to cliff erosion and a rising sea level.

In the Columbia Plateau people settled in the open forests of Douglas fir and western yellow pine. There they hunted elk and deer and by 9000 BC were fishing for salmon. However, seine nets came into common use only about 700 years ago. Bison were occasionally hunted up to the 19th century AD. In the summer, berries and roots (such as kause and camas) were gathered. By 1000 BC these people were beginning to build villages in the tributary valleys of the Snake, Columbia and Fraser Rivers. In later times people practiced cyclical settlement in winter villages and summer camps. Shellfish were common food, and by

1300 AD there was widespread trade in marine shells well into the interior east of the Cascade Range.

Sub-cultures developed north and south of the lower Snake River and north of the Okanogan highlands on the present-day border with Canada. Early northern houses were small, shallow and saucer shaped, with brush covering over poles which may have been tied at the top. Later, rectangular mat lodges up to 40 feet long were built. Large deep circular pit houses with benches were built for winter use. South of the Snake River the earliest villages of about 1000 BC contained large oval dwellings with floors which might be on or below the ground. These were timber-frame structures, 25 to 30 feet long and 20 to 24 feet wide, with walls made of bundles of bark or grass. Houses of this type were still in use when Lewis and Clark went down the Clearwater River in 1805.

Along the Pacific Coast people spread down the river valleys from the forested foothills, developing cultures adapted to the environmental peculiarities of each drainage. By 500 BC there was in the Fraser delta a rich slate-grinding industry as well as hunting and sea fishing. What is striking is the similarity in development on both sides of the Cascade Mountains; the foothills must have been a point of origin for both the people of the Coast and the Plateau.

In Puget Sound and along the Fraser Canyon the later food collectors used projectile points like those found east of the Cascades. Deer and elk were hunted in the woods which enclosed the prairies of Puget Sound and Vancouver Island. Later people improved early flake adzes by grinding new materials such as nephrite. They also switched to ground-slate points, collected and ate enormous quantities of shellfish and took migratory fish by building weirs across the big rivers flowing to the sea.

The pattern of adaptation to river valley conditions continued as far as the Pacific Coast, where a flourishing culture was in full swing by 1300 AD. Large plank houses, harpoons for deep-sea fishing and carved boxes and masks were known at the time on the Olympic Peninsula.

The Eskimos. In the far north the Eskimo-Aleut people were established along the Pacific Coast by 2000 BC. Larger populations were concentrated in the milder climate of the Aleutian islands (16,000 people in historic times) than ever developed on the mainland. Eskimos occupied the tundra as it developed into a major habitat after 2000 BC, and were

A buffalo hunt on snow shoes, by the 19th century artist George Catlin. Thousands of years earlier the Indians of the Great Plains were already living off the great herds of bison, often herding them over cliffs to their death.

Left: A reconstructed Haida Indian longhouse from Queen Charlotte Island. As early as 1300 AD a rich, highly-organized foraging culture emerged along the lush Northwest Pacific coast.

Right: A rare scene by John White, the Elizabethan artist, shows Eskimos in kayaks and with bows and arrows in an encounter with Europeans. At this time the Eskimo climax Thule culture was already hundreds of years old.

found everywhere by 1000 BC. The oceanic character of western Eskimo and Aleut culture may reflect a general pattern of coastal life spreading from Puget Sound to the Bering Strait. The early Eskimos and Aleuts in the Gulf of Alaska were hunters of sea mammals, birds and fish. They used bone to make harpoons, needles and pressure flaking tools, and made boats and floats from skins and bladders. Their tool-making techniques and styles (which produced fine blades and points of stone) are like those of related people in northern lands of the Old World. These similarities indicate a common environment and a widespread sharing of ideas and skills.

On the Alaskan mainland prehistoric hunters formed small groups for hunting caribou across the great barren grounds, using tents in the summer. On the Arctic slope a distinct culture evolved, characterized by the hunting of sea mammals, while in eastern Canada the use of small tools for hunting was a feature of the Dorset culture.

As in the dry regions of the West, a pattern of regional adaptation is detectable. Unlike the situation in the arid grasslands, the Eskimos developed a climax culture (known as Thule) on the tundra. This evolved about 800–900 AD and was the culture discovered by early Europeans who recorded the use of dog teams with sledges, the kayak and umiak and igloos in winter, the hunting of seals and the making of fine slate and ivory carving, tailored skin clothing, and barbed, toggled harpoons. The lowering of temperature, which minimized variations in precipitation, made a vast cold desert common to all Eskimos and this was the chief stimulus to their way of life.

It has often been assumed that the first appearance of small tools marks the initial spread of Eskimo groups, but the lanceolate points of the Arctic are clearly derived from the traditions of big game hunters in the arid western grasslands, known in the sub-Arctic by 3000 BC. Along the northwest coast it is possible that culture patterns spread north from Puget Sound after 6000 BC, to be developed regionally by those later people who came to be known as Eskimos. The makers of Arctic small tools would, in that case, have spread eastward as a result of population pressures and would have reached the Labrador coast somewhere around 1000 BC.

A miniature Eskimo mask from the early Dorset culture, radiocarbon dated to 720 BC. It is made of whale or narwhal ivory.

Agriculture. While later food collectors in North America were adjusting to the high temperatures between 5200 and 3000 BC, people in the central Mexican highlands were experimenting with plants. As large mammals disappeared and small mammals declined, men turned to cultivation.

The development of plant cultivation as a means of livelihood was slow and modest, both in Mexico and North America. It was not until 2300 BC that Mexican farmers had become self-sufficient food producers, although the earliest Mexican plants were under cultivation by 5000 BC and maize followed soon after. Despite this gradual development, the idea spread northwards rapidly.

By 3900 BC prehistoric dwellers at Bat Cave, New Mexico, were tilling the ground. The Bat Cave situation is so far unique in the American Southwest, yet it must illustrate the conditions of agricultural development in the arid regions. Bat Cave is nearly 7,000 feet above sea level and demonstrates the movement of people to higher altitudes in the period of greatest temperature. The beginnings of maize cultivation at Bat Cave coincide with a moderate increase in moisture and possibly some temperature decline. Bat Cave suggests that the earliest North American farmers were strung out along the forest margins of the southern Rocky Mountains on the Arizona–New Mexico border. These early farmers of the Southwest belonged to the Cochise culture. They had already been well established in the region as a food-collecting people for several thousand years. Being at home with the climate and vegetation, they appear to be the logical initiators of farming in the region. Yet this is hindsight, and we must wonder why other food collectors did not start farming too.

Part of the answer is certainly that the low-lying Southwest was too hot and dry. On the other hand, the mountain masses, extending northward, offered similar climatic conditions at slightly lower altitudes. People of similar ancestry and probably language occupied these habitats, so that the limits of cultivation do not appear necessarily to have been climatic or cultural. It is noteworthy that the early maize at Bat Cave underwent a gradual evolutionary change. The changes from very small corn with few kernels to large corn with many kernels, from pod-popcorn to modern Indian maize, imply a long period of experiment. Maize cultivation reached the Colorado Plateau about 2000 BC and the hot deserts of Arizona and Sonora about 1000 BC.

The Cochise culture was not much affected by farming, and it seems likely that these first farming people remained also hunters and harvesters of wild plants in high country, while more intensive farming developed to the north and southwest. Other domesticated plants, such as beans, gourds and squash, spread slowly in prehistoric times. Different varieties of corn were traded into the Southwest from Mexico as the development of agriculture accelerated far to the south. The differential acquisition of new plants

A auperb *Mimbres* bowl (11th century AD) found in a late Mogollon burial in the American Southwest. The bowl was deliberately broken to release the owner's soul.

may also explain the different rates at which farming began in parts of the Southwest, even where climate may not have barred the development of farming.

The success of agriculture among the Cochise people resulted in expanding populations which began to concentrate in villages of some size, by or shortly after 250 BC. These early villages were marked by pit houses, semi-subterranean structures around which new fields developed. By the 1st century AD the pattern of farm life was established over much, though not all, of the Southwest. With the addition of pottery-making brought from Central Mexico, the Cochise culture began to develop two new patterns. One pattern belonged to the Mogollon people, who remained in the mountains where their Cochise ancestors had lived; the second to the Hohokam people of the hot desert.

The Mogollon culture was notable for its pottery (red-on-brown and plain red ware), for pithouse villages which survived until 1000 AD and a random way of locating houses on hills. After 1000 AD they began to make spectacularly beautiful pottery called *Mimbres* ware and took to building masonry houses above ground. Although they are best known as farmers, the Mogollon were also bison hunters and may have hunted other big game. Many of their villages are found at altitudes above 4,000 feet, in open grassland or parkland areas. The economy and artifact types of this culture resemble those of prehistoric populations to the north, along the western slope of the Rocky Mountains and in the eastern Great Basin.

The Hohokam culture is characterized by large towns in later prehistoric times, but the basic living units were the rancherias, scattered in favored localities on or along the edge of the desert. The villages soon assumed a plan, with surface-built, rectangular houses. The Hohokam survived as farmers in a hostile terrain because they had mastered the technique of irrigation, using rivers such as the Gila and collecting runoff from summer rains. More than 100 miles of canals have been traced in the desert, a tribute to the sophistication of Hohokam farming. Their red-on-buff pottery was very similar to Mogollon red-on-brown in its earliest phases, but quickly developed distinctive forms and decorative styles.

In the mesas and canyons of the Colorado Plateau, the Basketmaker-Pueblo (or Anasazi) people lived in deep pithouses and caves. These people were so named because they made baskets which have been preserved in the arid conditions; they also cultivated tobacco and raised domesticated dogs. As farmers they took up irrigation and developed floodwater controls, involving simple materials but sophisticated techniques. For instance, they learned to put brushwood across canyons to trap sand, forming check

Hohokam pottery from Snaketown in southern Arizona, ranging in date from 100 BC to 1100 AD. Living in a desert environment, the early Hohokam farmers developed elaborate irrigation systems.

dams which reduced channel-cutting by spreading flood-waters. New sediment was added to flood plains to extend the area for potential farming. When erosion was severe, they farmed sand dunes where the water table was high, or alluvial fans where moisture collected. These skills permitted population growth even in a marginal farming area. In good times the Colorado Plateau had sufficient water, an adequate growing season and big game.

By 900 AD Anasazi communities had developed plazas, or squares around which houses stood, and a street system. They appear to have learned pottery-making from Mogollon and perhaps from the Hohokam people to the south. The pottery was distinctive, beginning in plain gray, but soon developing into a handsome black-on-white ware. In later prehistory the Anasazi used glaze paint for decoration.

About 400 AD conditions for, and knowledge of farming were sufficient to establish the Fremont culture in the eastern Great Basin. Desert culture food collectors began to cultivate maize, beans and squash. Their villages, pottery and fields were small-scale versions of Mogollon and Anasazi farm life in the Southwest. They continued farming until 1200 AD when they returned to food collecting and to bison hunting about 1500 AD, possibly due to the increasing aridity of the area. While farming they had continued their food collecting, so agriculture never completely replaced their old methods.

The farmers of the East became as precisely adapted to their habitats as the food collectors had been, living either in dispersed houses or, where circumstances permitted, congregating in villages of some size. Farming itself probably did not create towns in eastern North America but was the result of the population increase in the region. But the development of agriculture did not prevent the regional development of older food collecting cultures in the East. The variations correspond to vegetation patterns, and the people of the Gulf Coast plain belonged to a different pottery complex from those in the oak/deer biome to the north. The practice of farming was mainly restricted to flood plains and areas where annual floods supplied new silt and maintained disturbed land surfaces on which selected plants, such as amaranth and the seed-producing sunflower, might easily be cultivated.

In the oak–hickory woodlands prehistoric people continued to collect large quantities of acorns, hickory nuts and walnuts. The farmers probably did not introduce the use of storage pits, since these were already in use in non-farming regions, and were therefore taken up as a convenience for the greater storage requirements of developed agriculture. Outside the ceremonial centers of the time, population growth was apparently represented by additional, rather than by larger villages, until late prehistoric times. Large towns were not common until after 1000 AD.

In the eastern woodlands farming followed pottery, a reversal of the sequence in the Southwest. Pottery reached Florida by 2000 BC, 1,700 years before it was used in the Mogollon and Hohokam cultures, but the cultivation of

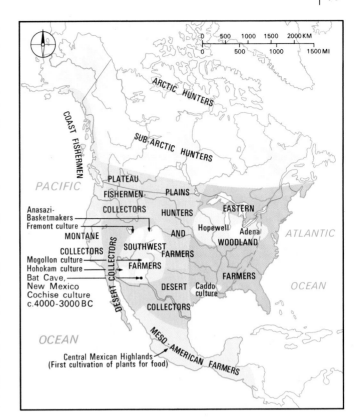

[Map 4] North American cultures, 2000 BC–1500 AD.

maize, beans and squash began as late as 1000 BC in the alluvial valleys of the East, almost 3,000 years later than at Bat Cave. Farming communities arose along the flanks of the Mississippi floodplain in the Illinois and Ohio valleys. In Florida the earliest maize may have been grown in drained fields. At Fort Center it is known that a circular ditch was dug, possibly to drain low-lying ground, which was then farmed. Along the piedmont of the Atlantic Coast region, early farming began on floodplains, only later spreading down the valleys towards the coastal plain.

Farming spread across the prairies from south to north and east to west. By the 3rd century AD a few people were farming in most of the river valleys, having adopted a version of Woodland culture which had appeared in the prairies by 500 BC. The start of this new culture was marked by the appearance of Woodland pottery, which spread westward to the foot of the Rocky Mountains, while on the northwestern plains in Montana and Alberta people were still driving bison over cliffs to get their principal food. There were soon well-established small villages on tributaries of the major rivers crossing the central plains – three to five circular houses built in saucer-shaped depressions. Cultivation marks in the fields of these villages seem to have been made with bison scapula hoes, and clearance of fields for planting may have occurred in areas where trees were felled for house timbers. Prehistoric man had already begun to modify his environment. These earlier farms reached west as far as the 100th meridian, but later ones were not established so far to the west because of a prehistoric drought.

In the 12th and 13th centuries the hunting of game declined sharply, owing to reduction of timber and erosion in parts of the prairie country. Deer especially were affected, making bison relatively more important even while the bison population was itself reduced in some areas. On the southern plains a concentration of farmers developed in the Oklahoma–Texas panhandle, maintaining trade relations with the Rio Grande pueblos. The last stage of prehistoric farming represented another movement of people in the south-central prairie. Villages developed on the Big Bend of the Arkansas where early Spanish explorers found Quivira, the province of the historic Wichita Indians.

A series of changes in prehistoric climate has been postulated by Reid Bryson and David Baerreis of the University of Wisconsin. These have been applied to the archaeology of farming villages in the northern plains by Donald Lehmer of Dana College. These studies show that the changing settlements of the central plains were paralleled in the Middle Missouri valley, where large farm towns were established in a tropical climate about 900 AD. These corn-growing communities reached west up to Missouri until 1250 AD, when a change to cool, dry weather forced an eastward contraction and dispersal of villages which were also reduced in size. Between 1450 and 1550 AD more favorable conditions allowed an increase in the numbers and range of farming communities, but this was followed by a period of cool summers so that villages were again restricted by a marginal economy until 1675. The first Europeans arriving in the 18th century found large palisaded villages containing great houses and populations of several hundred people.

It is significant that farmers were as sensitive as the food collectors to climatic change. Expansion into the prairies probably followed population increases in the woodlands and the acquisition of farming skills suitable for floodplain farming. This knowledge permitted effective settlement, but the precise requirements of agriculture placed its practitioners at the mercy of precipitation and temperature changes perhaps more than in the Southwest. No irrigation was practiced on the plains, so that changes in stream flow and in growing conditions forced farmers in the central grasslands to move about a great deal.

The effects of civilization. The rise of high civilizations in Mesoamerica had a strong impact upon later food collectors in much of North America. In the Southwest its influence came primarily after farming was well established, while in the Southeast Mesoamerican influences penetrated almost simultaneously with knowledge of agriculture. The source of new ideas and material goods for the desert regions was certainly central highland Mexico, but for the Gulf coastal plain these influences originated in lowland Mesoamerica or northern South America.

The nearby presence of civilization changed customs by altering men's perceptions of their world. Now they looked south, aware of distant power. The initial effect was to increase the difference between farmers and collectors. But the long-term effect was to blend together the cultural variations of the regions which had been evolving over millennia.

North Americans did not learn to use hieroglyphs or to build paved roads, like the Maya, but they did undertake an architecture which could be described as monumental by their own standards. Towns developed, but not cities, nor could 50,000 people congregate in these market places, as was possible in Teotihuacan in Mexico. There was no astronomy, no calendar and no hierarchical political system in either the Southwest or the Southeast. Yet the impact of an advanced culture is observable everywhere.

The first Mexican influences, if we discount farming, were probably felt about 3,000 years ago in the lower Mississippi valley, and 2,000 years ago in southern Arizona and northern Sonora or Chihuahua. In the southeastern coastal plain and the river valleys opening to the Gulf there was an environment akin to the subtropical lowlands of Yucatan, northern South America and the Caribbean.

The arrival of new culture elements in the Southeast appears to date from about 1200 to 1000 BC at Poverty Point, Louisiana and a few centuries later at Fort Center, Florida. The development of the Adena-Hopewell culture in the Ohio and Illinois river valleys also reveals these new influences. Burial mounds, temple mounds, earthworks of octagonal or round shape, concentrated numbers of burials on platforms, multiple types of burials and selected trade goods bear witness to the initial phase of civilized influence. Burial mounds were widespread. They are sometimes conical in shape, sometimes rectangular, often made of earth but occasionally of large rocks. They occur far beyond the limits of temple mounds, but burial mounds often had a small primary triangular mound as the starting point of construction.

The more complex early features occur in the lower Mississippi valley and the Gulf coastal plain from eastern Texas to northern Florida. Further north, architecture was simpler except that a local climax may have been achieved between 300 BC and 200 AD in the Ohio Hopewell culture area, which was ecologically restricted, comprising only the major alluvial valleys of the lower Great Lakes. Outside these selected areas later food collectors and farmers still lived in small villages or camps.

In the Ohio valley of West Virginia, western Pennsylvania, northern Kentucky, Ohio and Indiana there arose a distinctive early culture – the Adena culture. It has clear antecedents in late food collecting cultures of the region and predates the Hopewell culture, yet the Adena also has features that suggest Mesoamerican influence. Both the Adena and Hopewell cultures are variants of the Woodland culture. The Adena culture began about 1000 BC with low, simple burial mounds, houses supported by a single row of posts, and the use of simple tobacco pipes. New features emerged later, such as rectangular houses with double or single rows of posts, large oval burial mounds

with log chambers, earthwork enclosures, copper gorgets (ornamental plaques hung around the neck) and strings of freshwater pearls, incised tablets, tubular pipes and mica (used to make cut-out shapes). Social or class distinctions in the Adena culture, with accompanying ceremonies related to the patterns of the Southeast and beyond to Mesoamerica, have been adduced from the contrast between simple cremation burials and the sumptuously furnished burial mounds obviously built for more important people.

The evolution of the Hopewell culture coincides with an apparent population shift westward from the Adena cul-

ture area. There was some overlapping in the Ohio Valley but the main development area of the Hopewell culture extended from Ohio west to Missouri and even Minnesota. There were concentrations in the alluvial valleys most suited to the cultivation of maize and other crops. Ceremonial centers grew up in the early centuries AD. Burial mounds were sometimes built with multiple chambers of wood, sometimes without a roof. Far-flung trade provided copper for ear spools (spool-shaped ornaments inserted through the lobes of the ears), obsidian from the mountains of the west and grizzly bear teeth from the northwestern plains or northern Rocky Mountains. These goods were traded over the entire eastern woodlands and were often placed in Ohio valley burials.

This luxury trade illustrates the importance of ceremonial life in the Hopewell culture. Despite this great trade network, which seems to have resulted from the stimulus of contact with a higher culture, Hopewell life preserved many older traditions and passed them on to later people. By 400 to 500 AD Hopewell arts and crafts had declined, and the large burial mounds were no longer built. The small mounds which were built were set on bluffs, and stone slabs were used instead of log chambers.

In the Southeast, the period after 1000 BC marks the early period of burial mounds which were either built up with layers of earth, or consisted of log tombs covered by earth. At first only one body was interred in each, but later mounds contain several burials. Southeasterners maintained their regional differences, despite the impact of a higher culture bringing ceremonial activities and a wide-

Above: Reconstruction model of an Adena house in Ohio, with wattled sides, hearth and smokehole in the roof, based on the excavated postholes of an actual house. The Adena people were the first of the mound builders.

A Hopewell burial mound in White City, Illinois, after excavation. The Hopewell people traded extensively in goods coming from as far as the Rocky Mountains.

spread trade in luxury goods for burials. There were culture differences between those living in the southern Appalachian Mountains, the Georgia–Florida–Alabama region and the lower Mississippi valley, although stamped pottery designs, some rather complicated, were used in all three regions. In the Southeast people obtained or copied panpipes, platform pipes and copper ear spools, apparently from the Ohio valley. Towards 500 AD burial mounds became smaller but more numerous than before, with as many as 70 in one area.

Between the 6th and 11th centuries AD there emerged more clearly defined regional characteristics, but the use of ceremony also indicates much wider connections. Temple mounds appeared along with copper masks depicting long-nosed gods. Conch shells were widely traded and pottery, decorated with checks and complex stamp designs, was common. In the far Southeast a culture known as the Weeden Island culture appeared as a synthesis of earlier mountain and coastal traditions. In the lower Mississippi a firm Gulf tradition grew out of earlier developments. The most striking changes, reflecting new Mesoamerican influences, appear, however, on the southern plains in east Texas and adjacent areas. The Caddo culture, with its temple mounds, numerous well-built houses and pottery with engraved scroll and meander designs of clearly Mesoamerican stylistic origin, appeared suddenly about 500 AD.

Just north of the Mason–Dixon line a new culture pattern of great importance emerged. About 1000 AD this culture, known as the Mississippi Pattern, grew rapidly and affected the entire Southeast. It resembled the early Caddo culture except that its ceremonial centers were far larger. Towns developed with large temple mounds, plazas, burial mounds and semi-subterranean ceremonial centers. The largest of these was Cahokia, Illinois, but other great centers were established at Spiro, Oklahoma; Etowah, Georgia; Moundville, Alabama and a lesser one at Hiwassee Island, Tennessee. These centers imply the certain rise of a class or perhaps caste system and large populations. There were green corn ceremonies and apparently a more efficient farming system, using a new variety of maize.

Some communities were more affected by the Mississippi pattern than others. Most contained shell ornaments and pottery tempered with shell, as well as long-nosed god images, sun and eagle symbols, and new effigy pots and lobed pottery. Some centers also had palisades which were possibly fortifications, but ordinary villages kept their old ways, reminiscent of the Weeden Island culture. The symbols on pottery, the masks and multiple temple mounds, suggest a major religious development, often called the Southern Cult. This cult with its carinated (shouldered) pottery and new architectural styles, is clearly Mesoamerican in inspiration. For a brief period of a few centuries it dominated the region, a last flowering before the European conquest.

The Mississippi culture pattern appeared in the upper Great Lakes region and its farming complex reached north

Ceremonial pot in the shape of a head, from the late Temple Mound culture, Arkansas, which was clearly open to Mesoamerican influences from the great civilizations to the south.

out of the central Mississippi valley. By the 10th century farming villages had spread to the northern plains in the alluvial valleys of the middle Missouri. In Wisconsin effigy mounds of animals replaced the mounds of Illinois Hopewell type. Oval houses were common and elbow pipes replaced the handsome effigy platform pipes. Villages increased to 10 or 20 acres while ceremonial centers reached 100 acres in extent. Stone carving, the embossing of copper and engraving of shell are all components of this Southeastern complex in which the Mississippi culture reached its peak. In all areas the economy rested on a new type of maize and the use of flint hoes.

To the east the Mississippi culture had reached the middle and upper Ohio by 1400 AD. The effects were felt in Indiana. These northern and eastern groups were only poor relations of the southern centers of Mississippi culture, but they illustrate the far-flung influence of Mesoamerican civilization in eastern North America.

Mesoamerican influence in the American Southwest was probably felt earlier than in the Southeast, if one starts with farming at nearly 4000 BC. But brown-on-red pottery resembling Central Mexican wares was introduced to the Mogollon people about 250 BC, nearly 2,000 years later than the appearance of the earliest ceramics in Florida. Architecture and other elements of high culture also seem to have appeared later in the Southwest.

From the Hohokam culture of the hot desert of Arizona there developed a strikingly Mexican culture pattern exemplified by a large ceremonial center at Snaketown. This locality was a farming village in the 1st century AD but acquired a distinctive Mesoamerican flavor after the 6th century. Some elements are reminiscent of northern Mexico and others have more in common with central Mexican culture, but a few are uniquely Hohokam. As in the Southeast, the pattern of village farming persisted, despite centuries of influence from and trade with distant regions.

From 600 to 900 AD colonial Hohokam culture produced carved and plain stone bowls and mortars, partly and fully-grooved axes, burial and early platform mounds (apparently temple mounds), trough-type metates (millstones), small handstones and pottery designs remarkably Mesoamerican in appearance. Paint palettes and mosaic mirrors are distinctive in style. Designs on pottery, closely resembling Mexican motifs, include alligator-like monsters, twin deities, serpents with horns, big cats and turtles. Often these designs were laid out in quarters, with a god, a two-headed serpent with star symbols, an eagle and dancing twin deities in each. The designs were painted in red on a buff wash which was itself an innovation.

Small ball courts were introduced into Hohokam society and were followed by larger ones. Copper bells were being traded about 1000 AD. Cotton was grown and irrigation systems were established in the Gila River valley by at least 900 AD. The temple mounds were similar to South-eastern and Mexican ones in that they were rubble-filled and built up with layers of earth, but a new feature was plastering with caliche (nitrate-bearing gravel) on the platform and slopes. The engraving and sculpting of shell was also an important feature of the Hohokam culture, and the technique resembles that of the Mississippi culture. The etching of shell (using acid and a resist material) was unique to the Hohokam people so far as is known and craft specialists with separate workshops may have existed at Snaketown. Rectangular houses replaced square ones and rubbish was put on new artificial trash mounds instead of being scattered over the settlement. Cremation in pits was also an innovation. One of the most important results of Mexican influence was the northward expansion of Hohokam culture out of the desert between 600 and 900 AD.

To the northeast of the Hohokam the Mogollon people remained largely unaffected by events among the Hohokam or in Mexico. Not until about 900 AD did Mexican elements appear – primarily pottery designs and the use of red paint on a white background. Some of these ideas could have been borrowed from their Hohokam neighbors, but differences in pottery type and the geography of the Mogollon area suggest that civilization touched the Mogollon people directly if lightly. It may have been the Mogollon predilection for hunting and high country that made the social and ceremonial features of Mesoamerica less attractive to them.

About 900 AD the Anasazi village began to develop, and town plazas appeared. The plaza may have been Mexican

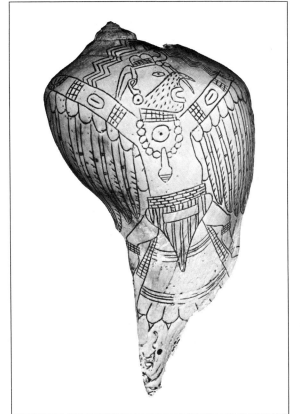

Left: Incised design of an eagle dancer on a conch shell from an Oklahoma temple mound. These were widely traded.

Below: Turquoise mosaic inlay, reminiscent of Aztec work, on ornaments of the Anasazi or Pueblo type, from Hawikuh, New Mexico.

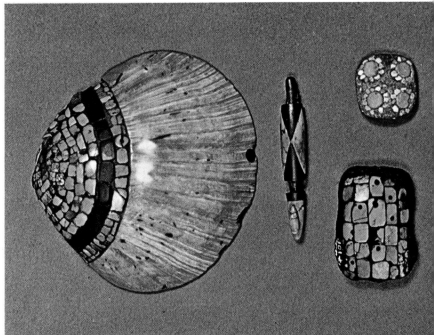

in origin, but no direct connection with Mexico can now be proved. Other developments reached Anasazi communities at almost the same time as they reached the Hohokam area.

It may have been through the sharing of ideas and trade that the Anasazi culture spread southward within the next 300 years, so that Anasazi and Hohokam people lived side by side. The Hohokam culture influence has been observed at Alkali Ridge, in south Utah, in the 8th century AD and is represented by trash mounds and a red-on-orange pottery whose paint, design and forms resemble some Hohokam pottery of that period. There were also marked similarities in men's but not women's clothing, which has led Albert Schroeder of the National Park Service to think that traders were responsible for the exchange of ideas between Anasazi and Hohokam people. It is possible but not proven that these were Mexican traders.

At the Chaco Canyon and Aztec National Monuments the later effects of civilization are plainly visible. Pueblo Bonito has a temple mound with steps and balustrades, square columns on a building front, and round towers; and copper bells, turquoise mosaics and conch shell trumpets of Hohokam type have been found. Mesoamerican influence may also be detectable in the great Kiva (the structure in which ceremonies were held) at Aztec.

Late Anasazi prehistory is marked by adjustment to regional climatic changes and by the development of great centers of farming and ceremony with considerable populations, as at the Mesa Verde, Aztec and Chaco Canyon communities. Mural paintings, polychrome pottery, sun symbols and an intense religious life provided the Anasazi people with a regional cultural climax of stunning proportions. They even built dwellings up to five stories high.

There are some similarities in the influence of civilization in the two affected regions of North America, the Southwest and the Southeast. These similarities are most striking

Taos Pueblo near Sante Fe, New Mexico. This ancient communal Indian dwelling, still flourishing, is the lineal descendant of the larger prehistoric cliff dwellings and pueblos of the Southwest.

in the late prehistoric period. A few great centers mark each regional climax. Temple mounds, house mounds, burial mounds, multiple burials, painted pottery, shell engraving, eagle and sun symbols, serpent designs and far-flung trade are common to both the Southwest and the Southeast. Both regions exhibit an increasing richness of culture southward towards Mesoamerica. Even the method of mound construction is more or less the same. Some communities have plazas and a concentration of ceremonial structures. Just as Mesoamerican ideas spread north to the Great Lakes and into the Dakotas, the influence of Mesoamerica also reached as far as the northern edge of the Great Basin. In each case some dilution of these new cultural influences occurred.

The Southwest and the Southeast are also similar in experiencing cult complexes which were introduced in the 14th and 15th centuries AD. In the Southeast this was the Southern cult. In the Southwest it has been referred to as a Quetzalcoatl or plumed serpent cult, which survived in a modified form among the Anasazi until the 19th century.

The Southwest was left in isolation by the collapse of the Guasave culture in the Sinaloa and Nayarit states of Mexico, which had linked what is now the southwestern United States with Mesoamerican civilization. When Europeans arrived in the 16th century the Hohokam area was characterized by small rancherias, while the Anasazi had abandoned Mesa Verde for more dispersed farming villages. Whether the Southeast had also lost the intermediaries between itself and the regions of high culture is not so evident, because the links have not yet been clearly established. Elements of Mesoamerican civilization may have been diffused by trade in specific goods, the spread of ideas, or by the actual migration of people.

Teotihuacan: Metropolis of Ancient Mexico

Unlike the jungle-covered ruins of the Maya zone, Teotihuacan (*below*) was never a "lost city." There was a later Aztec town on the same site, and Montezuma II (the last native ruler before the Spanish Conquest) made offerings among the pyramids of the ancient city, built, it was believed, in mythological times by a people whose name had not been preserved. As one Aztec informant told the Spanish friar, Bernardino de Sahagún: "It is called Teotihuacan. And when the rulers died, they buried them there. Then they built a pyramid over them . . . And they built the pyramids of the sun and moon very large, just like mountains. It is unbelievable when it is said that they are made by hands, but giants still lived there then."

The truth behind the myth has been revealed by archaeological excavation. The first small-scale occupation of the site belongs to about the first century BC, and sometime before 200 AD the city began to take on its present shape with the construction of the Pyramid of the Plumed Serpent, the Pyramids of the Sun and Moon, and the shrines which flank the Street of the Dead. The power of Teotihuacan was not to last. Around 750 AD much of the central zone was looted and burned; temples were partially dismantled and thrown down, material was deliberately buried. It is uncertain whether the city was destroyed by invasion from outside or by revolution from within, but its collapse changed the entire course of Mexican history.

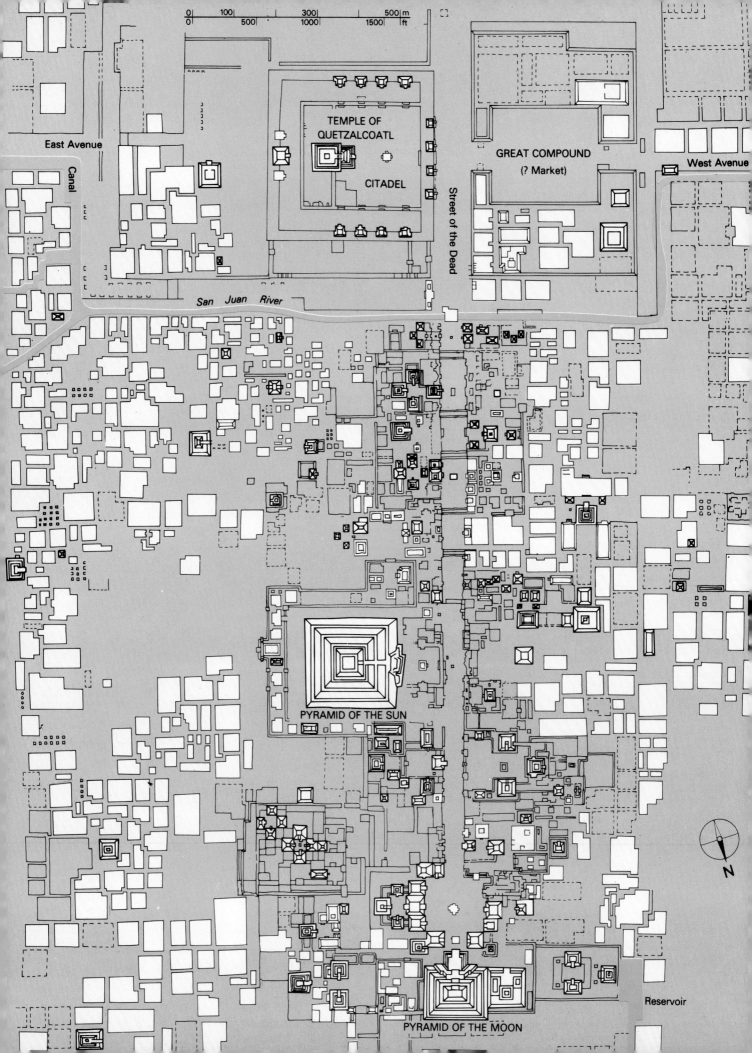

East Avenue

Canal

0 100 300 500 m
0 500 1000 1500 ft

TEMPLE OF
QUETZALCOATL

CITADEL

GREAT COMPOUND
(? Market)

West Avenue

Street of the Dead

San   Juan   River

PYRAMID OF THE SUN

N

Reservoir

PYRAMID OF THE MOON

Teotihuacan (ground plan, *left* and reconstruction, *above*) was both an administrative, commercial and manufacturing center and a temple city. In the 6th century AD its population could have been as high as 200,000 people. It was laid out on a precise grid plan, even the river being canalized to conform. At the center, where the East-West Avenue crosses the Street of the Dead, are the main temples, the principal market, the "Citadel" and some of the major palaces and mansions of the nobility.

The two great pyramids are temple platforms, not tombs. The great Pyramid of the Sun is just over 200 feet high and contains more than 30 million cubic feet of earth, rubbish and sun-dried mud brick. The shrine on the top has now disappeared. The city covered eight square miles (larger than Imperial Rome), with the houses of the ordinary people nearer the outskirts, and contained more than 500 workshops (of potters, weavers, sculptors) as well as colonies of "foreign" Mesoamerican merchants.

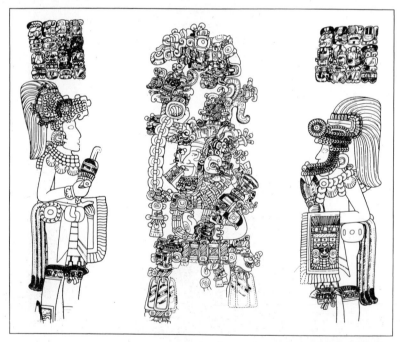

Left, above: Obsidian objects from Teotihuacan. Export of these objects of natural volcanic glass was a main source of the city's wealth. They included projectile points, knives, scrapers and even human-shaped figurines. Such objects, dated as early as 200 AD, have been found at a Maya site nearly 800 miles away.

Teotihuacan not only exported obsidian objects, but imported "Thin Orange" pottery made in southern Puebla, like the effigy pot above. This ware has been found all over Mesoamerica, from northwest Mexico to the southern end of Maya territory, proving that the centers of regional civilization at this time were in close touch.

Opposite page, above: Detail from a wall painting from Teotihuacan showing the figure of a priest wearing the eye mask of the Rain God. To his right are two undeciphered glyphs, possibly representing a headdress and an animal head. Another inscription of five signs, and single glyphs on pottery and frescoes have been found, but no other evidence of writing at Teotihuacan.

A Maya stela from Tikal betrays the strong influence of Teotihuacan on Maya art and culture. Flanking the richly-dressed Maya dignitary are two warriors in Teotihuacan uniform, one holding a shield showing a Rain God face similar to the one in the fresco at Teotihuacan (right).

Right: The Rain God, later called Tlaloc by the Aztecs, on a fresco from Tetitla palace. With a spectacle-like mask over his eyes and another, fringed or tusked, over his mouth he appears everywhere at Teotihuacan. Here sylized streams of water pour from his open hands.

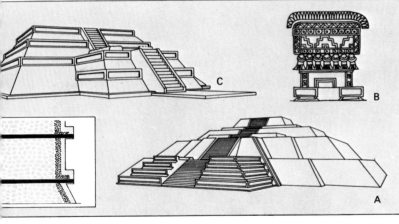

Teotihuacan architecture was notable for the use of a
rectangular panel with raised borders (*tablero*), placed above
a sloping zone (the *talud*). This *talud-tablero* device (*inset*) can
be seen on the Pyramid of the Moon (A), in the Tetitla
palace frescoes (B) and on a pyramid (C) at Guatemala City
belonging to a possible Teotihuacan colony.

Right: The Temple of Quetzalcoatl, the Plumed Serpent, is
centrally located in the Citadel compound, where the main
avenues intersect. The facade (here restored) is decorated with
alternating heads of Quetzalcoatl and a goggle-eyed
personage who may be the Rain God.

An undisturbed dish from a burial at Teotihuacan contains textile fragments, a few seeds, and parcels of straws or plant stems wrapped in bark cloth, preserved by incomplete charring from the hot cremation fire in the tomb itself. The burial, accompanied by over 1200 offerings, was unusually rich.

Below: The Palace of the Quetzal Butterfly, excavated and restored, gives an excellent impression of Teotihuacan architecture. The palace was probably the residence of the priests who served the attached shrine on the Street of the Dead. Rooms decorated with frescoes open onto a central patio.

Left: Reconstruction of a carved pillar from the Palace of the Quetzal Butterfly. These rectangular columns are made of rubble faced with dressed stone. The principal decorative motif, which gives the building its name, is a bird – a quetzal, or perhaps an owl – with stylized butterfly wings.

5. Mesoamerica

To the archaeologist, Mesoamerica (or Middle America) is a cultural unit rather than a geographical region. It consists of those parts of Mexico, Guatemala and the adjacent republics which were occupied at the time of the Spanish Conquest by the Maya, the Aztecs and various other civilized nations. In spite of local differences, these people shared in a common cultural tradition which had come into being by 1000 BC at the latest, and which persisted, with modifications and changes, until the arrival of the Europeans in the 16th century AD.

Early man in Mesoamerica. During his initial spread from North to South America, man must have passed through the narrow funnel of Mexico and the Isthmus of Tehuantepec. The date of this first migration is still unknown, but there is evidence that he had reached central Mexico some time before 20,000 BC.

The site of Tlapacoya, 15 miles east of Mexico City, was at that time an island or peninsula in the freshwater lake which filled the Valley of Mexico. Its shores offered suitable camping places for small migratory bands who hunted deer, cottontail rabbit, bear, waterfowl and various edible rodents. Traces of several camp sites have been recognized, all of them with radiocarbon dates clustering around 22,000 to 20,000 BC. Most of the artifacts from Tlapacoya were crudely chipped flakes and blades made from stone which could be picked up on the beach, but a few tools were made of good quality obsidian, quartz and basalt imported from some distance away.

After about 8000 BC, sites become more numerous and we get the first reasonably complete picture of life in a Pleistocene environment. Some of the discoveries can be directly linked with flint-working traditions already familiar in North America. The Mexican desert is ecologi-

Previous page: Warrior-columns in the Toltec capital of Tula.

Museum diorama of Stone Age hunters killing a mired mammoth in the Valley of Mexico at Tepexpan, about 7000 BC.

cally a continuation of the North American arid zone, and a scatter of fluted points demonstrates that Clovis hunters penetrated southwards into this area. Still further south, a fluted point has been found in the hills west of Guatemala City, and the fluting technique (though not the typical Clovis shape) was passed on to Panama and to South America where local varieties were invented.

None of the Mexican fluted points comes from a well-documented archaeological context, but there is clear evidence that the early inhabitants of Mexico, like their North American counterparts, were capable of hunting big game. The greatest concentration of kill sites is in the Valley of Mexico. Pollen analysis and geological studies show that the climate of the valley was cooler and more humid than it is today; the hills were covered with forests of pine and oak, and the floor of the basin was occupied by a shallow lake which was not drained until colonial times.

The climate was favorable to large game animals and to the hunters who preyed on them. At several points around the lake shore are kill sites where groups of hunters were able to drive mammoths into the marshy shallows. Here the creatures could be dispatched with spears and cut up on the spot. One such kill site was located at Santa Isabel Iztapan, where two separate mammoth skeletons were excavated in 1952 and 1954. From the jumbled position of its bones, the first mammoth had clearly been dismembered where it fell. Lodged between its ribs was a flint spearhead, and nearby lay the knives and scrapers used to butcher the animal. The second mammoth had also been butchered, and some of the bones showed deep cuts made by sharp blades of flint or obsidian. Among the bones were found a knife, a leaf-shaped spearpoint and a square-based lancehead. A radiocarbon date on the sediment surrounding the first mammoth places these events at about 7000 BC, and a comparable date of 7800 comes from another mammoth kill site at San Bartolo Atepehuacan.

To this period belongs one of the oldest human skeletons from Mexico, found at Tepexpan, less than two miles from Santa Isabel. The corpse lay face down, with the legs drawn up under the body, and was at the same level as the geological deposit which contains the mammoth kill sites. The Tepexpan skeleton was not excavated scientifically, and it is not clear whether it represents a deliberate burial (without any funerary offerings) or an accidental death by drowning in the swamps of the lake shore. In spite of these ambiguities the age is not in doubt, for the fluorine content of the bones closely matched that of the Pleistocene animal bones from the same locality. On the evidence of this skeleton, the mammoth hunters were indistinguishable from present day Mexican Indians.

The late Pleistocene may also have witnessed the earliest attempts at art. Mesoamerica has no early pictorial art comparable with the cave paintings of Europe, but in 1870 a Mexican naturalist discovered part of the pelvic region of an extinct llama 40 feet below ground surface at Tequixquiac, north of Mexico City. In its natural state the bone

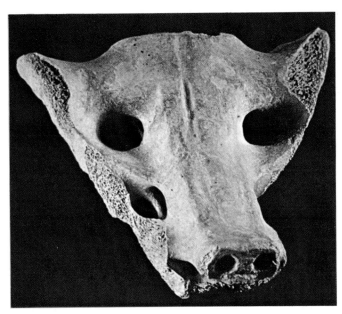

Pelvic bone of an extinct llama, carved to look like a dog or coyote; from Tequixquiac, north of Mexico City.

looks like the head of a dog or coyote, and this chance resemblance was enhanced by careful trimming and by the addition of nostril pits. The precise age is uncertain, but the general locality has yielded fossil animal bones of late Pleistocene age.

The mammoth kill sites represent the most dramatic aspect of Pleistocene life, but they give little idea of ordinary everyday activities. The home sites of the men who hunted in the Valley of Mexico have yet to be discovered, but tools of the kind found with the mammoth skeletons have turned up on very different – and much less spectacular – sites all over Mexico. Most of these are cave shelters and small open-air camps in the arid parts of the country.

Oval, leaf-shaped points have been found at the oldest sites in the Tehuacan Valley, in the highlands of the state of Puebla, where they belong to the Ajuereado period (10,000 to 6500 BC). The camp sites of the Ajuereado people have only two or three hearths, perhaps equivalent to a band of two or three families, and the little groups followed a nomadic round of hunting and of collecting wild plants as these came into season. Far from being big game hunters, 55 per cent of the food bones found in Ajuereado camp sites belonged to jack rabbits, followed by other small game such as fox, skunk, coyote, lizard, ground squirrel and turtle. Extinct horse and antelope were rare, and mammoth completely absent. Since mammoth bones have been found in non-archaeological contexts in the valley, we must assume that kill sites exist somewhere but that the meat was stripped off the bone before being carried back to the caves and rock shelters.

Leaf-shaped points, scraping tools and choppers similar to those made by the Ajuereado people have been discovered in the San Juan cave (Hidalgo) and in the canyon

and desert country of the Sierra de Tamaulipas, near the Texas border. The evidence is far from complete, but it all tends to show that the Pleistocene inhabitants of Mesoamerica were not specialist big game hunters, but foragers who made use of all available sources of food.

The first farmers. The end of the Pleistocene Ice Age brought with it certain climatic changes and the extinction of some of the larger game animals such as the mammoth, mastodon and horse. Between 7000 and 6500 BC the landscape of Mesoamerica took on its present form, with plants and animals similar to those of today.

In this new, post-Pleistocene environment the first experiments were made with the cultivation of plants, as we have seen in chapter 3. Probably such experiments took place all over Mesoamerica, but it is only in sheltered caves in the desert zones of Mexico that the remains of plants and other organic materials have been preserved. From Tamaulipas, Tehuacan, and the Valley of Oaxaca we have long sequences of deposits which span the period from 7000 BC to the introduction of pottery around 2000 BC, and which show how agriculture became more important as time went on.

In the early stages, cultivation was only a supplementary activity providing no more than five per cent of the diet. The small groups of people continued to follow a seasonal round, eating whatever came their way. Analysis of coprolites (desiccated human faeces) gives some idea of their food habits. During the El Riego period in the Tehuacan Valley (6800 to 5000 BC) the coprolites contained seeds of wild grasses, together with fragments of roasted maguey cactus, charred pieces of pochote root, seeds of chili peppers and fragments of meat. Faeces of a slightly later date from caves in Tamaulipas confirm the collection of a wide range of foodstuffs: plants, game, and also insects, worms, grubs, snails and grasshoppers. This broad-range collecting continued for thousands of years, but gradually some of the plants which had been eaten in the wild state were brought into cultivation. People in each area experimented with the plants which were locally available. The El Riego people began with avocados, squashes, and perhaps amaranth grains and chili peppers, while at about the same time the inhabitants of southwest Tamaulipas were beginning to grow pumpkins, bottle gourds and chilis.

Under cultivation, genetic changes took place in certain plants which made them much more productive than their wild forms. These were the crops which eventually became staple foods. Between 5000 and 3000 BC maize and beans became an increasingly important part of the diet. More and more species of plants were added to the repertoire, new and better races were developed, agricultural technology was improved, and all these changes led to an increasing reliance on cultivated plants at the expense of wild foods. The El Riego diet consisted of about 54 per cent meat, 41 per cent wild plants and only 5 per cent cultivated plants. By 3400 BC the proportion of cultivated foods in the Tehuacan diet had risen to 14 per cent; by 2300 it was up to 25 per cent; and by 1500 BC had reached 40 per cent. At this stage we can safely talk of farming communities rather than bands of hunters and gatherers.

The coprolites also show how culinary habits changed. Pumpkins and squashes were at first grown mainly for their seeds (usually roasted), later for their flesh. Beans were originally eaten green, and sometimes in their pods; later they were eaten mature, after soaking and boiling. Young and tender maize cobs were at first chewed whole to extract the juice; only at a later date were the cobs shelled and the kernels pounded into flour or made into gruel. Meat was roasted, steamed or eaten raw, and bones were scraped to extract the marrow.

As the productivity and reliability of cultivated plants improved, communities grew larger and were able to stay in once place for the greater part of the year, dispersing only in the dry months when food was scarce. This point marks the threshold between nomadism and settled village life, and is the first step towards civilization.

The dry conditions which preserved the botanical material here also preserved all kinds of perishable objects, so that a fairly complete picture can be reconstructed of life during the period of incipient agriculture. Stone was used for knives, scrapers, choppers, dart points and seed-grinders. Wood was employed for tool handles, dart shafts, fire-drills, tongues, snares and spring traps, rabbit clubs and the sticks used for digging up roots and turning over the soil. Cactus fiber was rolled by hand into string for bags, nets, snares and kilts. Strips of palm or cactus leaf were woven into sleeping mats and bags.

In one of the Tehuacan caves two burials were found belonging to the El Riego period. The bodies were wrapped in blankets and nets, and were richly furnished with baskets. One burial contained the skeletons of two children whose heads had been removed and changed over. The second burial included an old man, a middle-aged woman and an infant. The body of the man had been intentionally burned, and the heads of the woman and child were smashed. These elaborate burials must indicate complex ideas about the afterlife, and may be precursors of the ceremonialism which surrounded death and sacrifice throughout later Mexican prehistory.

Not all parts of Mesoamerica are dry and well adapted to the cultivation of maize, beans and squash. We must imagine a rather different line of development in the tropical lowlands (with a greater emphasis on root crops and forest products), and there is also evidence for a coastal

Oaxaca Valley, the Mexican highlands. Here, and in nearby Tehuacan Valley, evidences of settled communities and the transition from foraging to domestication of crops have been found.

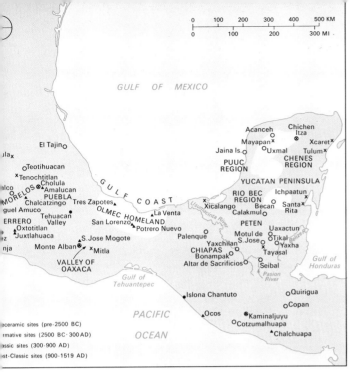

Scale bar: 0 100 200 300 400 500 KM / 0 100 200 300 MI

GULF OF MEXICO

El Tajin○
Teotihuacan○
✕Tenochtitlan
Cholula
Amalucan
MORELOS○✕
PUEBLA
Chalcatzingo Tres Zapotes▲
guel Amuco OLMEC HOMELAND
Tehuacan ▲La Venta
ERRERO Valley San Lorenzo● Potrero Nuevo
Oxtotitlan ✕ ●
Juxtlahuaca
nja Monte Alban■ ✕Mitla
VALLEY OF
OAXACA

Gulf of
Tehuantepec

PACIFIC
OCEAN

Acanceh Chichen
Mayapan○ Itza✕
Jaina Is.○ ○Uxmal Xcaret✕
PUUC Tulum✕
REGION CHENES
REGION
YUCATAN PENINSULA
RIO BEC Ichpaatun✕
REGION
Xicalango● Becan Santa✕
Calakmul○ Rita
PETEN
Palenque▲ Motul de Uaxactun○
S.Jose○ ○Tikal
Yaxchilan✕ ○Yaxha
CHIAPAS ○
Bonampak Tayasal
Altar de Sacrificios○ Seibal●
Pasion
River

Gulf of
Honduras

○Quirigua
○Copan

Islona Chantuto●
●Ocos ✳Kaminaljuyu
○Cotzumalhuapa
▲Chalchuapa

eceramic sites (pre-2500 BC)
rmative sites (2500 BC-300 AD)
assic sites (300-900 AD)
st-Classic sites (900-1519 AD)

[Map 1:] Ancient Mesoamerica.

and lagoon adaptation which incorporates fishing and shellfish collecting alongside hunting, gathering and a little farming. Mounds of discarded shells have been discovered along the Pacific coast from Islona Chantuto (Chiapas) to San Blas (Nayarit), and also on the Gulf Coast of Veracruz. The lack of pottery in these shell middens suggests a date before 2000 BC, but organic materials were not preserved, and investigation of these sites has hardly begun. Nevertheless it is safe to assume that the people of each ecological zone made the best use of local resources, and that several different ways of life were practiced within the boundaries of Mesoamerica.

The beginnings of civilization (2200 BC to 300 AD).
During the last 2,000 years before Christ, a distinctively Mesoamerican pattern of civilization began to take shape, and for that reason this era is often called the "Formative period."

Archaeologically, the start of the Formative is marked by the introduction of pottery, but more important are the social and technological changes which prepared the way for civilization. Farming became the basis of life. All the main crop plants were cultivated, and in dry areas the farmers practiced irrigation by means of wells and canals. Permanent year-round settlements were established, and some of them grew into large sites with temples, stone monuments and public buildings. Long before 300 AD there is evidence for class distinctions, hieroglyphic writing, long-distance trade, specialized crafts, fine art, religious cults and ceremonialism – in short, all the characteristic features of a state level of organization.

The oldest pottery vessels in Mesoamerica are from shell mounds on the Pacific coast at Zanja and Puerto Marquez, the latter with a radiocarbon date of around 2450 BC. At

more or less the same time, similar pottery came into use in the Tehuacan Valley, where the shapes of the vessels seem to copy those of the stone bowls used during the preceramic period.

The rate of change quickened in about 1500 BC, and during this early stage of the Formative period the most important developments took place in the lowlands.

In the Ocos region, where the Mexico-Guatemala frontier meets the Pacific ocean, little farming hamlets of three to twenty families were established just above the muddy banks of mangrove-fringed estuaries and lagoons. Pole-and-thatch houses with whitewashed mud walls were built on low earthen mounds to raise them above the summer floods, and the inhabitants gained their living by fishing, growing maize, catching turtles and iguanas, and collecting crabs, clams and oysters. One site had a large mound, 25 feet high, which may have been a temple platform. Ritual at household level is attested by solid, handmade female figurines of baked clay. We do not know what gods or beliefs these figures represent, but the custom of making terracotta figurines is one which persisted through the whole of Mesoamerican history.

Pottery similar to that of Ocos has been found at sites in the highlands of Chiapas and in the Gulf Coast lowlands, but these early farming villages were unspectacular and give no hint of the great developments still to come. The Ocós area, although an early starter, became a backwater, and the steps towards new levels of organization were taken elsewhere.

In Oaxaca between 1500 and 1250 BC some settlements were already more important than others. Most villages consisted of just a few houses grouped around an open square, but one site (San Jose Mogote) covered nearly four acres and had large-scale ceremonial architecture. By 850 BC San Jose Mogote was so much larger than its neighbors that it probably served as a local capital surrounded by smaller, dependent satellite communities. The township now covered 45 acres, with stone-faced rectangular platforms, a court for the ritual ball game, and an industrial zone occupied by part-time craftsmen.

A trade network linked Oaxaca with all the important centers outside the valley. Gray pottery manufactured in Oaxaca was exported to the Gulf Coast, Ocos and the Basin of Mexico; in return, obsidian was imported from at least six different sources scattered throughout Mesoamerica, and the Gulf Coast provided pottery, sting ray spines, shells, shark teeth, turtle shells and red pigment.

The Olmecs. While the people of Oaxaca were becoming urban, a different manner of life was developing in the hot and humid plain of the Gulf Coast, the homeland of a people to whom archaeologists have given the name Olmec. In these eastern lowlands rainfall may reach 120 inches per year, and the soil quickly loses its fertility if the forest is not allowed to regenerate after the land has been cropped for a few years. Except in special conditions (e.g.

Colossal Olmec head from La Venta, a principal Olmec center on the hot and humid Gulf coast plains, which flourished from about 1000 to 600 BC. The head was carved from a single block of imported basalt.

river levees, where fertility is restored by annual flooding), shifting cultivation was the rule. Populations were smaller than in the highlands, the farmers lived scattered in the countryside, and there were no large towns.

The main Olmec sites were ceremonial centers without suburbs or residential areas. San Lorenzo, during the climax of Olmec civilization between 1150 and 900 BC, consisted of platforms, courtyards, monumental stone sculptures, artificial lagoons and stone-lined drains, all laid out on a great artificial plateau more than 20 feet high. In spite of this architectural grandeur, only about 200 house mounds have been found, giving a resident population of 800 to 1,000 inhabitants – too few to have either built or maintained the center. La Venta, constructed between 100 and 600 BC, is an even more extreme case, for it was built on a small island surrounded by swamps where agriculture was impossible. Under shifting cultivation no more than 150 people could have obtained their food from the island itself.

The lack of cities in no way prevented the development of civilization. In agricultural technology and in socio-political organization the Olmecs may have been little more advanced than their contemporaries in Oaxaca, but through their art and architecture they made a unique contribution to Mesoamerican history.

Olmec centers were not random accumulations of buildings but were carefully planned temple communities. The nucleus of La Venta was a group of structures arranged symmetrically along a single axis. At the south end stood an unusual clay pyramid in the shape of a fluted cone rising to a height of over 100 feet. North of the pyramid stretched a series of courtyards flanked by low mounds made from colored clays brought from outside the island. La Venta also had a ball court and many rich offerings and tombs.

Imported serpentine was used for the buried pavements and the so-called "massive offerings," whose purpose remains a mystery. At the cost of enormous labor, huge pits were excavated and floored with stone blocks – then immediately filled in again. One such pit was 24 feet deep and contained more than 1000 tons of serpentine slabs. In the same non-functional category were three identical mosaic pavements, each consisting of nearly 500 oblong blocks of green serpentine laid out in the form of a stylized jaguar face with the open spaces in the design filled with yellow and orange sands. Like the other pavements, these mosaics were covered up as soon as they were finished and must be considered as offerings rather than as architecture.

The Olmecs were the first Mesoamerican people to handle large masses of stone, and they also created the first Mesoamerican art style. Monumental stone sculpture appeared suddenly in the Olmec heartland with no known antecedents, and at the same time Olmec craftsmen began to create small-scale masterpieces in jade and pottery.

The most spectacular sculptures are the colossal human heads from San Lorenzo, La Venta and Tres Zapotes. The heads are carved in the round from a single block of basalt, and depict heavy-featured, thick-lipped individuals wearing round helmets. The largest head stands more than nine feet high. Basalt was also used for stelae carved with scenes in relief, and for block-shaped altars with niches containing seated human figures.

Olmec art drew its inspiration from mythology and religion. At the core of the mythology seems to be the union of a woman with a jaguar, depicted on a monument from the little site of Potrero Nuevo. From this act sprang a race of "were-jaguars," half human and half feline, which combine the features of both parents in various proportions. The human element is usually infantile, paunchy and stubby-limbed, with puffy cheeks and toothless gums. Grafted onto this are jaguar characteristics: fangs, sometimes claws, and a snarling expression with the mouth turned down at the corners. Heads are frequently cleft at the top. These hybrid creatures appear in all media: large sculptures, delicately carved jade axes and figurines only a few inches high, on the walls of pottery vessels, and in a series of large, hollow clay figures.

There are strong hints that the jaguar-babies may be ancestral to the Rain Gods of the later civilizations. Other Olmec figures may represent deities which were still being worshiped when the Spaniards arrived: Xipe Totec (god of springtime), the Death God, and Quetzalcoatl (the feathered serpent). If these controversial identifications

Seated figurine of a woman from Tlatilco in the Valley of Mexico.
The handling of the features betrays strong Olmec influence.

are correct, the roots of Mesoamerican religion reach deep
into the Formative period.

Outside the Gulf Coast homeland there are no Olmec
temple-centers, colossal heads or massive offerings, but
the influence of Olmec culture spread over a wide area,
carried perhaps by traders, missionaries or military expeditions. A scatter of small jades and relief carvings in the
Olmec style marks a route along the Pacific coast of
Mexico and Guatemala, through Chalchuapa in western
El Salvador, and onwards to the sources of blue-green
jade in the Guanacaste region of Costa Rica.

Another route led northwards and westwards into the
states of Puebla and Morelos, where the local styles of
pottery and figurines are suddenly influenced by Olmec
designs around 1200 BC. A few centuries later, rock carvings in pure Olmec style appear in the highlands at
Chalcatzingo, a site which commands one of the strategic
routes of communication. From Morelos the trade route
continues to the rich mineral resources of Guerrero, and
is marked by an Olmec stela at San Miguel Amuco and
by a unique series of colored paintings in the caves of
Juxtlahuaca and Oxtotitlan.

The same mixture of local and Olmec elements can be
seen in the Valley of Mexico at Ayotla and Zohapilco
(near Tlapacoya) and at Tlatilco just across the lake. These
settlements were villages occupied by peasant farmers, and

have none of the ceremonial architecture and monumental
sculpture characteristic of the Olmec homeland. At
Tlatilco, a cemetery of more than three hundred close-
packed graves has been excavated, the skeletons lying face
up and surrounded by dozens of pots, roller stamps (for
making painted designs on the body), clay masks, and the
figurines for which this site is famous.

By about 900 BC changes took place in the Valley with
the founding of new settlements near the shores of the
lake at Copilco, Zacatenco and El Arbolillo. At these sites,
and in the most recent graves at Tlatilco, there is no longer
any sign of Olmec influence. The Valley of Mexico had
now an art style of its own, less urbane and sophisticated
than that of the Olmecs, but full of vigor and detail – a
peasant style rather than a metropolitan one. The local
element shows most clearly in the little solid figurines
from Tlatilco. The subjects are ordinary people: dancers,
ball players, pretty girls with short skirts and fancy hair-
styles, acrobats, hunchbacks, couples seated on couches,
women carrying children or pet dogs. There are also
representations of two-headed individuals and monstrous
faces divided vertically into fleshed and skeletal sections.
These lively portrayals are quite alien to the Olmec style,
and reflect none of the "were-jaguar" mythology or the
rituals of Olmec life.

The final stages of the Mesoamerican Formative period,
400 BC to 300 AD, witnessed no major new developments.

[Map 2:] The Basin of Mexico.

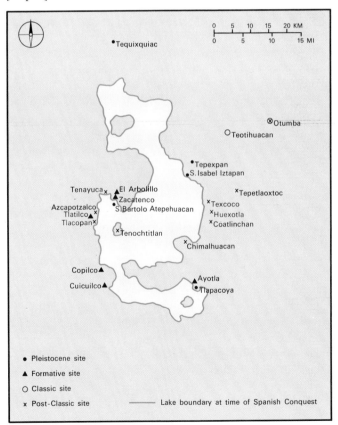

The lowland pattern of life, with ceremonial centers serving a scattered population, became firmly established in the Gulf Coast plain and the Maya lowlands. At this time, too, the Maya were moving towards their cultural climax as Olmec civilization declined and disappeared. In the highlands, towns became larger and larger. San José Mogote covered more than 90 acres, but lost its dominant position in the Valley of Oaxaca around 600 BC with the foundation of Monte Alban, the future Zapotec capital. In the Valley of Mexico the country cousins were rapidly catching up with their neighbors. Cuicuilco, near the southwestern shore of the lake, grew into a town with a circular, stone-faced temple platform, and at about the same time an important temple was built at Tlapacoya. Large towns, up to 300 acres in extent, have also been discovered in the eastern part of the Valley.

During the late Formative the balance of power gradually shifted from the lowlands to the central highland regions of Mexico, a process which culminated in the early centuries AD with the growth of an empire whose center was at Teotihuacan, in a previously unimportant side branch of the Valley of Mexico.

Astronomy, writing and arithmetic. The Formative was succeeded by the Classic period (approximately 300 to 900 AD) during which the greater part of Mesoamerica participated in a single culture with many regional variants. Each local civilization had its own ceramics, art and architectural styles, but underlying the diversity was a common intellectual and spiritual tradition involving a shared system of beliefs and attitudes whose roots can be traced back into the Formative period.

The basic unity of Mesoamerican culture is marked by a series of traits which recur throughout the area but are not generally found elsewhere in the New World. The diagnostic features include a ritual ball game played in an I-shaped court, the use of hieroglyphic writing and of books made from a single strip of leather or bark paper folded like a screen, temples on stepped pyramids, blood offerings (self-mutilation as well as human sacrifice), many of the same gods (worshiped under a variety of local names), a complex calendar based on interlocking cycles of time, and similar myths about the nature of the universe and the creation of mankind.

Two forms of calendar were in use. The 365-day calendar based on the solar year was divided into 18 "months" of 20 days, with the addition of five uncounted days which were considered unlucky. Each of the 20 days had a name which was represented by a hieroglyph. For divination, astrology and all religious purposes a second, quite different, calendar was employed, which bore no relationship with any astronomical phenomenon. This sacred calendar was a 260-day cycle in which each of the 20 day signs was combined with every number from 1 to 13. Each day sign and each number had its power for good or evil, and was watched over by one of the many deities.

These two calendars, solar and ritual, were combined into a 52-year cycle called the "Calendar Round" (52 years equals 18,980 days, the lowest common multiple of 260 and 365).

Astronomical observations were made by sighting through a pair of crossed sticks and noting the way in which the sun, moon and planets moved in relation to natural features on the horizon. The Maya were the supreme astronomers of ancient America. Although they never realized that the earth moves round the sun, they made precise measurements of the length of the solar year and were able to calculate the cycles of the moon and the planet Venus. The priests also composed tables which could predict eclipses, and had worked out a leap year correction formula which was more accurate than the one used in the Julian calendar of the Christian Church.

These calculations were dependent on two other inventions: hieroglyphic writing and an effective arithmetical notation. All Mesoamerican systems used a base of 20 (rather than the 10 employed in western mathematics), but the Maya also invented for themselves the concept of zero and the idea of place value. The Maya used only three symbols: a bar for 5, a dot for each unit up to 4, and a stylized shell for zero. The number 7, for example, was expressed by a bar and two dots. Numbers were written in a vertical column, with the place value increasing from bottom to top (not from right to left, as in our system). The lowest group of bars and dots gave the number of units, the one above it gave the number of 20s, and the one above that the number of 400s (i.e. 20 × 20).

Some Olmec symbols may have served as hieroglyphs, but the oldest bar-and-dot numerals are found on carved slabs from Monte Alban, Oaxaca, dating from around 500 BC. The hieroglyphic inscriptions on these slabs

The earliest dated writing in the Americas (abut 500 BC) is found on these carved stone slabs from early Monte Alban, Oaxaca. The righthand slab in the picture on the opposite page shows hieroglyphs and bar-and-dot numerals. On the slab next to it and in the picture above are distorted human figures, variously interpreted as dancers or as executed corpses.

Schematic rendering of an inscription from the east side of stele E, from the Classic Maya site of Quirigua in Guatemala, with its interpretation by the Maya expert, S. G. Morley. The inscription displays calendrical information which includes an initial and a supplementary series of glyphs. The Maya glyphs and calendrical system were first interpreted in the late 19th century.

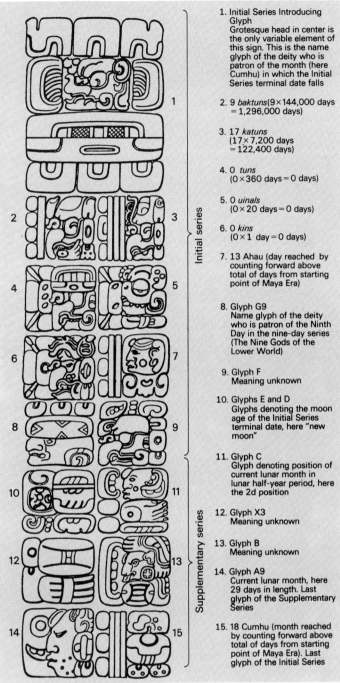

1. Initial Series Introducing Glyph
Grotesque head in center is the only variable element of this sign. This is the name glyph of the deity who is patron of the month (here Cumhu) in which the Initial Series terminal date falls

2. 9 *baktuns* (9 × 144,000 days = 1,296,000 days)

3. 17 *katuns* (17 × 7,200 days = 122,400 days)

4. 0 *tuns* (0 × 360 days = 0 days)

5. 0 *uinals* (0 × 20 days = 0 days)

6. 0 *kins* (0 × 1 day = 0 days)

7. 13 Ahau (day reached by counting forward above total of days from starting point of Maya Era)

8. Glyph G9
Name glyph of the deity who is patron of the Ninth Day in the nine-day series (The Nine Gods of the Lower World)

9. Glyph F
Meaning unknown

10. Glyphs E and D
Glyphs denoting the moon age of the Initial Series terminal date, here "new moon"

11. Glyph C
Glyph denoting position of current lunar month in lunar half-year period, here the 2d position

12. Glyph X3
Meaning unknown

13. Glyph B
Meaning unknown

14. Glyph A9
Current lunar month, here 29 days in length. Last glyph of the Supplementary Series

15. 18 Cumhu (month reached by counting forward above total of days from starting point of Maya Era). Last glyph of the Initial Series

suggest that the Calendar Round was also employed there, and by 300 AD this knowledge had spread over most of Mesoamerica.

Another system, the "Long Count," had a more restricted distribution. It made its appearance around the time of Christ on the southern and western fringes of Maya territory. From there it spread to the Maya of Guatemala and Yucatan, but was never adopted in highland Mexico.

The Long Count, like the Christian calendar, counts the number of days which have elapsed since a fixed point in past time, but instead of weeks, months and years it employs the following units:

1 kin	=	1 day
1 uinal	=	20 days (20 kins)
1 tun	=	360 days (18 uinals)
1 katun	=	7,200 days (20 tuns)
1 baktun	=	144,000 days (20 katuns)

The symbols for the tuns, uinals etc. were often missed out, and the date expressed simply as a column of bar-and-dot numerals.

The Long Count system reconciles the 360 "counted" days of the solar year with the needs of an arithmetic which works in 20s. The starting date for the Long Count seems not to have been a real event but a mathematical-mythological abstraction, the day 13.0.0.0.0 which ended the last Great Cycle of 13 baktuns and initiated a new era. According to the usually accepted correlation, this starting day was equivalent to August 12, 3113 BC.

The Maya were preoccupied with the passage of time, and many of their stelae were put up to commemorate the end of a katun, or 20-year period. On each slab was carved the Long Count date, the age of the moon, and the glyphs for the gods ruling at that time. The oldest stela from the Maya lowlands (stela no. 29 at Tikal) has a Long Count date which reads 8.12.14.8.15 – that is, 8 baktuns, 12 katuns, and so on. This figure gives a total of 1,243,615 days from the starting point of the Count; the stela was therefore erected on July 6 in the year 292 AD.

The appearance of Long Count inscriptions in the Maya zone is used by archaeologists as a time-marker for the start of the Classic period, and by extension the term Classic has come into use for cultures of the same date elsewhere in Mexico.

The rise and fall of Classic Maya civilization. The heartland of Classic Maya culture was the semi-tropical rainforest of the Guatemalan department of El Peten and the adjacent parts of Mexico and Belize. During the late Formative, the diagnostic traits of Maya culture appeared one by one in the archaeological record. By about 200 BC the first temples were being built at Tikal and Uaxactun. Shortly afterwards, architects in the Peten discovered the principle of the corbeled roof, in which each course of masonry overhangs the one below, narrowing the gap between the walls until it is small enough to close by a single slab. With the introduction of the Calendar Round, the Long Count and the stela cult around 300 AD, Maya civilization took on its definitive character.

Sculpture, architecture, jade carving and stucco modeling reached the height of artistry between 300 and 900 AD. The walls of buildings were decorated with stucco reliefs and colored frescoes, although (except at Bonampak) most of these paintings have been destroyed by the tropical climate. Some impression of the lost frescoes can be obtained from pottery, the finest of which was decorated with miniature painted scenes of gods, priests, merchants and nobles engaged in all kinds of ritual and ceremonial activities. In contrast to the formal art of the stelae, the scenes on the painted vessels give a more intimate view of aristocratic life and are full of information about dress, weapons, customs and everyday objects.

Rich tombs were a normal feature of Maya ceremonial centers, though few of them can rival the funerary crypt below the Temple of the Inscriptions at Palenque. A vaulted staircase led from the floor of the temple to a chamber 80 feet below. The walls of the crypt were covered with plaster reliefs representing the Nine Lords of the Night and the Underworld, and most of the floor space was occupied by a huge stone coffin with a carved

Above: The so-called Palace Structure at Palenque, one of the larger Maya centers. Towers are unusual in Maya architecture.

Below: Detail from the fresco wall paintings at Bonampak, Chiapas, Mexico, a Classic Maya site. It shows Maya dignitaries.

red cinnabar. At Jaina island the dead were accompanied by their personal ornaments, pottery and beautiful terra-cotta whistle-figurines in the shape of gods, warriors and Maya dignitaries.

The political history of the Classic period is still far from clear, but the influence of the Mexican city of Teotihuacan made itself strongly felt between 400 and 600 AD. Invasion of actual Teotihuacan armies cannot be demonstrated, except perhaps at Kaminaljuyu in the Guatemalan highlands, where a Mexican dynasty seems to have established its rule over a Maya population. The newcomers turned

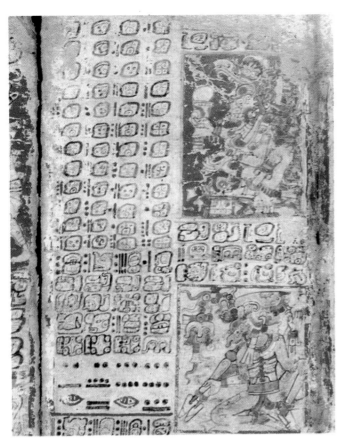

Right: The young maize (corn) god, depicted in a graceful statue of basalt from the Classic Maya site of Copan.

Detail from a Maya codex, preserved since the 16th century in a German library at Dresden. Using this codex, Ernst Förstemann inaugurated the deciphering of Maya writing in the 1880s.

lid. Within the sarcophagus lay the body of a middle-aged man. Each finger was adorned with jade rings; at his side were two figurines; another jade sealed his mouth, and he was buried with his necklaces, diadems and ear spools. His face was covered by a mosaic mask, and after the coffin was sealed the mourners had placed an offering of fine pottery and two stucco heads on the floor of the crypt. As the final stage in the ceremony, five or six youths were sacrificed and left to accompany the deceased on his journey to the afterlife.

The burials in the ceremonial centers were not grouped into cemeteries. As a general rule ordinary people were buried below the floors of their houses or in abandoned storage pits, while the rich were interred within the platforms of important buildings. An exception is the little island of Jaina, off the Campeche coast, which became a burial ground with several hundred tombs. The corpses were usually wrapped in mantles or mats, and their heads covered with bowls. The graves were then sprinkled with

this ancient Maya site into a smaller version of Teotihuacan, with foreign styles of architecture and Teotihuacan types of pottery. In highland Guatemala the use of the Long Count ceased, as did the custom of erecting stelae and large stone sculptures. Even so, Maya gods and figures continued to be painted on pottery, and the presence of imported Peten bowls shows that the old trade links were maintained.

In the lowlands the effects of Teotihuacan contact were widespread but less drastic, though a few Teotihuacan-style buildings were put up at Tikal and Acanceh. Warriors and Rain Gods in Teotihuacan costume were carved on stelae at Tikal and Yaxha, and Teotihuacan ceramics were imported or copied on a considerable scale, occurring even at rural house sites far from the main centers.

By about 600 AD, Teotihuacan influence waned, the foreign elements disappeared from lowland Maya culture, and the centuries from 600 to 900 were the climax period of Maya civilization. The Peten sites continued much as before, though on an even grander scale, but in the 6th to 8th centuries the Maya of Yucatan created the new, regional styles of architecture known as Chenes, Rio Bec and Puuc. All three share a taste for the flamboyant and showy. In the Rio Bec area palaces were adorned with false towers, roof crests and sky serpent masks. Further north, in the Chenes and Puuc regions, ornamentation became still more elaborate, and the facades of buildings were covered with a veneer of finely carved limestone slabs, with rows of half columns and with relief designs made up of thousands of separate elements forming geometric patterns, sky serpents, human and divine figures, and stylized masks of Chac, the long-nosed Rain God. Most of these sites were occupied for no more than 300 years, but they include Uxmal, Old Chichen Itza, and nearly all the notable sites of Yucatan. One of the rare exceptions is Becan, which has a history stretching back into the Formative period.

The most striking phenomenon in the whole of Meso-

Panorama of the ceremonial center of El Tajin, covering over two square miles in the Veracruz Gulf coast lowlands, Mexico. Unexcavated mounds concealing palaces, temple pyramids and ball courts lie on either side of the Pyramid of the Niches.

american history is the collapse of Classic Maya civilization during the century before 900 AD. Archaeologically the collapse is indicated by the apparent breakdown of Maya society, by large-scale depopulation of both the countryside and the ceremonial centers, and by evidence of invasion at sites in the Usumacinta-Pasion drainage. At all the major sites of the central lowlands the palaces were abandoned and fell into ruin, temples were not refurbished, carved stelae ceased to be erected, the Classic forms of writing and calendrics went out of use, rituals and ceremonies lapsed, and luxury items (painted pottery, carved jades etc.) were no longer made. In the countryside many hamlets were abandoned, and the population either died out or moved to such areas as the Belize valley or the Peten lakes where small concentrations of people lingered on.

The Maya collapse is easy enough to recognize, but has still not been satisfactorily explained. Many causes have been suggested (most of them not verifiable by archaeological means) but they fall into two major groups: internal breakdown, and invasion from outside.

There is some evidence that Maya civilization had reached a crisis point in the 9th century. With the increasing complexity of society, more and more people were withdrawn from farming to become administrators, craftsmen and priests, all of whom had to be fed from the produce of the land. Sites like Tikal had grown so large that they were near the limits of their food supply, and Late Classic skeletons show signs of malnutrition and of marked differences between rich and poor. These conditions in themselves may have led to unrest, and also to the breakdown of the delicately balanced agricultural system. Food production could not be indefinitely

increased, and the short-term expedient of reducing the fallow period could lead to long-term disaster as the impoverished soil became less and less fertile. This is a speculative explanation, but one which would account for rural depopulation as well as the abandonment of the centers.

There is also evidence for foreign invaders in the western part of the Maya lowlands, where the sites of Seibal and Altar de Sacrificios were taken over by one or more groups of outsiders. At about the same time, such Mexican features as phallic sculptures, non-Maya gods, and depictions of foreign weapons and costumes became more common at the Puuc sites of Yucatan, though there is no evidence for an actual takeover.

Rather than a single invasion there may have been multiple raids from many different quarters. Unfortunately the details cannot yet be worked out, and it is impossible at the moment to see whether these raids preceded (and in part caused) the Maya collapse, or whether internal breakdown came first and so weakened the lowland Maya states that they became easy prey to invaders. The problem is enormously complex, and any single-cause explanation is likely to prove inadequate.

The Classic civilizations of Mexico (300 to 900 AD). In artistic and intellectual achievements the Maya were supreme, but by 300 AD several other regions of Mesoamerica had attained a comparable standard of life.

In the Valley of Oaxaca the ancestors of the present-day Zapotec Indians enlarged their hilltop center at Monte Alban into a true city with residential suburbs surrounding a nucleus of public buildings, temples, carved monuments and rich tombs. Other Zapotec towns, some of them quite large, were scattered on the slopes and floor of the valley.

On the other side of the country, in the lowlands of Veracruz, El Tajin became the dominant power in eastern Mexico and the capital of a regional civilization with strong local characteristics. The site was set among low

hills in a hot and humid zone where shifting cultivation is the rule, and (like the Maya sites, in a somewhat similar environment) was a religious and governmental center rather than a city. Nevertheless, El Tajin was a large site. Unexcavated mounds cover at least two square miles, and at the heart is a 150-acre ceremonial zone with palaces, temple pyramids and ball courts. The finest building at El Tajin was a six-tiered platform whose facade was ornamented with recessed niches, one for each day of the year.

Tajin sculptors created a highly individual art style based on interlocking scroll patterns which are reproduced on pottery, stone objects and panels of architectural decoration. The ritual of the ball game seems to have had unusual significance for the people of El Tajin. There are no less than 11 courts in the central zone, and some of them have finely carved relief sculpture. The carvings on the south court depict ceremonies connected with the game itself, and include sacrificial scenes in which two men dressed in the padded costume of ball players are cutting out the heart of a third player while the skeletal Death God looks on. Other carvings, on the column drums of one of the palaces, show priests, winged dancers, warriors in eagle costumes, and also bar-and-dot numbers with day signs of non-Maya type.

The highland Mexican pattern of urban life is best exemplified at Teotihuacan, in a side branch of the Valley of Mexico, where the late Formative town grew into a metropolitan city during the early centuries AD. Until its violent destruction in about 750, Teotihuacan controlled central Mexican politics and commerce. Cholula, in the Puebla Basin, became a Teotihuacan colony; the obsidian quarries at Otumba supplied tools and raw material to sites all over Mesoamerica, and Teotihuacan pottery was traded to all the centers of civilized life.

It is difficult to say just how much territory was under the direct control of Teotihuacan. If there was ever such a thing as a "Teotihuacan Empire" it may not have extended much outside the highlands of central Mexico. Elsewhere (at Monte Alban, El Tajin and in the Maya lowlands) the Teotihuacan elements appeared alongside, and sometimes blended with, purely local styles of architecture, ceramics, figurines and sculpture.

It would be more accurate to think of Mesoamerica between 300 and 750 AD as a vast common market in which objects, ideas and people moved freely from any one center to all of the others. Colonies of foreign merchants or ambassadors have been recognized at Teotihuacan; Tajin scroll decoration occurs on altar slabs at Cholula and on pottery at Teotihuacan; rich Zapotecs were buried in tombs decorated with frescoes in which the hieroglyphs and iconography were native, but the treatment of the figures derived from the art of Teotihuacan. Literacy was widespread, though only the upper classes could read and write. Certain gods were worshiped all over Mesoamerica alongside local, regional deities, and the Calendar Round was in regular use, although every regional culture had its own version of the 20 day signs. Of the major sites, only Teotihuacan has failed to produce carved inscriptions, but it is inconceivable that a city with such widespread trade contacts could have remained ignorant of writing and calendrics.

In this situation, new and eclectic art styles came into being at Xochicalco (Morelos) and the Cotzumalhuapa region of highland Guatemala, drawing something from neighboring styles but reassembling the elements in original and distinctive ways. At Xochicalco the facade of the main temple had a Mexican feathered serpent with Maya dignitaries seated among the coils of its body, and the calendrical glyphs showed both Mixtec and Zapotec influences. In the mountains of Guatemala, which remained a predominantly Maya area, Cotzumalhuapa and a few nearby sites formed a little enclave characterized by stelae with non-Maya hieroglyphs and gods of Mexican appearance.

The high quality of cultural and artistic life may, however, have concealed political instability, for the 8th and 9th centuries were a time of upheavals and of changes in the balance of power. Teotihuacan, the most powerful city of all, was the first to succumb, destroyed (probably by invaders from the north) in about 750. Between 800 and 900 the lowland Maya centers fell into decay, and in the 10th century Monte Alban also fell into disrepair when large parts of the Valley of Oaxaca came under the control of Mixtec dynasties from the surrounding mountains. Of all the principal centers in Mexico, only El Tajin remained undisturbed, but this respite was only temporary and the site was destroyed by fire in the 12th century.

Mixtecs and Toltecs. The period immediately after the fall of the Classic civilization was a time of warfare, confusion and the movement of peoples. As the old order was swept away, new states arose to fill the power vacuum.

Native manuscripts trace the history of the Mixtecs back to the 7th century AD, but for a long time their activities were confined to their homeland in the mountains of western Oaxaca. By a mixture of force, diplomacy and royal marriages into Zapotec dynasties they eventually infiltrated the Valley of Oaxaca, and brought most of the northern part of it under their sway. The Zapotec capital at Monte Alban was deserted and never occupied again, although the newcomers re-used some of the Zapotec tombs for the burial of their own dead.

One of these graves, Monte Alban tomb 7, has yielded one of the greatest treasures ever unearthed in Mexico. In the tomb was the body of a Mixtec lord surrounded by his slaughtered servants. Beside the corpse lay a wealth of funerary offerings: beads of amber, jet, crystal, jade and coral, pieces of jaguar bone engraved with mythological and historical scenes, silver bowls, thousands of pearls, and gold objects weighing almost eight pounds. The dead king was provided with every kind of jewelry: pectorals, finger rings, necklaces, nose and ear ornaments, lip-plugs,

Part of one of the palace buildings at Monte Alban, Oaxaca, the Zapotec capital. The architecture shows strong Mixtec influences.

tweezers, diadems, false fingernails and miniature masks.

These objects illustrate Mixtec craftsmanship at its finest. The Mixtecs were not great architects and sculptors by Mesoamerican standards, but they excelled in the minor arts of goldworking, turquoise mosaic, manuscript painting and pottery-making.

The influence of the Mixtec art style was felt all over Mesoamerica, and extended far outside the area under direct Mixtec control. Cholula became a center for the manufacture of pottery in the Mixtec style, and export pieces or copies are abundant at sites along the Gulf Coast. Individual Mixtec designs were adopted outside the southern frontier of Mesoamerica as far south as the Nicoya region of Costa Rica. The style of figure painting used in the Mixtec books was copied on a larger scale in a wall fresco at the Maya site of Santa Rita, and can still be seen in almost pure form in some of the carved stone monuments from the Aztec capital at Tenochtitlan. Although most of Mixtec territory eventually came under the control of the expanding Aztec empire, the art style remained alive and was still flourishing at the time of the Spanish conquest.

Meanwhile, after a period of warfare and disunity, a new state emerged in north-central Mexico as the heir of Teotihuacan. The Toltecs were a coalition of nations. In part they were the descendants of old established peoples, but their ruling group (the Tolteca-Chichimeca) was composed of immigrants from north or west Mexico. Led by a semi-mythical chief called Mixcoatl (Cloud Serpent), the Tolteca-Chichimeca appeared on the scene just after 900 AD, and under their second ruler, a historical figure named Topiltzin, established their capital at Tula in the year 968 or 980.

Aztec myths look back to the Toltec period as a golden age. The Toltecs, whose name means "artificers" or "craftsmen," were (wrongly) believed to be the first to work metals and to use the ritual calendar. Their city had palaces of gold and precious feathers; maize cobs grew as big as milling stones; cotton grew in every color; life was one long round of pleasure.

The truth is more prosaic, but archaeology has confirmed that Tula was indeed a great city whose ruins cover at least three square miles. Its buildings were constructed in a distinctive style which shows several technical innovations. On the north side of the main square was a large rectangular hall with a painted frieze and three rows of columns to support the roof beams. Behind this was a terraced pyramid on which stood a temple with a roof held up by stone pillars of different forms: columns in the shape of warrior figures, round pillars carved with feathered serpents and square columns with reliefs depicting soldiers. The facade of this pyramid was decorated with limestone panels showing a procession of jaguars, feathered serpent faces, and birds of prey tearing at hearts. In later times eagles and jaguars were the symbols of the Aztec warrior orders, and a new militaristic spirit is evident everywhere in the art of Tula. Benches and platforms were adorned with military figures, the facades of altars were decorated with carved skulls and bones, and there were scenes depicting serpents devouring human beings.

Mexican legends also say something about the political history of Tula, though in a form which is difficult to interpret. Topiltzin seems to have identified himself with Quetzalcoatl, the Feathered Serpent, and to have adopted the god's name as his own. Rivalry between the followers of Quetzalcoatl and the devotees of Tezcatlipoca (Smoking Mirror), the patron deity of warriors and sorcerers, led to a palace revolution and to the exile of Topiltzin-Quetzalcoatl from Tula. According to one version of the legend, Quetzalcoatl and his followers journeyed to the Gulf Coast, from which they sailed away eastwards on a raft of serpents, promising to return and claim the kingdom again – a threat which greatly perturbed Montezuma II in 1519 when the Spaniards sailed out of the west and landed on this same stretch of coast.

Under new leadership the Toltec state continued to flourish, controlling a large part of northern and western Mexico until Tula, in its turn, was violently destroyed by a new wave of barbarian invaders sometime in the 12th century.

The final centuries of Maya civilization in Yucatan. The effects of these events were felt in Maya territory where, after the collapse of the Classic-period states of the central lowlands, the balance of power shifted to Yucatan. Maya legends tell of the arrival of foreigners in the year 987, led by a man called Kukulkan (Feathered Serpent) who conquered the peninsula and set up his capital at the site which later became known as Chichen Itza. Unfortunately the history of this event is confused by the mention of another, perhaps later, group of foreign invaders called the Itza, whose descendants were still living at Lake Tayasal when the Spaniards first penetrated the interior.

It may be coincidence that the exile of Quetzalcoatl from Tula coincided with the arrival of a war chief of the same name at Chichen Itza, but archaeology has confirmed that the invaders were either Toltecs or people who had come under strong Toltec influence. Old-established centers like Uxmal were abandoned, and political power was concentrated at Chichen Itza where the invaders constructed a new administrative center in a hybrid Maya-Toltec style.

Highland Mexican gods shared temples with local Maya deities, and architectural ideas originating from Tula made their first appearance in Maya territory. In this hybrid culture the ruling party was undoubtedly Mexican. Scenes showing Toltec victories over Maya forces were painted on walls and engraved on gold disks thrown into the cenote (a huge natural well); relief sculpture portrayed human sacrifice and warriors wearing Toltec dress and weapons; a stone platform was carved into a representation of a typically Mexican tzompantli (the wooden rack on which the heads of sacrificed victims were dis-

Left: The Mixtec god of death, an example of fine Mixtec craftsmanship in a gold-copper alloy. The pectoral came from the remarkable treasure discovered in tomb 7 at Monte Alban. The rectangular panels below the face bear calendrical dates.

Right: The main temple at the Toltec capital of Tula. The columns, carved in the shapes of feathered serpents and warriors, originally carried the roof beams of a wood and thatch temple. In the foreground stood a colonnaded hall.

played). Toltec feathered serpent columns were used to support the lintels of temple doorways, and the same god appears (with eagles and jaguars identical to those of Tula) on the altars beside the skull rack. But the Maya element was not submerged. Yucatec remained the language of the population; the Maya type of corbeled roof persisted alongside the foreign column-and-beam technique, and Rain God masks continued to adorn some of the main temples.

The secular power of Chichen Itza was reinforced by its importance as a center of pilgrimage. The focus of the cult was the cenote, the well, into which offerings and sacrificial victims were thrown. The dredging of its bottom has produced a rich haul of pottery, jade, copper bells, gold objects (some from as far away as Panama), and also wooden items, textile fragments, and balls of copal (resin) incense preserved by the wet mud.

The later history of Chichen Itza is obscure and confused, but native chronicles agree with archaeological sources that sometime in the 13th century the neighboring city of Mayapan emerged as the ruling power in Yucatan.

Unlike the dispersed and scattered centers of earlier times, Mayapan was a true city bounded by a stone wall with six gateways. Within the wall lived about 12,000 people. Although Mayapan was strong enough to extort tribute from a wide surrounding area, the quality of craftsmanship was in decline. There was no attempt at town planning, and the buildings were a poor imitation of those at Chichen Itza – badly constructed, with shoddy masonry hidden by a thick layer of plaster. Temples were fewer and poorer than at any previous time and were overshadowed by the palaces of the nobility, each with its own domestic shrine. The military aristocracy seems to have gained influence at the expense of the priesthood, and household rites had partially replaced public worship.

Smaller walled towns were founded at Tulum, Xcaret and Ichpaatun along the east coast of Yucatan, and Mayapan-style remains have been found as far south as the Peten and Belize. One of the Belize sites (Santa Rita) had a wall painting which combines Maya calendrical signs with figures drawn in the style of the Mixtec painted books.

Among the deities in the Santa Rita fresco is a Merchant God, and, even during the period of decline, trade remained an important activity. The whole of the Maya zone formed a single economic unit, with ramifications into highland Mexico and southwards to the Isthmus of Central America. Certain coastal towns served as ports of trade, redistributing goods brought from all over the Maya world.

A canoe route around the Yucatan peninsula linked the ports on the east and west coasts, and historical records show that resident colonies of Maya traders maintained warehouses at towns on the Gulf of Honduras. Along this sea route passed every type of regional speciality, including commodities not preserved under archaeological con-

ditions. From Yucatan came salt, feathers, embroidered cotton mantles, wax, honey, flint tools and slaves. Honduras provided metal ingots, copper bells, marble vases, and the cocoa beans which were used as currency all over Mesoamerica. Xicalango, on the coast of southwest Yucatan, was the point where the Maya trade network met that of central Mexico, and through this port came metal objects, rabbit fur, obsidian and other highland products. Overland trade routes linked the Peten with the highlands of Guatemala. Pottery, cocoa and tobacco from the lowlands were exchanged for jade, obsidian, green quetzal plumage, red pigment and corn-grinding stones made of volcanic lava.

This trade survived the fall of Mayapan in the mid-15th century, and was still flourishing when the first Spanish ships explored the coasts of Yucatan in 1517. By that time Yucatan was in a state of disunity, divided between 16 rival states. The Conquest began in earnest during the 1520s, and all parts of the Maya zone, except the jungles of the interior, quickly came under Spanish control.

The Aztecs. The prehistory of highland Mexico is a story of political unification followed by periods of fragmen-

The Castillo, a Toltec-Maya temple at Chichen Itza in Yucatan. In the foreground is a Chacmool figure, a type of altar. Offerings were placed on his stomach.

tation into small and warring states. After Tula was destroyed, the Valley of Mexico was once more invaded by semi-civilized tribes. They were known collectively as the Chichimecs, and they established their own little states at Tenayuca, Azcapotzalco and a number of other towns. Chichimec rulers married into Toltec families, and the newcomers learned the arts of civilization and urban life from the descendents of the settled peoples.

The last of the barbarian tribes to enter the valley was

the one which we know as the Aztecs, though they referred to themselves as the Mexica or Tenochca. They came to the Basin of Mexico in the 13th century, only to find that the land had already been divided up among the earlier arrivals. For a while the Aztecs existed as vassals and mercenaries of the more powerful states, until in 1345 they were allowed to settle on a muddy island in Lake Texcoco. They called the place Tenochtitlan.

Tenochtitlan was at first subject to the city of Azcapot-zalco, but in 1428 (with the help of the neighboring towns of Texcoco and Tlacopan) the Aztecs defeated their overlords and won their independence. The allied cities were now the strongest military force in the Valley, and they quickly reduced the other states to subjection. By 1440 the allied armies had begun to campaign outside the Basin of Mexico, and in less than a century they conquered the greater part of Mexico and controlled the routes leading into Maya territory.

The Aztec period was a time of rapid population growth and of pressure on food resources. With the best agricultural land already taken up, new settlements were established in the marginal terrain on the upper slopes of the hills. At the same time, a massive drainage scheme was undertaken by the Texcocans to convert the waterlogged plain on the eastern shore of the lake into prime farmland. These ecological changes were accompanied by political changes. Texcoco became an important city during the early 15th century, and in the eastern part of the Valley the minor towns of Chimalhuacan and Tepetlaoxtoc grew into the capitals of new states which shared power with the older foundations of Huexotla and Coatlinchan.

Tenochtitlan also participated in this general growth. As its power and importance increased, it was quickly transformed from a village of reed huts into an imperial capital covering nearly five square miles. Because of its island locality, land was scarce and the Aztecs were forced to drain the surrounding swamps in order to provide more building land and garden plots. Canals were cut through the reed beds, and the debris piled up between the canals to make artificial platforms. Alternate layers of mud and reeds were added to raise the level, and the platforms were consolidated by driving in wickerwork hurdles around the sides and by planting trees whose roots anchored the platforms to the lake bottom.

A final layer of mud converted the artificial islands into chinampas, long narrow garden plots separated by canals and rising only two or three feet above the lake. Moisture for the growing plants was provided by natural filtration and by hand irrigation, while soil fertility could be renewed at any time by dredging up fresh muck from the lake bottom. By means of nursery beds and constant transplanting, the chinampas were kept in production throughout the year, and a single acre of best chinampa land could provide a subsistence diet for six to eight people.

The low-lying chinampas were vulnerable to flooding and to pollution from the salty waters of the eastern part of the lake. To prevent disaster, a dyke ten miles long was built across a narrow neck of the lake and was provided with sluice gates to control the water level.

Sealed off behind this dyke, Tenochtitlan stood like a Mexican Venice in an artificial lagoon fed by streams of fresh water. Causeways linked the city with the mainland, and aqueducts carried water from springs on the shore. A grid of canals reached to all parts of Tenochtitlan, dividing it into rectangular blocks. An anonymous conquistador, a companion of Cortes, has left this description of the scene:

"The inhabitants go for a stroll, some in canoes and others along the banks, and keep up conversations. Besides these, there are other principal streets entirely of water, and all travel is by barks and canoes, without which they could neither leave their houses nor return to them."

At the heart of the city was a walled precinct. Within it, sharing a single tall pyramid, were the twin shrines of Tlaloc (the Rain God) and Huitzilopochtli, the tribal god of the Aztecs. Nearby stood a round temple dedicated to Quetzalcoatl, and here too were the priests' quarters, ball courts, a skull rack and all the paraphernalia of sacrifice. In his memoirs, the conquistador Bernal Diaz gives an eye-

A model of the central precinct and main temple of the Aztec capital of Tenochtitlan, now Mexico City. The reconstruction is based on extensive archaeological and documentary evidence.

witness account of this precinct and its shrines, commenting that the place smelled like a Spanish slaughterhouse.

Close by the precinct was the palace, which served both as the ruler's private house and as the administrative center of the empire. Besides the rooms occupied by the royal household, the building contained a council room, law courts, treasury, storerooms where tribute was kept, a jail, an arsenal, guest rooms, a hall for music and dancing, and quarters for more than 3,000 servants and palace workmen.

Around the civic-ceremonial nucleus of Tenochtitlan

was a zone of more ordinary housing, with suburban temples and administrative buildings maintained by the calpullis (clans) into which the city was divided. Every freeborn Aztec belonged to one of these calpullis by right of birth. The calpullis may have begun as kinship groups, but by the 16th century were primarily land-holding corporations organized on a communal basis. Under normal circumstances a calpulli occupied its own ward of a town or else constituted a single rural community. At the time of the Conquest there were between 80 and 90 calpullis in Tenochtitlan, each of which was responsible for administering its own local affairs. Some calpullis were made up of workmen practicing a single craft or profession – metalworkers, feather workers, merchants, etc. – all of whom lived together in their own part of the town;

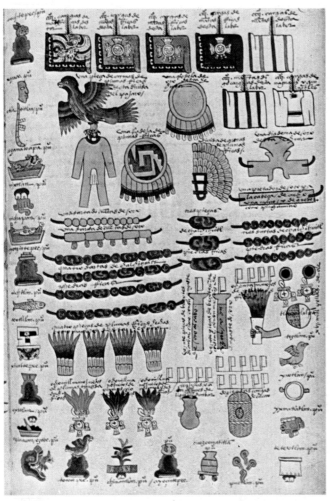

An early Spanish copy of a page from the codex Mendoza, the tribute list of the Aztec emperor, Montezuma, at the time of the conquest. The copy was made for the Spanish viceroy Mendoza who wanted the tribute for himself. Down the left side are symbols for the tributory cities. The remaining symbols indicate the items which each city was required to send to the Aztec capital, including cotton blankets, warriors' costumes and shields, strings of jade beads, gold ornaments and bunches of tropical feathers.

other calpullis were mainly agricultural and controlled blocks of farmland which were shared out among their members. Around the outer edge of the city was a ring of chinampa suburbs, in places more than half a mile wide, divided up into individual lots owned either by the calpullis or by private landlords.

The rise of Tenochtitlan from small town to metropolitan city was accompanied by rapid social changes of the kind associated with the formation of states. The ruler, the warriors and the nobility gained power and status at the expense of the common people. A class of professional civil servants came into existence, much of the land passed into private ownership, and religion became more formalized with continued military success, for the Aztecs had good reason to feel especially favored by the gods.

Human sacrifice became increasingly important. The best estimates suggest that 10,000 to 50,000 victims were sacrificed each year, mostly war captives, but also slaves and children obtained by purchase. For the Aztecs, and for the other nations of Mexico, human sacrifice was a sacred duty. According to Mexican mythology, the universe and mankind itself were created by the voluntary sacrifice of the gods, and it was man's duty to repay this debt. The shedding of blood reenacted this original sacrifice at a symbolic level, but it also had a practical purpose. The god Huitzilopochtli was a warrior god, identified with the life-giving sun, and to help him in his daily struggle with the forces of darkness and night he had to be nourished with hearts and blood. Death in battle or by sacrifice became something to look forward to, and was the subject of many Aztec poems and songs.

Psychological, religious and economic pressures all combined to make constant warfare a necessity. War offered a young man his chance of glory and promotion, but it also provided the captives needed in ever greater quantities by the gods. In spite of its rich chinampas, the new Aztec "superpower" had grown so large that it could no longer feed its population, and the city became dependent for its survival on imported foodstuffs, raw materials and manufactured goods. Some of these were obtained by purchase, but a great deal was extorted in the form of taxes from subject provinces. Copies of Aztec tribute lists have survived the Spanish Conquest and show that the cities of the triple alliance were obtaining more than 20,000 tons of basic foods from the provinces of the empire in the 16th century, not to mention cloth, metal and luxury goods from the tropical lowlands. Having learned that aggression pays, Aztec policy became one of continuous conquest.

In 1519, when Cortes landed on the Gulf Coast of Mexico, the Aztec empire was at the height of its glory and was still expanding the territory under its control. Two years later its power was broken and Tenochtitlan lay in ruins – to rise again in a new guise as Mexico City, colonial capital of New Spain.

Machu Picchu: Inca Architecture and Engineering

The Inca city of Machu Picchu presents an astonishing sight to those who are hardy enough to negotiate the narrow stone road, sometimes stepped, that leads along the crest of the Andes to the city. Situated at some 9,000 feet elevation, Machu Picchu tops a narrow saddle of rock between two mountains, with precipitous drops on either side, as shown in the aerial view below. Over 100 acres of stone buildings in fine Inca masonry of granite exhibit the engineering skill of those who built the city. Despite its glamorous situation, Machu Picchu has all the salient features of a typical Inca provincial city – a central plaza flanked by the palace, the Sun Temple and various public buildings, a defensive wall, an efficient water system supplying numerous baths and fountains, and terraced hillsides for the intensive growing of crops. But there is one difference: it is by far the best preserved Inca city left to us. For centuries after the Spanish conquest it was totally forgotten until it was dramatically rediscovered in 1911 by the American explorer, Hiram Bingham.

Right and opposite page: The city of Machu Picchu was a natural fortress, protected by steep slopes and a mountain on three sides and open only to the south, where the main road entered. Here was a defensive wall with a dry moat, and on the highest part of the ridge was the city gate (*right*). It was built into a defensive salient, and as in the reconstructions on the opposite page it was probably secured by massive wooden beams and a cross bar, all lashed to the stonework.

Below: This plan of Machu Picchu shows clearly the typical arrangement of an Inca city, with the main road leading into an oblong plaza to the right, the royal palace at one end, and the Sun Temple directly behind it (the Inca king was considered the son of the sun).

1. Sacred Plaza
   a. Priest's House
   b. Temple of the Three Windows
   c. Principal Temple
2. Intihuatana Hill (Stone marked)
3. Central Plaza
4. Royal Inca Palace
5. Temple of the Sun
6. Baths and Fountains Staircase
7. Ingenuity Group
8. Three-Doorway Group (residential)
9. Storehouses
10. Residential Groups
11. Workmen's Dwellings (construction workers?)
12. Acllahuasi
13. Barracks
14. Main Road
15. Lookout Tower
16. The Wall
17. City Gate
18. Agricultural Terraces

Below: A view of the city, looking north along the main plaza, with the houses of nobles built into the hill to the right. The hill has been terraced and outcrops of rock have been cleverly moulded into the building pattern. At the far end of the plaza is the Acllahuasi, or "house of the chosen women," a kind of convent where the most attractive girls were housed for eventual sacrifice, for the use of the royal harem as concubines, or for making the royal clothes. Most larger Inca cities had an Acllahuasi.

Below: The sacred plaza, lying on the west side of the central plaza and at the foot of the stairway leading up the Intihuatana hill. Two temples, both open-fronted, face onto the plaza as well as the priest's house (background, with two doorways) which was probably the dwelling of the High Priest or his deputies. Its interior is lined with niches and has a large stone bench on one side. The High Priest, who was always a close relative of the Inca, or Emperor, must have only occasionally visited Machu Picchu.

Left: The temple of the three windows on the sacred plaza. It lies on heavy foundations built up from the steep terrace below. Excavations revealed no objects inside the building but numerous potsherds in the central plaza, outside and below the windows, perhaps thrown out as offerings to the gods.

Below: The Intihuatana temple with its stone altar and post, whose purpose is not known. However, the name means "place to which the sun is tied," and similar altars are found in other Inca centers, suggesting a connection with the rising of the sun at the June solstice, the beginning of the Inca ceremonial year.

Above: The royal palace, at the southern end of the central plaza. Behind it are the Sun Temple, linked to the palace by a gateway, and the largest of the baths. The palace was used to house the Inca and his family or subordinate officials when visiting the city.

Below: A burial cave, one of many found within and outside the city. These were natural fissures in the rock, often modified with masonry, as here, and sealed with a wall (here it has disappeared). The mummies, flexed, were usually laid in niches inside the caves.

Below: All caves in the city had been looted, but Bingham excavated many outside, finding numerous artifacts such as the Aryballus pot, below, and the remains of 173 mummies. Of these 150 were women, suggesting a large and permanent Acllahausi.

Left: A fine example of Inca polygonal masonry in Tampu Machay, another Inca town. No mortar was ever used, and so close is the fit between these massive stones that it has often been said, and with truth, that a knife cannot be inserted between them. The stones were prepared by patient pecking with stone mauls, and then abrading and sanding for a fine finish. The finest masonry is found in the capital, Cuzco.

Opposite page: A view from the city south across the main terraces (which probably belonged to the Inca) to a barrack block of gabled houses, some reconstructed, others not. The walls of these superbly-built terraces were about 15 feet high, but with only about 10 feet appearing above the next lower terrace. Topsoil was laboriously brought up the mountain by hand and laid on a gravel base to form the fields. The produce no doubt went to the Inca and his retainers.

Below: The so-called "ingenuity" group of buildings, probably residential, because excavations yielded much domestic pottery, mortars for grinding corn and so forth. The block is enclosed within a wall with one massive entrance, and within this each house is self-contained. Hiram Bingham named the group "ingenuity" because it was "characterized by particularly ingenious stone-cutting." It lies near one end of the central plaza.

Below: The photograph shows how the Inca engineers utilized every bit of space and every natural feature to build their city on the barren ridge of Machu Picchu. This building, part of one of the residential compounds on the eastern side, takes advantage of a jutting outcrop for support.

Below: Reconstruction of a gabled building, like the barrack block buildings in the picture above, to illustrate how the wooden-framed thatch roof may have been secured to the building. Ingenious lashings fastened the roof structure to stone pegs built into the masonry of the building itself.

Above: One of the 16 baths of Machu Picchu, built of heavy granite. The Incas were masters at water engineering for agricultural and domestic uses. A narrow conduit brought water into Machu Picchu, crossing the moat on a stone aqueduct, piercing the wall, then flowing down past the Sun Temple through a series of baths and fountains.

Below: One of the so-called barrack blocks at Machu Picchu. The Incas were a militaristic people and it seems most likely that a garrison would have been stationed at the city. The Incas maintained a small standing army, but for the frequent campaigns raised larger armies by conscripting regular quotas from each town and province.

GREATER ANTILLES
LESSER ANTILLES
CARIBBEAN SEA

ATLANTIC

OCEAN

90° 80° 70° 60° 50° 40° 30°

20°

Point
Gallinas

Gulf of Venezuela

Cartagena
Caracas
Gulf of Darien
Lake
Maracaibo
Orinoco
Delta

-10°

Isthmus of Panama

Gulf of Panama

Medellín

VENEZUELA

Orinoco

GUIANA

Bogotá

COLOMBIA

Rio Branco

Rio Negro

Mouths
of the
Amazon

ECUADOR

Japurá

Amazon

Quito
Cotopaxi
Equator

GALÁPAGOS
ISLANDS

Guayaquil Riobamba

Tumbes Tomebamba

Marañón

Iquitos

Manaus

Amazon

Cape
Sao Roque

Point Pariñas

Purus

Juruá

Madeira

Tapajós

Xingu

Tocantins

Parnaíba

Recife

Cajamarca

Chan Chan

SELVAS

Huánuco Viejo

SERRA DOS PARECIS
Guaporé

BRAZIL

-10°

Paramonga
Tarma
Lima Jauja
Pachacamac
Tambo Colorado

Machu Picchu
Cuzco

BOLIVIA

Titicaca
Island of the Sun
La Paz
Tiahuanaco
Poopó

Salvador
All Saints
Bay

Brasília

Rio São Francisco

Cuiabá

PACIFIC

Arica

Salar
de
Uyuni
Porco

Paraguay

Paraná

Paranaíba

Chaco

Pilcomayo

BRAZILIAN
HIGHLANDS

-20°

Tropic of Capricorn

San Miguel
de Tucumán

Paraguay

Asunción

São Paulo

Rio de Janeiro

Cape Frio

Tropic of Capricorn

Copiapó

Salinas
Grandes

Uruguay

Porto Alegre

OCEAN

Aconcagua

Santiago

Córdoba

Mendoza
Rosario

Paraná

Talca

Buenos Aires

Montevideo

Rio de la Plata

-30°

110°

Rio Negro
Lake
Nahuel
Huapi

Rio Negro

Blanca B.

PAMPAS

ARGENTINA

ANDES MOUNTAINS

CHILE

PATAGONIA

Atacama Desert

-40°

Cape
Tres Puntas

FALKLAND
ISLANDS

SOUTH AMERICA
AND THE
INCA EMPIRE

Strait of Magellan

Tierra del Fuego

SOUTH GEORGIA

approximate extension of
the Inca Empire

Inca road system

-50°

Cape
Horn

Drake Passage

SOUTH
ORKNEY ISLANDS

■ Porco Inca towns

● La Paz modern place names

SOUTH SHETLAND
ISLANDS

0   500   1000 k

0   500 st. miles

90° 80° 70° 60° 50° 40°

In 1525, on the eve of the Spanish conquest, South America was chequered with a multitude of different cultures, some quite primitive, others socially and politically advanced. Our knowledge of the ancient civilizations of South America is very uneven because most archaeological work has been concentrated in those areas, such as Peru and Colombia, where one can expect to make spectacular finds of gold, silver and copper objects as well as fine decorated pottery, carvings and substantial architecture. Very little work has been carried out in the Amazon basin, not only because the ceramics are of no great market value but also because the jungle makes sites difficult to locate and excavate, and the remains are poorly preserved in the humid soil. For this reason this brief survey will trace the prehistory of the most culturally advanced area of the continent, the Central Andes of Peru and Bolivia.

Early hunters. The date of man's migration southwards from Mesoamerica through the Isthmus of Panama can only be estimated with reference to the earliest "human-associated" archaeological finds in South America. The earliest recorded material has come from Flea Cave, in the Ayacucho basin in Highland Peru, where, in the lowest eight-inch layer of the cave, some animal vertebrae and a rib bone from an extinct species of ground sloth have been found, together with four stone chopping tools and a few flakes. Above this, a further four feet of deposit revealed a continuation of the same crude tools made by striking a core of volcanic tuff with a hammerstone. They were large and roughly shaped into choppers and scrapers for use in processing meat and wood, and into spokeshaves, or grooved tools for sharpening and shaping spears. These tools were also found in association with burned and fossilized ground sloth bones.

Several of these bones have been dated by the radiocarbon method and have produced a range of dates for this culture of "Core Tool" Hunters from 17,600 ($\pm$ 300) BC to 12,700 ($\pm$ 1400) BC, and MacNeish, the excavator, has estimated that this hunting tradition was typical of the area from 25,000 to 15,000 years ago.

Around 13,000 BC there was a distinct change in the tool inventory of the Andean hunters. A new method of stone tool production became important, that of shaping small flakes of stone or bone into lighter and easy-to-handle tools. After being struck from a core of rock, the flakes were chipped and worked into the desired forms, such as scrapers, spokeshaves, spearpoints and perforators.

With the final retreat of the glaciers between 9000 and 8000 BC the flora and fauna of South America began to adjust to new dynamic conditions. Man's lifestyle, too, had to readapt itself to the changing environment in order to exploit plant and animal resources effectively. In the

Page 117: In the high Andes, heartland of the Inca Empire. The llamas loiter on an Inca terrace high above the Urubamba River, near Machu Picchu.

[Map 1:] *Left*: South America and the Inca Empire.

warmer conditions Ice Age animals found it increasingly difficult to survive. Species of ground sloth, horse and mastodon were characteristic in the early phases of this post-glacial period, but by 7500 BC they were extinct. In contrast, species of modern deer and camelids (such as llama and alpaca) expanded their range. Their bones make up an increasing proportion of the refuse at archaeological sites up to 7500 BC after which they became the dominant animals.

The technology of these hunters had to be adapted to the new species of game, and a new type of small spearpoint (with a stemmed or fishtail base, so that it could be easily hafted to the shaft), became common. These were specialized hunting weapons shaped by precision flaking and designed to be efficient killers. Other common implements were the scrapers, burins, knives and gravers used for skinning and butchering animals. Similar remains are widely distributed throughout South America, and are almost always found in association with animal bones. The economy seems to have been solely a hunting one, yet there is no evidence of any modern hunters living solely by means of the kill. Such groups have a more generalized diet including wild berries, seeds and roots. The Andean hunters probably had a similar economy. The excavated sites do not appear to be the homes of permanent settlers but rather the seasonal shelters of migrant bands which moved in an annual cycle following the wild herds to pastures in the puna (treeless plateau), mountain valleys and lower flanks of the western Andes. They made their camps in particular seasons at localities where they could exploit specific plants for food, fiber and fuel.

About 7000 BC definite regional variations in the hunting and gathering economy can be detected. In Venezuela large pressure-flaked projectile points and scrapers are associated with mastodon and ground sloth. In the mountains and plateaus of northwest Argentina, northern Chile, Bolivia and Peru spearpoints were shaped from blades and were used to hunt llama and deer. There are several sites scattered throughout this area which also show tools, such as mortars and pestles, for grinding seeds. On the coast of Peru the tool kit contained flaked stemmed spearpoints as well as scrapers and other llama butchering tools, but there are also many core tools and a few grinders. Some sites were also littered with broken shells. The economy and diet of these bands were quite diverse.

The transition to agriculture. The emergence of agriculture took place gradually over several thousand years. Between 9000 and 7000 BC man experimented with technology in order to improve his food procuring ability in the changing environment. He developed better spearpoints and arrowheads for greater hunting efficiency and used grindstones and other tools to improve plant processing. The regular seasonal movements enabled him to assess the foods available, and over the next few millennia this intimate knowledge of his surroundings helped him to

domesticate, that is to control and alter, certain species of plants and animals for his own needs.

An English botanist, Barbara Pickersgill, has studied the early cultivated remains of chili peppers, beans, cotton, corn and peanuts found on the coast of Peru for the period 3000 BC to 150 AD and the present-day distributions of their wild ancestors. She suggested that agriculture may have begun in the Andes, or even further east in Amazonia. Until the late 1960s there was no evidence from the mountains to confirm Pickersgill's hypothesis, but recently Thomas Lynch has investigated a series of late Stone Age cave and open-air living sites situated at different altitudes and in different vegetation zones in the Callejon de Huaylas. He concluded that seasonal migration was still taking place because there was a marked difference in activity between sites from different zones. Those shelters located over 12,000 feet on the puna grassland were characterized almost entirely by spearpoints and llama and deer bones. These he called "butchering stations." The sites at around 9,000 feet could exploit two different zones, river valleys and desert scrub, and contained mixed deposits of plant and animal remains and only a few spearpoints. He called these "seasonal base camps."

One of these lower camps, Guitarrero Cave, has been extensively excavated and has revealed the nature of the economy between 8000 and 5500 BC. A few spearheads were found, characteristic of the Andean hunting tradition, but the predominant stone tools are scrapers and knives which could be used both for butchering wild animals and making wooden implements. In the lower levels a mortar and pestle have been found, indicating that

Desert landscape at Moche on the central coast of Peru. In this hot, dry region and in the highlands of Ayacucho archaeologists have traced the earliest transition from a hunting and collecting society to the first settled farming communities.

seeds were brought to the cave for crushing, but this does not necessarily mean that plants were cultivated. However, in the upper levels some small cobs of pop corn and two species of bean were recovered. The beans were definitely cultivated, for they have undergone genetic change. The seeds are larger than those of the wild ancestor and the pods do not shatter and cause the beans to be lost during harvest. They were found in a layer carbon dated 5730 ± 280 BC and probably represent a long period of domestication in the Santa Valley. However, hunting and gathering of wild animals and plants and seasonal migration up to puna pastures and back continued despite the development of cultivation. The changes in food yield brought about by agriculture were, at first, insufficient to make it the dominant activity, but over the next 3,000 years plants were improved and provided a greater share of the diet.

MacNeish has recorded similar seasonal migration, diversity of occupation and experiments in domestication at seasonal base camps in Ayacucho. During the period 6400 to 5000 BC llama were living with men in their caves, judging by the amount of llama excreta in the domestic refuse. In the next phase (5000–3800 BC) there are definite changes in the bone structure of the llama that suggest domestication. The guinea pig, still a delicacy in Peru today, was also brought under man's control as a food animal. The first definite evidence of cultivation, however, appears during the 5th millennium BC with squash, amaranth and quinoa. From 3800 BC onwards crop plants gradually increased in importance in the diet and new ones such as various fruits, cotton, corn, beans and manioc were domesticated. The importance of migratory hunting and collecting decreased and the population began to live in larger, more permanent villages as their food supply became more stable. The transition to agriculture in the sierra can be seen as a slow process of economic and social reorientation which lasted about 4,500 years.

On the central coast of Peru this transition took place rather differently. For 3,500 years prior to 3700 BC a general hunting and gathering economy sustained man's occupation of this hot dry desert. The folk camped on hillsides in the winter months where the moisture from permanent fog enabled plants to grow. This dense, lush carpet of vegetation, called lomas, allowed intensive gathering of wild plants – berries, roots, leaves and seeds. Llama and deer were hunted at the height of the winter when these animals came down from the highlands to graze in the lomas, and in the summer the people moved down into the river valleys to hunt the animals in the glades on the river banks. They collected wild grass seeds and roots there and gathered protein-rich shellfish from the seashore. These folk also cultivated the bottle gourd for use as a container and cooking pot into which hot stones were dropped to cook the food.

The next 1,200 years witnessed a change in emphasis in the economy. Hunting declined and the bulk of protein was now gained from shellfish collected from the shores of sandy bays and rocky headlands. It was much less effort to gather shellfish than to pursue and kill animals, nor could beds of shellfish be over-exploited to the point of extinction by such small, although increasing, populations. Thus a better protein supply was assured than could be provided by hunting. Large black rubbish dumps or middens covered in shell and containing crude houses of stone, whale bone and reeds line the bays and headlands. People still collected wild plants in winter from the lomas and went in summer to the valleys to gather berries and roots and cultivate gourds and squash.

After 2500 BC the population on the coast expanded very quickly and fishing provided a new and even more stable protein supply. Earlier fishing had been only a minor activity, but after 2500 BC nets, hooks and lines were used to exploit the inshore fishing grounds. People continued to live along the coast and collect shellfish, building up middens, and sea mammals which had been stranded on the beach were clubbed to death. Very few people now made the long trek to the lomas hillsides, as life revolved around coastal fishing; but a few moved to temporary summer campsites in the lower reaches of the rivers to grow beans, squash, chilis and fruit as well as cotton (for twining into clothes), using summer floodwater to irrigate their crops. The number and size of settlements increased year by year and in some villages over a thousand people lived in tightly-packed, flimsy houses made from cane anchored to the ground by stone footings.

Some 600 years later cultivated plants had become as important in the diet as fish and shellfish, but there was no staple. Maize first appeared on the coast around 2000 BC. In dietary terms it forms, together with beans, a complete protein-rich food, thus a rival to fish. As a result of this, settlements as large as those on the coast were permanently located on river flood plains to house farmers whose protein came from both agriculture and fishing. Further up valley, small villages were built for farmers who used small canals to bring water to their fields. This constant reorientation of economy away from hunting and gathering took place slowly, under conditions of an expanding population and demands for a more assured food supply. The delay in introducing agriculture on the coast was due to the success of shellfish gathering and fishing. But by the time the so-called Initial Pottery Period began on the coast, about 1800 BC, agriculture had become the most important subsistence activity.

Throughout this 6,000-year period society also underwent radical changes in organization. Hunters and collectors generally form small bands of about 100 people, who separate into family units in times of scarcity, but gather

A very ancient agricultural tool of the high Andes, the *taclla* or foot plow, recorded in a sketch by Poma de Ayala (1584–1614) of the potato harvest in June. De Ayala was himself a native Inca.

together in seasonal base camps to exploit a particularly abundant resource. There are no leaders or chiefs in this type of organization which was typical of the hunting and gathering folk of the central Andes, and even in the seasonal base camps there is no archaeological evidence of difference in status between individuals of the same group.

By 2000 BC, under the pressure of a dense, village-dwelling population, there was a need further to assure food production through religious ceremony, and a new type of social organization emerged based on class stratification. The people at the top of the hierarchy were priests who commanded not only the supernatural but the earthly life as well. Farmers brought produce as offerings to the gods of agriculture, rain, rivers and mountains. This was used to feed the priests and the gangs building the temples and was the origin of the tribute system, which was also administered by the Inca more than 3,000 years later.

The power wielded by priests can be seen quite dramatically in elaborate ceremonial pyramid centers. These must have taken a considerable amount of time and labor organization to construct. On the central and north-central coasts temples were built in areas of dense farming and fishing populations. In the Ancon-Chillon area of the central coast the sites of Rio Seco and Chuquitanta comprise cobble and earth pyramids flanked by lower structures or wings to form a plaza and ceremonial routeway.

The mound was built by filling in some rooms and constructing other rooms on top. These were then filled in with rubble and the mound was built up. The function of the wings has yet to be determined by excavation but they were probably the dwellings of the priests and storerooms for the offerings. In the mountains, the temple complex of Kotosh was begun by agricultural folk under the direction of a priestly organization.

The first appearance of pottery (1800–1000 BC). Pottery first appeared in Peru between 1800 and 1400 BC. Archaeologists see it as a major cultural divide and the beginning of a new period, but it caused little change in the way people lived except that the crudely-made jars could now be used for storing seeds, keeping them dry and free from destruction by rodents. Many were cooking pots, yet food was still cooked with a pot-boiler rather than by direct heating over a fire. In some areas local potters decorated their jars and bowls with incised designs of lines and dots, or with small balls or snakes of clay stuck on the outside. These have been found in association with elite occupation and burials, particularly around ceremonial buildings where offerings were made. The earliest pottery made in

An early terraced temple-pyramid, made of earth faced with cobblestones, at Chuquitanta, Peru. This was virtually the first major public building on the Peruvian coast (2500–1800 BC).

South America comes from Colombia and Ecuador, and is over 1,000 years older than that found in Peru.

At approximately the same time, the heddle loom was invented. It speeded up the production of woven cloth but in its early stages produced no better quality fabrics than those made by the older method of twining. It was only later that the loom, like pottery, was to have a major impact on prehistoric life style.

The economy continued much as it had before the introduction of pottery, and agriculture continued to gain ascendancy. Maize, already a staple food in the mountains, became a staple on the coast and spread rapidly while cultivated peanuts, first grown in the eastern Bolivian lowlands, were added to the coastal diet to supplement the protein content. Manioc, a tropical forest root crop, also made its first appearance on the coast at this time, which probably indicates contact with Amazonia as manioc has never been cultivated in the highlands. Bones of domesticated llama have also been found here though llama were not used for food but for sacrifice, being part of a cult in the Central Andes. Its remains occur in the earliest levels of the Kotosh temple and in a small shrine in a coastal midden in the Viru Valley.

With the emergence of permanent agriculture, life became more settled throughout the Central Andes. The number and size of villages increased as well as the number of ceremonial centers to serve and control the population. New centers were built on the north-central and central coasts and in the central and southern highlands. In the Chillon area of the central coast the earlier pyramids of Chuquitanta and Rio Seco were abandoned and a larger complex called La Florida was built in the Rimac Valley.

The vast site of Las Haldas in the desert south of Casma on the north-central coast also had a substantial residential area. Here the main focus was a large terraced platform and other mounds arranged around three plazas and approached via a wide, mile-long ceremonial roadway. The whole complex must have taken many years and much labor to construct. It was located several miles from the nearest cultivated land which shows how powerful the priests were in organizing labor gangs to build it, and in maintaining a tribute system. The power of religion may have therefore caused the first major status differences among the population.

At Kotosh in the central highlands improvements and extensions were made to the earlier temple complex. The size of the main pyramid was increased by filling in the ceremonial rooms on the old mound and building new ones on top. The rooms were faced with stone and had niches in the walls and several bas-reliefs, one of which shows a pair of crossed hands. This particular temple has been dated to 1450 BC and was the third oldest at the site.

The Chavin cult (1000–300 BC). During the Initial Pottery Period different regions showed similar subsistence characteristics and a similar pattern of ceremonial centers, but quite different pottery, sculpture and architecture. By contrast, the subsequent period, characterized by the Chavin cult (1000–300 BC), was one in which for the first time the formerly disparate regions were united under a common cultural banner.

The sphere of Chavin influence was widespread in the Central Andes. The cult was particularly dominant in the north and there are even traces of it in southern Ecuador, while in the Ica and Nazca Valleys to the south a distinctive contemporary culture was built up which had experienced strong influences from Chavin.

Chavin de Huantar was the main site of this period, and is situated high in the Andes in the Marañon drainage. The site comprises several stepped masonry platforms, terraces and sunken plazas. The original platform, the Old Temple, known as the Castillo, consists of a terraced building and two masonry wings, a U-shaped pattern which dates back to the first appearance of religious buildings in Peru. It is honeycombed with passages and inside one of them was found the Lanzon stela, a 13-foot tall carved obelisk of white granite. In front of the temple was a sunken plaza. The temple was gradually expanded and the old south wing was enlarged to form the New Temple. This too was galleried and shrines were built on top. On one of the outer terraces there is a row of sculpted deified heads tenoned into the wall. The pyramid was also approached between

[Map 2:] The Chavin cult, 1000–300 BC.

two detached wing-platforms and through a sunken plaza. A large monumental gateway made of white granite and black limestone gave entrance into the gallery system of this pyramid. It is decorated with a finely carved mythological creature, half man, half eagle, which was probably the guardian of the temple. The chief image inside this building has long since gone, but it was probably the so-called "Staff God."

The basic criterion by which archaeologists have distinguished Chavin culture is art style. This derived from the monumental stone sculpture at the site of Chavin de Huantar itself, but its characteristics have also been noted on massive mud-plaster carvings on bone and shell, incised or modeled on pots and metal, and woven into lengths of cloth. It is an art style which reflects a cult whose gods were mythological men and beasts. The most common device used on all figures is the snarling mouth of a jaguar with its canine teeth overlapping its lips. The extremities of the body, such as the arms and legs, are shown

At Chavin most sculptures are found in the form of heads projecting from the outer walls and in relief friezes set in the walls, cornices and doorway columns. There are two principal deities – the "Staff God" and the "Smiling God." The Smiling God is probably the elder of the two and the Staff God may derive from it. It is carved on the Lanzon stela and was probably the chief deity of the Old Temple. The carving is of a human with a large mouth, upturned as if smiling, with only the upper canines showing. He wears spools which distend the ears, a necklace and a belt of faces, and his hair is a mass of snakes. The god is also carved on three heads which project from the temple wall and in a frieze in the patio in front of the black and white gateway to the New Temple, where he is shown carrying a spondylus shell. Throughout Peruvian prehistory this shell was a most important religious offering and a symbol of status.

The Staff God (probably more important than the Smiling God) was also a deified human, but he is not

The Smiling God at Chavin de Huantar. This god and his companion, the Staff God, along with a range of mythological creatures, marked the spread of the Chavin cult throughout the central Andes.

Right: A schematic drawing of the Chavin Staff God with downturned mouth and canine teeth. He holds a staff in either hand.

as tongues issuing out of mouths. Even when the main figure is a bird or a cat, the mouth and tongue device is used to portray wings and tails. Hair and whiskers are represented by snakes, and this device is sometimes used to illustrate ears, birds' feathers, and feather-headdresses. The mouth, however, is the commonest feature. It was believed to be the strongest part of the body and consequently a row of mouths was used to illustrate bone structure.

smiling. His mouth is downturned, with all his canine teeth showing, and he carries a staff in each hand. He was first identified on a frieze which was found at Chavin in the 19th century, but which was removed immediately to a Lima museum, so we do not know exactly where in the temple it came from.

The origin of the Chavin cult and its iconography have not really been determined. Some scholars have argued that it crystalized on the north-central coast in the Casma and Nepeña Valleys where there was a history of stelae carving and temple building, but this is unlikely because the animals portrayed are the most powerful ones from the tropical forest, the jaguar, eagle, anaconda and caiman, and have always been revered by tribes from that area. It is probable, therefore, that the cult grew out of contact with a tropical forest culture.

Whatever its origins, the Chavin cult spread very rapidly throughout the northern part of Peru in the 10th and 9th centuries BC mainly as a result of missionary activity. Fort-like hilltop enclosures, located near some temples, indicate the importance also of military conquests. Wherever the cult has been found it was superimposed on the local cultures and is generally quite distinct from them in terms of pottery and iconography. Chavin pottery is fine-grained and generally of a single color, red or black, and is decorated with incised or scratched mythological designs. The most characteristic forms are the stirrup-spouted bottle and open bowl.

Metal-working now became common in Peru and it too was a medium of expression for the Chavin art style. Designs were engraved or embossed on thin sheets of hammered gold or copper. The most common metal items in graves are ear spools, tweezers, rings and belts. Another invention of this time speeded up the production and variety of textiles – the backstrap loom.

Life was not significantly altered, apart from these two additions. The ceremonial center was the focus not only of the supernatural life but also the economic, for tribute continued to be paid to the priests and gods. Small cities were built around some pyramids, although most had no attendant population. In these districts the common people lived in the countryside, adjacent to the lands they farmed, in small villages of conjoined family huts with their own small shrines and cemeteries, but under the domination of a ceremonial center. The idea of the temple complex being the focus of life spread widely with the diffusion of the cult in the northern area.

In southern Peru, in the Ica and Nazca Valleys, the Paracas culture existed without any major temples and the population was concentrated in fairly large settlements. This area was not devoid of Chavin influence, however, for its deities and mythological creatures appear on pottery and embroidered into textiles. The designs on pottery were both incised and painted and have been found in profusion in one cemetery known as Paracas Cavernas. Here mummies were discovered in 25-feet deep, dome-shaped chambers cut into the rock, and in one of these alone there were 55 crouched corpses wrapped in many layers of cloth. Irrigation systems on the coast were extended during this period as the population expanded and became more and more dependent upon maize agriculture.

By 700 BC all evidence of the Chavin cult had disappeared from the central coast but it remained strong in its northern heartland and around Paracas until about 200 BC when it finally disappeared.

Regional sub-cultures (200 BC–900 AD). With the end of the Chavin cult, uniformity of culture over much of the central Andes was lost and intense regional differences emerged. Six major nations have been delimited by their distinctive pottery, architecture and art styles. These are Mochica on the north coast; Cajamarca in the northern Highlands; Recuay from the Callejon de Huaylas; Lima from the central coast; Nazca from the south coast; and

Detail of a Paracas-Necropolis shroud from the southern coast of Peru. This fine textile shows an anthropomorphic deity, perhaps the hawk god, symbol of political dominance.

Tiahuanaco on the Bolivian antiplano. These remained intact for approximately 1,000 years, during which time technology was developed and significant aesthetic advances were made in all art forms including pottery, textiles, metallurgy, sculpture and architecture. Art historians believe that the central Andes achieved a cultural apogee in this period and have termed it the Classic or Florescent period.

Society, economy and government were still strictly ordered by religion. The temple complex with its attendant theocratic hierarchy continued to dominate the landscape and the people. Around it, large urban residential areas were built.

The Mochica culture of the north coast is the best known of all the cultures of this period because of the commercial and ethnographic value of its fine grave pottery, and the large amount of archaeological work which has been carried out in its area. The Mochica state covered the lower, coastal parts of nine river valleys stretching from Lambayeque in the north to Nepeña in the south. Each valley is separated from its neighbor by up to 40 miles of barren unoccupied desert and the entire state was linked by a series of roads.

Mochica pottery evolved out of local cultures, such as Salinar, which came briefly to the fore when Chavin influence waned. Phases one and two (of the five developmental phases) are contemporary in the Chicama Valley in the center of the cultural area but absent from the southern valleys. At this time there existed another small state in the south characterized by a negatively-painted pottery style (light on dark background) and known today as Gallinazo. It is related stylistically to both the Mochica and Recuay styles.

Along the whole of the north coast the dominant landscape feature was the pyramid or platform made from rectangular, canemold-marked adobe bricks. These pyramids were located in flat areas on the edge of cultivated land, and on the sides and tops of hills. In the Chicama Valley there is a small adobe pyramid known as Huaca Facala, perched on top of an isolated hill, a truly revered position, and approached by a long adobe and natural rock ramp. The people who built it and worshiped there must have lived scattered in the countryside because there are no houses around the hill, but their dead were buried in two cemeteries at its foot. In both the Moche and Viru Valleys similar small hilltop temples were built, but the sherds found around them are of Gallinazo origin. The Gallinazos built their capital near the coast on the northern edge of the Viru Valley. It comprised six terraced adobe pyramids of which the largest stood on a platform, 440 yards by 200 yards, and was 220 feet long by 290 feet wide and over 75 feet high. There were several subsidiary mounds which were honeycombed with galleries and rooms and surrounding the complex a large resident urban population. Gallinazo rural settlements had small pyramids and adjacent farming villages.

Phases three and four in the Mochica pottery seriation are also contemporary. During this period the Mochica state expanded, overwhelmed the Gallinazo nation and also spread northwards, but the community pattern and way of life changed little.

The new Mochica capital was typical of the period. It was built in the desert around a Gallinazo platform at the foot of the Cerro Blanco on the south side of the Moche

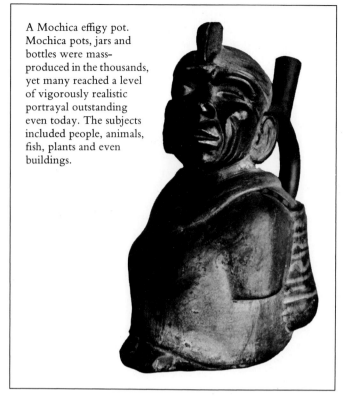

A Mochica effigy pot. Mochica pots, jars and bottles were mass-produced in the thousands, yet many reached a level of vigorously realistic portrayal outstanding even today. The subjects included people, animals, fish, plants and even buildings.

Valley. This temple, known today as Huaca de la Luna, was enlarged into a series of inter-connected platforms and plazas and upon them were built large rooms. This part of the site is very similar to the new Viru capital, Huancaco, which has been described as a temple with secular palace functions. Huaca de la Luna was covered with a thick mud plaster, and polychrome friezes depicting men and war scenes were painted on the outer walls. The main pyramid stood over 70 feet high. The other platforms were lower and probably carried storerooms or the residences of the priests.

About 600 yards across the plain from this temple, the Huaca del Sol was built. This was the largest mud-brick building in the prehispanic New World. It comprised a large rectangular platform 750 feet by 450 feet and 60 feet high and on top of this, in the southern half, a 340-foot square platform was raised a further 15 feet above the ground. This large edifice was approached by a 20-foot wide ceremonial ramp from the north which was over 100 yards long. The whole pyramid was built of vertical columns of rectangular adobe bricks bonded with layers of cane and wood, and the outer face was plastered. Over 130 million bricks were used, and it must have taken a vast labor force many years to build – the product of advanced engineering skill and organization. Between these pyramids are the remains of many rooms where a fairly large population lived. Today the lower slopes of Cerro Blanco are red with broken pottery left by looters who have ransacked the extensive cemeteries contemporary with the temples.

In all Mochican valleys ordinary people lived and were

buried not only in the shadow of the massive temples, but also in small rural villages where they engaged in agriculture or commerce. Their houses were built of cane and stone on terraces where the land was steep, in the desert near to irrigated land or alongside roads. The farmers grew a variety of crops and the whole range (maize, beans, potato and avocado) has been modeled in effigy pots and bottles. The irrigation systems in each valley were expanded to accommodate the needs of a growing population and a large religious organization, and in so doing the Moche people engaged in other massive public works schemes. Canals were dug and fields carved out of the desert. Aqueducts of earth and sand were constructed across the dry side valleys which enter the main valley. The Ascope aqueduct in the Chicama Valley was built to lead a canal directly across a side valley more than a mile wide. The aqueduct is over 50 feet high and contains over 200 million tons of earth, sand and adobe. It was truly a magnificent feat of engineering skill and avoided the construction of a ten-mile contour canal between the same two points.

The final phase of the Mochica state saw an increase in size of the urban population but a lessening in importance of the temple complex. The new pyramids were smaller, enclosed by walled courtyards and associated with secular, palace-like structures, under the influence of the Huari culture, which diffused more secular ideas over the whole country. Society no longer comprised only a theocratic oligarchy and peasantry. There was a class of local lords who performed certain religious functions, but were not strictly priests.

Mochica grave pottery is generally of two types: effigy stirrup-spouted bottles, and jars and bottles which are painted in a cream slip and onto which scenes of everyday life and the supernatural are drawn in black and red. The pots were made in molds and mass-produced. The magnificent effigy vessels were modeled on a variety of subjects. They include heads of important people, heads with special afflictions or diseases such as a hairlip or leprosy, death masks, full figures of men and women performing various sexual practices, hunting, fishing or fighting, and animals, fish and plants important in the Mochican diet or ritual such as deer, potatoes and spondylus shells. Some of the modeled pots represent buildings on top of pyramids or structures, probably throne rooms in which one man is sitting.

The painted ceramics are equally useful for the picture they give of everyday life and of the gods. Some show the aftermath of battle with corpses and naked prisoners being taken to the victorious lord who is sitting in a house on top of a pyramid. They show that the local chiefs were carried in litters. Scenes of religious or mythological significance with human figures in animal clothing or headdresses are common. One god is painted with the body, pincers and some of the legs of a crab but with the head and two legs of a man. Another, the "sun-god," appears in a variety of animal forms but always wears a semicircular headdress.

Huaca del Sol on the desert Pacific coast at Moche, the ceremonial capital of the Mochicas. The central pyramid, now half destroyed, was terraced, with graves on the terraces and probably a shrine at the top.

[Map 3:] Regional sub-cultures, 200 BC–900 AD.

During this period metallurgy became highly developed. Gold, silver and copper were smelted and cast into ornaments such as ear spools, nose ornaments, crests and pendants, by using the lost wax (cire perdue) method. In the Mochica realm, copper was also used for tools such as digging sticks, maces and lances. Various gilding techniques were employed to give a gold surface to objects made of copper or low grade alloys.

A similar pattern of cultural achievement and life style can be detected along the whole of the coast. On the central coast the important temple-city of Pachacamac was built comprising a large hilltop pyramid surrounded by a small city, and dedicated to the goddess mother-earth. On the south coast similar temple cities were built, and the characteristic pottery of the Nazca area showed many scenes of daily life and the local gods. Julio Tello in 1929

made to appease the gods or to accompany one of their priests in his afterlife.

Near the southern shores of Lake Titicaca at an altitude of almost 13,000 feet the temple city of Tiahuanaco was built during the first centuries AD. It comprised two avenues which met in a "T" near the main temples. The Akapana was a stone pyramid 50 feet high which rose in terraces and on top of which there was a shrine. Nearby there was a long, low rectangular platform called the Kalasaya surmounted by several shrines and a sunken court. Entrance to the temple complex was via a large gateway carved out of a single block of gray andesite, and is now known as the Gateway of the Sun. It is about 10 feet high and over 12 feet wide with a large doorway cut in the center. Carved above the entrance in bas-relief is a feline-mouthed god with weeping eyes, carrying two staves. He seems to

Right: The "Gateway of the Sun" at Tiahuanaco in Bolivia, entrance to the temple complex. The figure above the gate may be a version of the Chavin Staff God.

Left: A Mochica gold cult mask in the form of a puma with two condors, reversed, on either side, symbolizing strength. A feline mythology marks all Peruvian art from Chavin to the Incas.

[Map 4:] Tiahuanaco cultural influence, 600–1000 AD.

found a large cemetery at Paracas Necropolis in the Nazca Kingdom. He excavated deep rectangular pits filled with over 400 mummies. Each body, crouched, was wrapped in a finely embroidered multi-colored shroud depicting gods, animals, birds and fish, and every skull was deformed. These bodies were probably highly honored sacrifices

be a geometric version of the Chavin Staff God.

Tiahuanaco pottery is characterized by polished polychrome painting of mythological figures. The designs are geometrically rigid, unlike the life-like Mochica pottery.

The state of Tiahuanaco stretched southwards throughout highland Bolivia and into northwestern Argentina and

In the middle Mantaro Valley a local regional culture was dominant, characterized by cities and pottery reflecting influences from the larger state of Nazca. Some pots were painted with typical Nazca polychrome designs of mythological creatures believed to be the gods of that culture. Then after 600 AD the first pots depicting the Tiahuanaco Gateway God were used as burial goods at Conchopata. At this time too the local Nazca-influenced wares experienced minor changes and the feline mouth and bared teeth were included. These innovations imply the introduction of the Tiahuanaco cult, probably as a result of missionary activity or trading contact.

Over the next 50 to 100 years the Tiahuanaco religion was consolidated in this region and particularly in the city of Huari. The city was quite large, with many plazas and great rectangular enclosures forming a central core for both religious and secular functions. Around these were smaller urban residential buildings. A series of very large buildings with rectangular rooms and corridors but very few doors or windows functioned as storerooms for tribute. During this period Huari influence expanded on to the southern and central coasts and as far north as the Callejon de Huaylas, carrying with it its characteristic iconography and pottery. The distribution of two types of pottery – keros painted with religious motifs and modeled effigy bottles with double spouts and connecting bridge handles – indicates that the expansion had some religious significance, because these wares are found not only in Huari but are associated with grave goods at Pacheco in the Nazca Valley and even near Lima. A third kind, a cruder, more utilitarian pottery, mirrors the distribution of the other two and suggests that the expansion must have involved some form of military conquest or colonization.

Between 750 and 850 AD there was a marked change in the nature of the Huari empire but no physical expansion. On the basis of pottery analysis it appears that the religious control wielded by Huari began to be challenged on the coast by vigorous, but related, sects whose centers were in the Nazca Valley and Pachacamac in the Lurin Valley. All three centers continued to make use of earlier mythological figures but incorporated local gods and designs. Even the domestic pottery used at Huari now displayed certain religious symbols which up to this time had been confined to high status pots, mummy wrappings and public architecture, thus demonstrating the universal acceptance of the cult. The pottery of Huari was still the most widespread throughout the empire, the two local styles being restricted to their home provinces.

Politically this period is difficult to interpret. There were no military campaigns and conquests, but within the state the power of Huari seems to have been weakened by the emergence of the coastal sects. Yet the city of Huari grew in size and population at the expense of rival cities which were abandoned and never reoccupied. In the heartland, therefore, the power and the administrative ability of the capital remained strong.

northern Chile, but in Peru it was confined to the Titicaca basin and the area around modern Arequipa. It was a trading nation in basic products – maize, llamas and coca.

The spread of Tiahuanaco religion and the Huari empire (600–1000 AD). This was a time in Peruvian prehistory when much of the Andes area was unified by similar archaeological traits in pottery and iconography and thus, by implication, religion and empire, originating in the city and state of Tiahuanaco.

Zone of Tiahuanaco influence

Zone of Huari influence

Zone of Pachacamac influence

The next 150 years (850–1000 AD) witnessed the rapid expansion of the Huari empire, both to the north and to the south. In the north it established itself in the Basin of Cajamarca and had some influence on the coast, and in the south the frontier stretched between Secuani, Arequipa and the Ocoña Valley. The city of Huari continued to flourish as a great ceremonial and secular center housing a large population and controlling the administration of the empire and the collection and storage of tribute. Large secular cities were also built to administer the newly conquered provinces, and storage complexes in the urban area indicate the importance of tribute in the empire. Two such identical storage areas were built over 600 miles apart at Viracochapampa near Huamachuco in the north, and at Pikillaqta near Cuzco. In these new areas the objects of Huari origin were restricted to the nobility and local officers of the state and had very little influence on local peasant styles.

Society in the Huari empire was now organized along more secular lines. Its leaders were no longer priests alone but nobles and warriors who, in the name of the Tiahuanaco religion, conquered for aggrandizement and prestige. The Marañon Valley in the northern highlands must have been taken after a long struggle and after the men from Huari had sacked the fortified cities of Kollor and Marca Huamachuco. The defensive walls of the new city of Viracochapampa would seem to indicate that the conquerors found it difficult to maintain control of this area.

During this expansion period Pachacamac became the major focus of the Tiahuanaco religion on the coast as the prestige of Nazca was eclipsed. The city adjacent to the temples increased in size, as did the nearby cities of Cajamarquilla and Vista Alegre in the Rimac Valley. Eagle designs were used here on pottery and textiles alongside the basic Tiahuanaco iconography. The distribution of this new style is coastal from Chicama in the north to Nazca in the south. It seems that Pachacamac was carrying on its own traditions and religion from earlier times, with Huari influences, and it remained an important center of religious pilgrimage until the Spanish Conquest over five centuries after the collapse of the Huari empire.

The north coast provides an interesting contrast to much of Huari-Pachacamac-dominated Peru. There, the Mochica culture continued quite vigorously until about 1000 AD, but it never became part of the Huari empire. The Huari-style pottery found on the north coast was either from Cajamarca or copied locally. Even so, these wares form only a small fraction of the high status grave goods. Nevertheless, the Mochica kingdom was considerably influenced by the Huari expansion in two respects. Warfare became an important aspect of life, and city architecture became more secular as is indicated by the appearance of palace-like structures alongside temples, and even by a reduction in the size of temples.

By 1000 AD Huari had been abandoned and its empire

The important Temple of the Sun at Pachacamac, a revered pilgrimage center for all Peru from about 400 AD right up to the Conquest, when the Spaniards looted it.

had disintegrated. On the coast the city of Cajamarquilla suffered the same fate. Many reasons have been proposed for the collapse of this empire, such as a peasant revolt, barbarian invasions (as in the Roman Empire) or an ecological crisis. It seems more likely, however, that the size and multi-ethnic character of the empire caused administrative problems for the capital, hence the promotion of provincial centers at Pachacamac and in Nazca. The second wave of expansion, particularly in the north, must have placed a tremendous strain on state resources, in terms of administration and tribute. Cajamarca appears in the ceramic record to have had quite a widespread culture (c. 800 AD) and its resistance could have brought about the eventual collapse of the empire.

Local states and empires (c. 1000–1475 AD). The demise of the Huari empire witnessed the resurgence of local regional cultures. Each area developed its own distinctive pottery style out of existing local traditions and Huari forms. Andean society had been radically altered by the spread of the Tiahuanaco religion and the militaristic warlike attitudes of the rulers of Huari. Trends towards a more secular social order, urban lifestyle, state organization and warfare continued throughout this period, and these became manifest in changes in settlement form and architecture. The large ceremonial centers, dominant features of the settlement pattern of the earlier theocratic cultures, were no longer constructed. Cities were now built in which the space occupied by religious buildings was small in comparison with that devoted to palaces, administrative buildings and storehouses, and residential building showed differences in form and elaboration reflecting social stratification. Society was now ordered into a hierarchy of classes, each with its own tasks to perform in the running of the state, in agriculture, economics and administration as well as religion. The rulers were god-kings who performed the duties of high priests as well as pursuing more secular ambitions of aggrandizement and kingly authority.

Archaeological interpretation is now joined by documentary material collected by Spanish chroniclers and law courts in the 16th century. This information takes a variety of forms, ranging from legendary histories, lists of rulers and battle descriptions to precise details of the social, economic, political and cosmological order in particular areas in both pre-Inca and Inca times. From this, a concrete picture of the extent of local states and of interstate relations and warfare can be built up. On the coast there were four regional ceramic styles, named in the documents after the states of Chimu, Cuismancu, Chuquismancu and Chincha. In the Sierra, archaeological material of this period is limited, but the documents tell us of Cajamarca in the north, many small and warring nations around the Cuzco basin, and the large Lupaqa kingdom on the shores of Lake Titicaca. Since 200 BC most had been, in fact, centers of strong regional traditions.

The Chimu kingdom developed in a coastal region of the former Mochica nation. Archaeological knowledge of it derives from the political collapse of its predecessor under the military, political and social stresses of the last centuries of the 1st millennium AD. In cemeteries at this time not only the painted funerary pottery of Mochica phase five has been found, but also black pieces known as Chimu, and ceramics which show definite affinities to those of Huari, Pachacamac and Cajamarca. In the southern valleys of Nepeña, Santa and Viru, relatively high proportions of pots show Tiahuanaco themes, which must have come directly from Pachacamac or Huari; others were locally made imitations. These valleys therefore may have fallen under the Huari yoke for a short time.

By contrast, in the valleys to the north the proportion of pieces actually imported is much smaller, but the imitations of Huari designs and forms in black Chimu pottery are common. All are found in association with the finest local Mochica-style pots. It seems, therefore, that these valleys were subjected to some form of contact or missionary activity from Cajamarca or Huari but resisted military domination. The impact of the Huari empire on the Mochica state was, on the whole, one of social and political pressure under which the nation lost cohesion as each individual valley asserted itself independently in the face of the invader. The Chimu kingdom emerged from these remnants and comprised initially a series of local developments. Within a couple of centuries these local traditions had crystalized into two major groups centered on the valleys of Moche-Chicama and the Lambayeque oasis.

The documentary history of the north coast is meager, consisting merely of legends, dynastic history, a dictionary, and 16th-century descriptions collected by Spanish priests. But these do allow a reconstruction of the major events of political life and give some impression of the organization of society.

The first event recorded in the legends of both areas is the landing on the coast of an important chief, called Taycanamu in the Moche-Chicama area, who came from across the sea with a retinue of relations and courtiers and founded the new state. First he conquered the lower Moche Valley and established a new city, learning the local language from the Indians and taking the name of Chimor Capac, King of Chimu. His son, Guacricaur, according to legend, "acquired more power than his father, conquering the Indians and important men of the valley." His son, Ñançenpinco, became even more powerful. He conquered the upper reaches of the valley from the local rulers and expanded the kingdom along the coast, probably in about 1370 AD. There is then a gap of approximately 65 years in which no king names are given. During this time the

Gold hands from Chimu. Gold was a symbol of high status, and the figures on the back of the hands wear feathered headdresses, a symbol of the sun. Otherwise, the purpose of the hands is unknown.

Lambayeque oasis was brought under Chimu control and a southern frontier was established in the Fortaleza. By the first half of the 15th century the Chimu kingdom had become one of the most powerful in the central Andes and a rival to the Inca state.

The next ruler, we are told, was Minchançaman, who reigned from about 1440 to 1464. He extended his frontiers north to Tumbes and south into the Cuismancu state while the Chancay and Chillon valleys fell to his general. At the same time (1460) the Incas under Pachacuti had begun to conquer the central Sierra and a head-on clash of the two expanding powers was certain. The Incas by chance made the first move and eventually captured Minchançaman, who was replaced by his own son, a puppet ruler for the Incas.

The history of the Lambayeque speaks of a legendary leader called Ñamlap who landed with his wife and court and founded a settlement and shrine at Chot a few miles from the coast (possibly the present-day Huaca Chotuna). From him a succession of rulers descended who conquered the plains of the Lambayeque oasis. Around 1300 AD the king, Fempellec, decided to transfer power from Chot to a new capital, which entailed removing the Ñamlap idol from Chot. The legends then tell that in a vision he saw a temptress whom he seduced. This provoked the wrath of the gods and it rained for 30 days, ruining the crops and bringing famine, whereupon Fempellec was assassinated by the priests of the idol.

This myth almost certainly reflects contemporary events. It is known that many towns were founded during the first few centuries after the collapse of the Mochica state and the first part of the legend could be an indication that the authority, religious and secular, wielded by Chotuna had been challenged. A power struggle ensued which left the valley without any effective leadership and probably reduced it to a series of small states. This political vacuum was then filled by the expanding Chimu kingdom. The reference to rains, floods and famine described one of the occasional "El Niño" periods which occur about every 30 years or so in the area, bringing widespread destruction and famine. One of these may have helped to cause the disintegration of power in Lambayeque.

The whole period in Moche-Chicama is dominated by the expanding city of Chan Chan. It contained nine compounds, each enclosed by a high adobe wall. Within each of these there were exclusive residential areas, a royal tomb, myriads of storerooms and administrative units, kitchens, and some low-class housing for retainers. A recent study of the royal tombs has shown that the nine compounds were not built simultaneously but in a sequence, which can be related to the king list of the Moche-Chicama area until just after the Inca conquest. Sacrifice to the dead rulers continued for a long time and extensions were made to accommodate new victims. Collection, storage and redistribution of foodstuffs and luxury goods were major functions of the city, enabling economic and

The so-called Hall of the Arabesques at Chan Chan, the vast ruined capital of Chimu in Peru. The painting is after a careful drawing by the famous 19th century scholar-traveler, Ephraim G. Squier.

political control to be exercised over the whole kingdom. The rest of the city comprised lesser administrative and storage areas and much residential building, as well as four small pyramids. The population of the city in about 1450 has been estimated at between 40,000 and 200,000, but the lesser figure seems nearer the truth.

Many other cities with smaller populations (10,000 to 20,000) were founded during the Chimu hegemony, such as Manchan in Nepeña, Pacatnamu in Jequetepeque and Patapo, Collique and Apurlec in the northern oasis. In all of these the large rectangular compound forms an inherent part of the urban plan along with the storehouses and low pyramids. These were Chimu regional capitals and were linked to Chan Chan by roads.

In the countryside life was dominated by agriculture. The houses of the common folk were built on infertile sand dunes or steep mountains adjacent to the irrigated plains. The individual peasant did not own land but worked on that of his community, on royal lands and state construction projects. The fields were a mass of tiny ridges and furrows watered by canals. In some irrigated fields there were government administrative buildings for the supervision of agricultural work and the collection of produce.

According to the documents the supreme leader was a god-king whose chief officers were members of his family, and below these were local lords and the mass of farmers and craftsmen. The Ñamlap legend described the king's retinue. This included Pituzofi, the Blower of the Shell Trumpet; Ñinacola, Master of the Litter; Fonga, Preparer of the Way, who scattered shell dust on the ground in front of the king; and Occhocalo, the Royal Cook. In Chan Chan a layer of crushed shell has been found in a wall bench at the entry to a royal tomb, providing possible evidence of Fonga. The rigidity of society is evidenced in the early Spanish court cases and records.

The Chincha kingdom was a loose confederation of local rulers under the suzerainty of the cacique or lord of Chincha. The main city was La Centinela in the lower Chincha comprising an urban core of pyramids, terraces and courts surrounded by storerooms and the dwellings of the nobility. Chincha was not a powerful military state, but it was the wealthy economic center of the Andes and engaged in trade between the coast and highlands. Llama caravans of fish, guano, cotton and maize were transported from the coast and exchanged in Colla and Chucuito for gold, silver and copper, and the highly prized narcotic, coca. Chincha also acted as an entrepôt for it had a fleet of rafts used for trading with Chimu and coastal Ecuador. In Ecuador salt and copper axes were exchanged for emeralds, gold, cotton shirts and the ceremonially important spondylus shells; and some of these were sent into the southern highlands as items of barter.

The kingdom of Chincha grew wealthy and populous. There were 6,000 merchants as well as many others who were also metalsmiths, potters or fishers. The Incas in their first phase of major expansion tried to get a foothold on the coast in 1440 by attacking Chincha and it held out until 1476. But by then it had lost some of its prestige, for the Incas held Ecuador and had their own sources of spondylus shells and emeralds.

The capital of the Lupaqa kingdom was Chucuito,

situated on the southwestern shore of Lake Titicaca. Its archaeology is not very spectacular save for stone burial towers or chullpas, and the pottery known as decadent Tiahuanaco. Most of our information is therefore documentary. With the fall of the Tiahuanaco empire, the southern Sierra became a conglomeration of small nation states – Inca, Chanca, Quechua, Colla and Lupaqa – each vying for political supremacy. The Colla and Lupaqa states of the Titicaca basin were bitter enemies. During the ensuing struggle for power Lupaqa allied with the Inca and gained a victory over the Colla. Thus began a long period of Inca influence over the Lupaqa.

A *Visita* prepared by a Spanish Inspector describes the Lupaqa kingdom in 1567 and alludes to the time before Inca domination. The lakeshore was densely populated and potatoes and quinoa were grown in drained fields and on terraced hillsides. Llama and alpaca were herded on the high grasslands. Colonists were sent into the tropical forests to grow coca, tropical fruits and vegetables, and also to the coastal valleys of Moquegua and Sama, where they raised maize and cotton and collected guano for fertilizer. These products were then carried by people or llamas back up to Chucuito. The social organization resembled that of the Inca. There was a small powerful oligarchy in each province, led by the chieftains of the two clans (or hatha). The common people were clan members and had to supply labor and services as and when required by the rulers. The hatha owned the land and organized communal labor parties to work it and herd animals on it, in order to produce their tribute quota. The two leaders of Chucuito ruled supreme over the political, social and economic affairs of the seven provinces, controlling the tribute system and storing enough to alleviate famine or support an army.

The Inca Empire (1438–1532 AD). The Incas originally formed one of the small city states in the southern Sierra struggling for political power. By 1438 they became supreme in that area; and in less than a century they conquered an Empire 200 miles wide that stretched 2,000 miles from north to south. Its northern limit was approximately the modern Ecuador–Colombia border and its southern, the Maule River in central Chile. The spread eastwards was thwarted by the impenetrable Amazon jungles. Throughout the empire the Incas spread their own culture like a veneer over native traditions and ruled their new territories from purpose-built new towns with Inca-trained officials.

Inca history was never written down by those who made it. Stories about rulers, battles, conquest and catastrophes were passed on by word of mouth. Consequently, to a people who worshiped natural phenomena such as the sun and the earth, history became entangled with mythology. Their founder was Manco Capac who, according to legend, emerged from a cave with his three brothers, their sister-wives and the people of ten ayllus or clans. They were commanded by their father, the sun, to establish a

1. Chimu
2. Cuismancu
3. Chuquismancu
4. Chincha
5. Chanca
6. Inca
7. Colla
8. Chucuito

[Map 5:] Local states and empires, c. 1000–1475 AD.

Inca feather work, probably a headdress. Goods made from the feathers of exotic birds were a status symbol and were reserved for the well-born.

capital at the spot where a golden rod could be plunged into the ground until it disappeared, in other words where the soil was deep enough for agriculture. Manco became chief after murdering his brothers during the search in the mountains for a suitable site. At Cuzco the rod disappeared into the ground and the capital was founded. Thus according to this account the foundation of the capital was sanctioned by Inti, the sun, the principal god of the Incas.

Frequent raids were made on other tribes, but once the immediate area around Cuzco had been conquered such campaigns did not produce long-term territorial gains. It was not until the reign of the eighth Emperor (or Inca), Viracocha, in about 1410, that the state of Cuzco used alliances with neighboring lands for political and territorial expansion. By 1437, less than 100 years before the Spanish conquest, the Incas had made their first substantial territorial gains. In particular, one of Viracocha's sons – Yupanqui – conquered Chanca, the strongest of the mountain states.

In view of his father's age and the incompetence of his brother, the heir, Yupanqui had had himself crowned with the multi-colored llauta or headband of the Emperor and assumed the name Pachacuti or "cataclysm." He realized

that the Inca could not administer such a large territory by the traditional method of appointing his brothers and cousins as governors, generals, tribute collectors and so on. He therefore founded a new class of administrators known as Incas-by-privilege, chosen from among the most intelligent or brave commoners. To give them status Pachacuti depopulated the area around the capital and presented each appointee with land to support his office. He also began to reconstruct Cuzco with magnificent palaces and the fortress of Sacsahuaman.

Having thus consolidated his own country, Pachacuti marched his armies northwards and took many minor provinces. Though repulsed by Chincha, he defeated the Colla and took the Lupaqa kingdom, thus completing the conquest of the Titicaca basin. The Inca nation was now strongest in the mountains and only rivaled by Chimu. The eventual conquest of Ecuador, Chimu and the rest of the coast as far as Pachacamac was carried out by Pachacuti's son and heir, Topa. Later, near the end of his father's reign, he led an army against Chincha and overwhelmed it. During Pachacuti's reign Inca success was due to their administrative ability as well as fighting skill. Their policy of provincial government preserved local culture and only diverted tribute, formerly paid elsewhere, to Cuzco.

In 1471, when Topa became emperor, he immediately embarked upon further conquests. He crushed an insurrection in the Titicaca provinces and then moved his forces through Bolivia and into northern Argentina, sweeping across northern Chile as far south as the Maule River. But here his advance was halted by the ferocious Araucanian tribes. Since communications and supply lines were strained in the southern half of the Empire, Topa consolidated his gains by building roads, garrison towns, such as Talca, and smaller road-side rest houses or tambos in between. This was a typical Inca means of consolidating a province. The towns and tambos served as centers for Inca government and were supported by tribute from the local tribes.

In 1493 Huayna Capac became the next Sapa Inca. Like Topa, he was concerned with administration, although he did enlarge the Inca province of Chachapoyas in the Upper Amazon, built another capital at Quito in Ecuador and undertook campaigns to the north and around the Gulf of Guayaquil, where he quashed all resistance. He died suddenly in 1527 without announcing an heir. His son, Huascar, seemed best equipped to take office and was crowned by the High Priest in Cuzco, but another son, Atahuallpa, was promoted by the Quito hierarchy. The empire was divided and civil war ensued. Eventually Huascar was defeated and Atahuallpa became Sapa Inca. But, at exactly the same time, 1532, Francisco Pizarro with 150 buccaneering Spaniards was advancing quickly through Cajamarca, where Atahuallpa was garrisoned. The Emperor was captured and ransomed for gold, but Pizarro dared not free him, fearing he might rally Inca forces against the Spaniards. Atahuallpa was finally put to death. Thus ended native rule in the Central Andes.

The Sapa Incas ruled by divine right. Their first king, Manco Capac, was believed to be a son of Inti, the sun. Inti was the principal god and the Inca was his representative on earth. The emperor's relatives were given major government offices, and the Sapa Inca was married to his sister although he also had many concubines, chosen for their beauty. From his many sons he nominated the wisest and ablest as his successor. The descendants of each emperor belonged to his personal clan which after his death kept his mummy in the palace and continued to administer his lands and collect the produce from them to maintain the palace and the clan. Each new Inca built his own palace within Cuzco.

Cuzco was dominated by the hilltop fort of Sacsahuaman. In the center was a large plaza called Huacapata, or Holy Place, and from this ran the main roads to the four corners of the empire. Around it were the palaces of the last six Incas. On or near the plaza were also the Acllahuasi, the building where young virgins were kept for the emperor or for sacrifice, and the Yachahuasi, where children of the nobility were educated. The sun temple, Coricancha, was located further away and its portals were

Inca trapezoidal doorway at Machu Picchu, leading into a small room with trapezoidal niches. The Incas were outstanding builders, and to this day Inca walls stand up to earthquakes when more recent structures collapse.

veneered with sheets of gold. The main buildings were built of large blocks of closely fitted masonry. Cuzco was a city inhabited only by the court and the priests, but the suburbs contained houses belonging to the provincial governors and curacas or lords. These were built of stone and mud but still had the characteristic Inca-style trapezoidal niches, doorways and windows. On each of the four main roads to the provinces there were counting houses where tribute was checked before being sent to the palaces or to the storehouses situated on a hillside above Cuzco.

The provinces were administered by Incas-by-privilege who served as governors or by curacas who had been trained in the Cuzco system. They levied tribute to support Cuzco itself, the local administration and the army if it passed through the district, and also raised labor forces from the ordinary ayllus in order to build canals, terraces or cities, and even mustered an army. In each province the focus of government was the Inca new town or the former capital, such as Chan Chan. In the Sierra and on the coast the new towns, such as Huanuco, Pumpo and Tambo

The Inca quipu, sketched by Poma de Ayala. The Incas, despite their high civilization, had no real writing, and the quipu, a string counting device, was their only method of recording messages.

was used to fill the storehouses. The clans had to provide a quota of men each year to farm and maintain these lands as well as to construct new canals or terraces and repair old ones. Craftsmen had to send a quantity of goods to the provincial capital, and some workers were even transported to Cuzco to work for the Inca himself. Every year, too, each province and clan had to supply men for the army as part of the tribute system. In return for his labors, the common man received the protection of the sun god and Inca ritual to ensure plentiful harvests, and in times of famine food from the storehouses.

Inca religion, however, was not forced upon the conquered as Catholicism was after the Spanish Conquest. Each province was allowed to worship its traditional gods, provided Inti was acknowledged. One group did not belong to a clan but worked as yana, or indentured labor, on the private lands of the Incas or Incas-by-privilege. In order to maintain peace and loyalty in the provinces a labor-transport system, known as mitmaq, was established. Entire villages were uprooted by the Inca and moved into loyal provinces where their protests would be rendered harmless, and loyal groups from Cuzco were substituted.

All parts of the empire were linked to Cuzco by road, and since there was no form of wheeled transport messages were taken by chasqui runners, and goods were carried by llamas or men. Messages were passed on by the spoken word and numerical records were kept by a device of knotted strings called the quipu, because there was no form of writing. Information was sent to Cuzco where there were special buildings in which the quipu were kept and the bookkeepers worked. This information was used in the calculation of the tribute requirement from each province.

The Incas were great engineers. When a new province was conquered it was first surveyed and plans drawn up for new lands or land improvement schemes to augment the tribute quota. These schemes included new irrigation and terrace projects and river straightening to drain marshes. The Incas grew maize, beans and cotton on the coast, potatoes and quinoa in the highlands, and other foods and the narcotic coca in the tropical forests. The tools they used were hand hoes, digging sticks and foot plows. The amount of land under cultivation must have been very great and its production rates very high to sustain an empire of this size. Pastures were also improved for the grazing of the vast herds of llama and alpaca, kept for porterage and for their fine wool.

In 1532, when the Empire was at the height of its powers culturally and administratively, the Spaniards came and in the course of ten years virtually destroyed Inca civilization. Some Cuzco nobles retreated into the Vilcabamba jungles and put up a spirited resistance, but by 1580 Inca rule had been broken once and for all.

Colorado were built on the Cuzco model containing a central plaza surrounded by a palace, acclahuasi barracks and administrative buildings. In the plaza itself was an usnu, or platform, on which Inca ceremonies and rites were performed. Around this core cruder buildings housed the construction and maintenance gangs and craftsmen, and on hillsides storehouses were built.

The impact of the Incas on the archaeological record in the provinces is marginal. Typically Inca artifacts such as polychrome pottery in the shape of the aryballus, kero and flat-bottomed plate and Incaic building techniques such as trapezoidal niches and well-fitted masonry have been found only in the urban core. The artifacts of the commoners were hardly affected.

Life for the common people was dominated by the tribute system. Each clan farmed its own lands from which it sent a tribute quota to the provincial capital. If the local governor or Inca himself held lands in the area the produce

Further reading

GENERAL

MacNeish, R. S., editor, *Early Man in America: Readings from Scientific American* (San Francisco, 1974).

Willey, G. R., *An Introduction to American Archaeology.* Volume 1: *North and Middle America.* Volume 2: *South America* (Englewood Cliffs, N.J., 1966 and 1971).

Willey, G. R., and **Sabloff, J. A.,** *A History of American Archaeology* (London, 1974).

NORTH AMERICA

Driver, H. E., *Indians of North America* (Chicago, 1961).

Giddings, J. L., *Ancient Men of the Arctic* (London, 1968).

Griffin, J. B., editor, *Archaeology of the Eastern United States* (Chicago, 1952).

Martin, P. S., and **Plog, F.,** *The Archaeology of Arizona* (New York, 1973).

Quimby, G. I., *Indian Life in the Upper Great Lakes: 11,000 BC–1800 AD* (Chicago, 1960).

MESOAMERICA

Bray, W., *Everyday Life of the Aztecs* (London and New York, 1968).

Byers, D., editor, *The Prehistory of the Tehuacan Valley.* Volume 1: Environment and Subsistence (Austin, Texas, 1967).

Coe, M. D., *Mexico* (London, 1962).

Coe, M. D., *The Maya* (London, 1966).

Sanders, W. T., and **Price, B. J.,** *Mesoamerica: The Evolution of a Civilization* (New York, 1968).

Thompson, J. E. S., *The Rise and Fall of Maya Civilization,* 2nd edition (Norman, Okla., 1966).

Wauchope, R., general editor, *Handbook of Middle American Indians,* 13 volumes (Austin, Texas, 1964–1973).

Weaver, M. P., *The Aztecs, Maya, and their Predecessors* (New York, 1972).

SOUTH AMERICA

Bushnell, G. H. S., *Peru* (London, 1956).

Hemming, J., *The Conquest of the Incas* (London, 1970. Also Abacus paperback, 1973).

Kendall, A., *Everyday Life of the Incas* (London and New York, 1973).

Lanning, E. P., *Peru Before the Incas* (Englewood Cliffs, N.J., 1967).

Lathrap, D. W., *The Upper Amazon* (London, 1970).

Moseley, M. E., *The Maritime Foundations of Andean Civilization* (Reading, Mass., 1974).

Acknowledgments

Unless otherwise stated all the illustrations on a given page are credited to the same source.

J. M. Anderson 33 left

Arizona State Museum 45, 78 right

F. Guaman Poma de Ayala, Nueva Coronica y Buen Gobierno 121, 136

G. H. A. Bankes 124 left

D. Barnard 87, 88 top left, 89 bottom left, 111 top, 113 bottom right, 115 bottom right, after E. G. Squier: *Peru: Incidents of Travel* (1877) 132

Bodleian Library, Oxford 108

W. Bray 18 left, 25, 85, 88 bottom, 94, 100 top, 102, 110 top, 120, 122, 127 top

Trustees of the British Museum, London 13, 19 top left, 23, 26, 47 bottom, 101 bottom

Chaco Center, National Park Service, N.M. 43, 55, 59, 60 center and bottom, 61, 62, 63, 64

T. Charlton 51 top

Columbus's letter to Sanchez, Barcelona, 1493. 2

M. Compañon: *Trujillo del Peru a fines del Siglo XVIII* (Madrid, 1936) 28, 29

Denver Museum of Natural History 12

Elsevier, Amsterdam 20 top, 66, 70, 73, 79, 89 bottom right, 95, 97 right, 118, 123, 126, 127 bottom, 129 bottom, 133

Gallery André Emmerich, New York 128

Etnografiska Museet, Stockholm 90 top right

I. Farrington 56, 57, 112 top

J. Fisher 130

W. Forman Archive, London 9, 11, 15, 16, 18 right, 49, 69 left and right, 71, 76, 77 right, 78 left, 82, 96

J. R. Freeman, London 21, 24, 34, 65, 75, 77 left

R. Gorringe 46, 86, after S. G. Morley 99 right, 110 bottom, 124 right

S. Griggs/Woolfitt 58

R. Harding, London 10, 67

A. A. M. van der Heyden, Amsterdam 17 left, 90 left and bottom right, 91, 98, 99 left, 104, 105, 106

Holle Bildarchiv, Baden-Baden 100 bottom, 109, 129 top, 131

R. Hubbard 52

Idaho State University Museum 35, 36, 37, 38, 39, 40, 41, 42

Illinois State Museum 81 bottom

Instituto Nacional de Antropologia e Historia, Mexico 44, 92, 93, 97 left, 107

A. Kendall 50, 111 bottom right, 113 top and bottom left, 115 bottom left, 116, 135

V. Kennett 111 bottom left, 112 bottom, 114, 115 top

Photo Leimbach 19 bottom

Lindenmuseum, Stuttgart 134

The Mansell Collection 31 bottom

Milwaukee Public Museum, Wis. 72

Museo Regional de Oaxaca 105 left

Museum of the American Indian, New York 17 right, 32, 83, 88 top right

Museum of St. Louis, Mo. 89 top

Museum für Völkerkunde, Vienna 22

The Natural History Photographic Agency 47 top

Ohio Historical Society 81 top

Robert S. Peabody Foundation for Archaeology, Andover, Mass. 51 bottom

Radio Times-Hulton Picture Library 20 bottom, 27

W. Reiss and A. Stübel: *The Necropolis of Ancon in Peru*, 3 vols, (1880–1887) 31 top

M. Rivero y Ustariz and J. J. von Tschudi, *Peruvian Antiquities*, (1854) 54

Sächsische Landesbibliothek 101 top

Spectrum, London 84, 117

State Records Center, Sante Fe, N.M. 33 right

E. Swanson 60 top, 69 center

Textile Museum, Washington, D.C. 125

University of Pennsylvania Museum, Pa. 88 center left

After G. R. Willey 53

Glossary sketches:

Backstrap loom: drawing by Eva Wilson
Mochica design: drawing after Karen Olsen Bruhns
Tlaloc, Quetzalcoatl: drawing after Mary Beth Stokes
Twining: drawing after Judith Newcomer

The Publishers have attempted to observe the legal requirements with respect to the rights of the suppliers of photographic materials. Nevertheless, persons who have claims are invited to apply to the Publishers.

Glossary

Acllahuasi The building in which the "chosen women" of the Incas lived and were educated.

Adobe Unfired mud-brick, dried and hardened in the sun.

Alluvium Sand and silt carried in suspension by a river and later redeposited in valleys and deltas. See also **Floodplain**.

Alluvial fan A mass of sediment deposited along a river at a point where there is a decrease in gradient (e.g. where the river flows out of mountains and onto a level plain).

Almagro, Diego de (1475–1538) A partner, and later a rival, of Pizarro in the conquest of Inca Peru. In 1535 Almagro led a brutal raiding and exploring expedition into Chile. His conflict with the Pizarro family brought about his execution.

Alpaca (*Lama pacos*) An Andean camelid. A smaller relative of the llama, it was raised mainly for its wool and, to a lesser extent, for meat. See also **Camelid**.

Alpaca

Amaranth (pigweed) Related species of amaranth are cultivated for food in many areas, from the southwestern United States to the Andes of South America. Each plant produces enormous quantities of small seeds. The seeds, and also a dough made from ground amaranth, were used in certain Aztec rituals.

Amerindian The peoples (other than the Eskimo) who inhabited the Americas before the European conquest. They were, and are, of Mongoloid stock, like their Asiatic relatives.

Anasazi The Anasazi region comprises southern Utah and Colorado, with northern Arizona and New Mexico. Shortly before the start of the Christian era, some of the tribes in this area began to practice rudimentary farming. This phase of development (the Basketmaker period) ended around 700 AD when the Anasazi people began to construct pueblos. The modern Pueblo Indians of this area (the Hopi and Zuñi) are the direct descendants of the prehistoric Anasazi peoples. See also **Pueblo**.

Andesite A fine-grained volcanic rock.

Apache An Athapaskan-speaking tribe which invaded the American Southwest in the late prehistoric period, sometime between 1000 AD and 1500 AD. Unlike their settled Pueblo neighbors, the Apache were mobile hunters and collectors, though their present way of life incorporates many Pueblo and European features.

Araucanian Araucanian-speaking Indians occupied central Chile west of the high Andes. The Incas failed to conquer them, and these warlike Indians were not finally subdued until the 1880s.

Archaic culture The way of life (based on hunting, plant-collecting and shellfish-gathering) of the peoples of the eastern woodlands of North America from 6000 BC until the development of effective farming in about 1000 BC.

Aryballus A characteristic Inca pottery form, consisting of a large jar with a conical base, tall narrow neck and flaring lip. It was designed to be carried by means of a rope which passed through two loop-shaped handles low down on the body and around a projecting nubbin on the upper body.

Atlatl (spear thrower) A device which increases the force with which a spear can be hurled. The atlatl consists of a rod or narrow board, around one to two feet long, with finger grips at one end. At the other end is a hook which engages with the butt of the spear. This device artificially lengthens the thrower's arm, allowing him to maintain contact with the spear shaft for a longer time, and thus to transmit extra power to his throw.

Ayllu Village community. Quechua term, used in Peru and Bolivia, for a social and administrative unit consisting of a number of associated families (usually related to each other) who communally owned and cultivated a section of land. The Ayllu formed the basis of Peruvian social organization.

Aztec A Mexican tribe whose capital was at Tenochtitlan, present-day Mexico City. The Aztecs and their allies ruled over most of Mexico during the century before the Spanish conquest of 1519–21.

Backstrap loom A form of handloom. The warp threads are stretched between two parallel rods. One rod is tied to a post or branch, the other is attached to a strap or belt which passes behind the weaver's waist. To alter the tension on the warp threads, the weaver has only to move her body backwards or forwards. See also **Heddle**.

Ball game/ball court A game played in Mexico, the Maya zone, the West Indies and

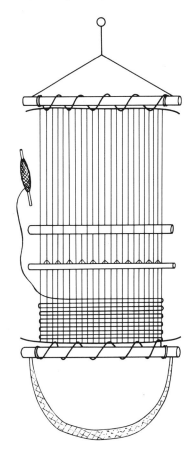

Backstrap Loom

parts of the American Southwest. The players propelled a heavy rubber ball around a walled court, using only their hips and thighs. In Mesoamerica the court was shaped like a capital I, with exaggerated end pieces. In one version of the game stone rings were fixed to the side walls, and the team which passed the ball through one of these rings won the game outright. The ball game had a ritual as well as a sporting significance, and goes back to the first millennium BC in Mexico.

Bark paper A paper-like material made by beating out the inner bark of certain trees belonging to the fig family.

Basalt A dark-colored, fine-grained volcanic rock.

Basketmaker culture The culture of the early, pre-Pueblo stages of the Anasazi tradition of the San Juan and Little Colorado drainages of the American Southwest. See also **Anasazi**.

Biface A chipped stone tool (or sometimes a preform) made by removing flakes from both faces of the object; hence the term "bifacial working" is used for this technique of manufacture. See also **Preform, Core, Flake**.

Biome An ecological community of plants and animals extending over a large natural area.

Bluff Headland or cliff, usually overlooking a river.

Burin A chipped stone tool with a pointed or chisel-ended tip, made by removing one or more flakes from the side edge. Used for incising and engraving.

Cacao (cocoa) The cacao tree grows in moist tropical regions of Central and South America. In Mesoamerica the centers of production were in and around lowland Maya

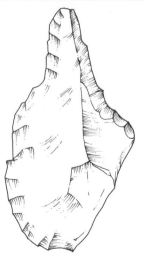

Burin

territory. In Mexico and the Maya zone the beans were used as small change in the market places, and cacao was also made into a prestigious and expensive drink.

Cacique Native word (of West Indian origin) meaning chief or lord.

Calendar round 52-year calendrical cycle produced by the permutation of a 260-day ritual calendar with the 365-day solar one.

Camas (*Camassia esculenta*) A lily-like plant with edible bulbs. Native to parts of North America.

Camelid Belonging to the *Camelidae* family, which includes the domestic llama and alpaca, and also the wild vicuña and guanaco.

Camera lucida An instrument by which the rays of light from an object are reflected by a prism to produce an image on a sheet of paper. This image can then be traced by the artist or draftsman.

Canadian Shield The geological region of North America which lies west of the Appalachians and north of the Great Lakes.

Carination An angle or ridge, where the profile of a vessel wall sharply changes direction.

Cascade point A bifacially chipped spearhead, pointed at both ends and shaped rather like a willow leaf. Used by the early hunters of the mountain and plateau country of western North America.

Catherwood, Frederick (1799–1854) London-born architect. As a young man he traveled in Egypt, North Africa, Palestine and Classical lands, making drawings of ancient and modern buildings as well as topographical sketches. In 1839 he joined forces with J. L. Stephens and served as artist in his Maya expeditions. In his later years Catherwood worked more as a surveyor and civil engineer than as an architect, and he became a pioneer railway builder in British Guiana. See also **Stephens**.

Cenote A kind of natural well on the arid plateau of Yucatan. A cenote is formed when the overlying limestone crust collapses to expose the groundwater below it.

Chac Lowland Maya name for the Rain God or group of rain deities, usually depicted with long, pendulous noses and toothless mouths. The four major chacs were linked with the cardinal directions and with the colors red, black and yellow.

Chasqui Runner who carried messages along the Inca road system. The runners were

organized in relays, each man carrying the message for about a mile before handing it on. At the changeover point small huts (chasqui posts) were built to house the runners.

Chavin The first of the great Peruvian civilizations (c. 1000–300 BC), named after the site of Chavin de Huantar in the northern Andes. The Chavin art style, with its distinctive mythology and religious symbolism, spread over much of Peru.

Cascade Point

Chimu A powerful empire which emerged as a political entity on the north coast of Peru during the 14th century AD, though the characteristic black Chimu pottery and other archaeological materials were in use some centuries earlier. Chan Chan, the Chimu capital, held about 40,000 to 200,000 people. The Chimu kingdom was overthrown by the Incas in about 1464.

Christy, Henry (1810–1865) Wealthy British businessman who traveled all over Central and North America from 1850 onwards, accumulating what was in its time the finest private ethnological collection in the world. From 1863 Christy and Edouard Lartet carried out important excavations in the Palaeolithic caves of southern France.

Chullpa Cylindrical or square burial tower, made of stone or adobe, found in parts of the southern Andes.

Cieza de Leon, Pedro de (1520–1554) He took part in the conquest of Colombia and Peru, and his book is a mine of information on the native cultures of the Andes. The geographical part of his *Cronica del Peru* was published in 1553, but the section on Inca history remained in manuscript until 1880.

Cinnabar Mercuric sulphide, a red-colored ore of mercury. In powdered form it was used as a paint or pigment.

Cire-perdue casting (lost wax) A technique of metal casting, particularly useful for producing complex shapes which are difficult to cast in a multi-piece mold. The item is modeled in wax (sometimes over a clay core), and then encased in clay. Next, the whole thing is heated so that the wax vaporizes, and molten metal is poured into the cavity formerly occupied by the wax. When the metal has cooled, the clay casing is broken open to remove the metal casting – an exact copy of the original wax model.

City State An independent political unit based on a capital city with its own royal dynasty. The territory of the state consisted of the capital plus a number of rural villages and hamlets which owed it allegiance and paid taxes to its ruler.

Classic Period The term was originally coined for the stage of Maya civilization characterized by the development of hieroglyphic writing. By extension, it came to be used for other Mexican cultures with a comparable level of excellence (Teotihuacan, El Tajin, Monte Alban etc). All these civilizations were roughly – though not precisely – contemporary, and the phrase is now used in a general sense for the period of Mesoamerican archaeology falling between 300 and 900 AD.

Clovis point A type of fluted point made in many parts of North America, mainly between 10,000 and 9,000 BC. The shape is lanceolate, with a concave base, and fluting flakes which rarely extend more than halfway towards the tip. See also **Fluted point**.

Cobble River or beach pebble.

Coca (*Erythroxylon coca*) A shrubby plant whose leaves are the source of cocaine. The main coca plantations lay on the moist eastern slopes of the Andes, but the leaves were widely traded. A quid, consisting of coca leaves mixed with lime, is held in the cheek while the juice is swallowed. This process liberates a minute quantity of cocaine, the effect of which is to dull the senses slightly, helping the chewer to bear hunger and fatigue.

Columbus, Christopher (Cristobal Colon) (1451–1506) Discovered the New World under the mistaken impression that he had reached Asia. He made four voyages between 1492 and 1504, exploring the West Indies and the Atlantic coast of Central America and Venezuela.

Conquistador A person who took part in the original Spanish expeditions which conquered the native civilizations of Central and South America.

Continental divide (watershed) Boundary line which separates the headwaters of river systems which flow towards opposite sides of a continent.

Copal An incense consisting of the resin of various tropical trees. It played an important part in Maya ritual.

Coprolite Dried or fossilized excreta.

Cordillera A mountain range.

Core A lump of stone from which flakes or blades have been removed. Sometimes it is merely a by-product of tool making, but it may also be shaped into an implement in its own right. See also **Core tool**, **Flake**.

Core tool A stone tool made by the removal of flakes to leave a finished object of the desired form.

Coricancha The principal temple of the Inca religion, the Coricancha was located in Cuzco and housed images of all the sky gods, including Inti (the Sun) and Viracocha (the Creator God). There were similar temples in provincial capitals.

Cornice A horizontal molding running around a building or the walls of a room.

Cortes, Hernando (1485–1547) The conqueror of Mexico and the Aztec empire. Between 1519 and 1526 he wrote five long letters to Charles V of Spain describing the subjugation of the Aztecs and his subsequent journey overland to Honduras. Besides political material, these letters contain important information about native life.

Crossdating Method used to discover the date of an object or culture of unknown age by linking it with one whose date is already known. The links are established either by actual imports from one area to another, or by close stylistic similarities between the products of the two regions.

Daguerrotype An early photographic process in which the impression was taken on a silver plate, sensitized by iodine, and then developed by vapor of mercury.

Deposition The laying down of solid material (dust, soil etc.) carried from elsewhere by a natural agency such as wind or water.

Desert Culture A way of life adapted to the arid conditions of the Great Basin of North America and to the dry intermontane zone of that continent. Subsistence was based on the collection of wild seeds and nuts, plus the hunting of small game. This mode of life can be recognized archaeologically by the fifth millennium BC, and may be even older. In some inhospitable areas, a variant of the Desert Culture persisted until European contact.

Diaz del Castillo, Bernal (1492–1581) Took part in Grijalva's Mexican expedition of 1518 and accompanied Cortes throughout the conquest of the Aztec empire in 1519–21. In his old age Diaz wrote a *True History of the Conquest of New Spain*, in which he vividly described his experiences.

Ear spool Round disc or spool-shaped ornament worn in a hole through the ear lobe.

Ecosystem A community of organisms (from man down to the simplest forms of life) which inhabit a single environment, and which interact with one another and with the non-organic elements of the environment in which they live.

Effigy pot Jar made in the form of a figure, usually human or animal, with a spout. Common among Andean cultures. The finest effigy pots were made by the Mochica.

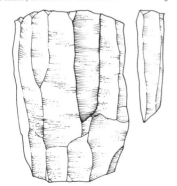

Core and Blade

Effigy Pot

Elbow pipe A smoking pipe in which the bowl is set at right angles to the stem.

El Dorado This Spanish phrase literally means "The Gilded Man," and refers to 16th century reports of an Indian lord who covered his body with gold dust which he then washed off in a sacred lake. The factual basis for this story probably lies in certain rituals of the Muisca (or Chibcha) tribes of Andean Colombia, but popular belief located the source of the legend in many different parts of northern South America. The search for the land of "El Dorado" stimulated exploration and conquest of much of Venezuela, Guyana and Colombia.

El Niño An ocean current of warm water which occasionally flows southwards along the Pacific coast of Peru, overriding the cold waters of the Humboldt or Peru current. When this happens, the fish and sea birds (which are adapted to cool waters) quickly die, weather conditions change, and the normal balance of nature is upset. The outcome is destructive to the coastal peoples who gain their livelihood from the sea.

Ethnobotany The study of the botanical knowledge of indigenous peoples.

False color infrared film Used in air photography to reveal the difference in absorptive and reflective properties of water, bare soil, buried structures or pits, different types of vegetation etc. On the processed transparency or print, each of these features comes out in a distinctive color, though the colors themselves bear no relationship to natural colors.

Fire drill (fire stick) Used in kindling fire by friction. A stick or rod (the fire drill) was rotated between the hands, with the lower end resting on a board of soft wood. Enough heat was generated to create fire.

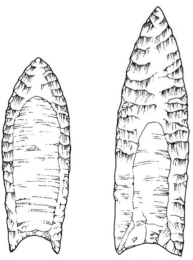

Folsom Point (left) and Clovis Point

Flake A fragment removed from a larger piece of stone (the core or nucleus) by percussion or pressure. Flakes often served as blanks from which other tools (knives, scrapers, etc.) were made. Such artifacts are called flake tools. See also **Biface**, **Core**, **Core tool**.

Flake scar Concave scar left on a chipped stone object by the removal of a flake.

Flexed burial Burial in which the corpse was interred with the legs bent and the knees drawn up towards the chest.

Floodplain The flat area, adjacent to a river, where floodwaters have deposited alluvium. Floodplains often have deep, rich soils and are prime farmland. See also **Alluvium**.

Floodplain

Fluorine Bone buried in damp earth gradually and cumulatively takes up fluorine from the soil water. The rate at which it does so depends on local conditions, and there is no universal standard. But, at any one locality, the relative age of buried bones can be determined; the oldest bones will contain the most fluorine, and those most recently deposited will have the least.

Fluted point A bifacially worked spearhead, thinned on one or both faces by the removal of long flakes (channel flakes) from the base towards the tip. This flaking helps to thin the base, and the shallow grooves or channels allow the point to be held firmly in a split shaft. See also **Biface**, **Clovis point**, **Folsom point**.

Folsom point Folsom, in northeastern New Mexico, was in 1926 the scene of one of the first discoveries in the New World of a man-made tool in the same deposit as an extinct animal. The site gave its name to a type of fluted spearpoint, used around 9000–8000 BC. Folsom points are lanceolate, concave-based, and with channel flakes or flutes running almost to the tip. See also **Fluted point**.

Formative (or Preclassic) Period Term used in Mesoamerican archaeology for the period from the introduction of pottery (between 2400 and 1500 BC, according to the locality) and the start of the Classic Period around 300 AD. It was during the Formative Period that Mesoamerican civilization took shape.

Frieze A band of painted or carved decoration.

Gene Unit of the material of inheritance through sexual reproduction, responsible for transmitting heritable biological characteristics from parent to offspring.

Glaciation A period of cold climate during which the area covered by glaciers and ice caps increased.

Glaze Glassy vitreous surface-coating applied to pottery, etc.

Goodman, Joseph (1838–1917) Began as a businessman and newspaper owner (one of his claims to fame being the discovery of Mark Twain). In middle age he became interested in Maya hieroglyphs and made important contributions to their decipherment. The most generally accepted formula for converting Maya dates to Christian dates is known as the Goodman-Martinez-Thompson (or GMT) correlation.

Gorget Ornamental plaque worn on the chest and suspended by a cord around the neck.

Grave goods Offerings put with the corpse into the tomb.

Griddle See **Manioc**.

Grijalva, Juan de (1489?–1527) In 1518 Diego Velasquez, Governor of Cuba, sent a fleet to explore the newly-discovered peninsula of Yucatan. Under the command of Grijalva, this expedition visited Yucatan and much of the Gulf Coast of Mexico, obtaining gold to the value of 20,000 pesos. The success of this expedition prompted Velazquez to send out another mission, commanded this time by Cortes, the conqueror of Mexico.

Guano The excrement of sea birds. There are rich guano deposits on the islands off the Peruvian coast, and the material was used as a natural fertilizer by Indian farmers.

Heddle Device used on a loom (in pre-European America, usually a backstrap loom) for raising selected warps to create a space (the shed) through which the weft thread could be passed in a single movement. See also **Backstrap loom**.

Hieroglyphic writing A method of writing in which objects, ideas (and sometimes also sounds) are represented by stylized pictures known as hieroglyphs, or glyphs. Hieroglyphic writing was employed in ancient Mesoamerica, and reached its finest development among the Maya.

Hohokam A farming culture of the southern Arizona desert, beginning during the late centuries BC and lasting until about 1400 AD. The modern Pima Indians may be the descendants of the Hohokam people.

Homo sapiens The modern form of man, to which all present-day races belong. He had evolved by about 40,000 BC in parts of the Old World.

Hopewell A Woodland culture centered on Ohio and Illinois. It reached a climax in the late centuries BC and early centuries AD. See also **Woodland culture**.

Hopi A Pueblo Indian tribe of northeast Arizona. See also **Pueblo**.

Housemound Raised mound or platform on which a house or other structure was built.

Huaca A Quechua (Peruvian) Indian word implying sanctity, applied indiscriminately to ancient ruins, mounds, tombs and their contents.

Huari (or Wari) The capital of an expansionist empire which controlled much of Peru from the 6th to the 10th centuries AD.

Kero Beaker

Huitzilopochtli National god of the Aztecs. He guided the tribe during its nomadic days and, at the time of military success and imperial expansion, he became the patron deity of the warriors. He was identified with the sun.

Humboldt, Alexander von (1769–1859) A Prussian aristocrat who became one of the greatest explorers and scientists of his age. He traveled widely in Central and South America, and was the first to climb Mount Chimborazo. The data he collected on his journeys laid the foundations of modern physical geography and the study of plant distributions. His knowledge was encyclopedic, and for him archaeology was never more than a fringe interest.

Iconography The study of the subject matter, meaning and symbolism expressed in representational art.

Igloo Dome-shaped Eskimo winter house, made from blocks of snow.

Inca Originally an unimportant Quechua-speaking tribe of the south Peruvian Andes. During the century before the Spanish arrival they built up a conquest empire which stretched from Ecuador to Chile.

Incised decoration/incision Pottery decoration in which lines are cut with a sharp instrument into the soft surface of the clay before the pot is fired.

Initial Period In Peruvian archaeology, the centuries between the first introduction of pottery (1800–1400 BC) and the spread of the Chavin style in about 1000 BC.

Inti The Inca Sun God, one of the most important servants of Viracocha (the Creator). Inti was the divine ancestor of the Inca royal house, and was usually represented as a gold disc with a human face surrounded by rays.

Kame A mound of gravel and sand formed by deposition of sediment from a stream as it runs from beneath a glacier.

Kayak One-man Eskimo canoe, made from a light wooden framework covered with skins. The kayak is decked, except for a circular hole in the center.

Kero A beaker with straight or concave flaring sides. In wood the shape was popular among the Incas, though it is older in pottery.

Kidder, Alfred Vincent (1885–1963) One of the pioneers in the study of Pueblo archaeology in the American Southwest, his research forms the basis of nearly all later work in this area. In 1929 he became director of the Maya program of the Carnegie Institution of Washington, which sponsored interdisciplinary studies of all aspects of Maya culture. Kidder himself excavated the Maya sites at Kaminaljuyu and Uaxactun.

Kiva An underground room in a Pueblo village, usually circular, used as a men's clubhouse and for the performance of religious ceremonies. See also **Pueblo**.

Kroeber, Alfred Louis (1876–1960) One of the scholars whose work helped to form New World archaeology as a scientific discipline. He worked in ethnology, folklore and linguistics, as well as North American and Peruvian archaeology. In his later years he examined theoretical aspects of anthropology, especially the processes of culture change.

Lanceolate Lance-shaped (referring to projectile points).

Landa, Diego de (1524–1579) A Franciscan friar who became Bishop of Yucatan and wrote an encyclopedic study on the 16th century Maya. Although written in about 1566, his manuscript remained in a Madrid library, unpublished until the mid-19th century.

Levee A natural raised bank formed along the edge of a river by deposition of sediment during flooding. When the flood subsides, the sediment remains, and the levee is the highest part of the river's floodplain. Each time the river floods, more sediment is left behind. See also **Floodplain**.

Lignite A type of dark brown coal.

Lip plug An ornament worn in a hole cut through the lower lip.

Llama (*Lama glama*) Andean camelid, domesticated in Peru by 6500 BC. Used as a beast of burden, for its wool and, to a lesser degree, for meat and hides. Dried llama dung was also used as a fuel. See also **Camelid**.

Llama

Long Count Maya system of dating by counting the number of days which have elapsed since a mythological starting point (3113 BC) in past time.

Macroband A hunting and foraging band made up of several families. A macroband is often formed by the temporary fusion of a number of microbands coming together to exploit seasonally-abundant foodstuffs. See also **Microband**.

Maguey (agave, century plant) One of the most useful all-purpose plants in the New World. The leaves can be roasted for food, and they also provide fibers for cordage and cloth. A fermented drink (pulque) is made from the sap. The dried flower stalks make durable poles; the spines serve as needles and for ritual blood-letting. The maguey cactus will grow on poor land, unsuitable for maize. Planted in rows across hillslopes, it also helps to check soil erosion.

Mammoth Extinct Pleistocene form of elephant.

Manati (manatee) A large, aquatic, herbivorous mammal which lives in the rivers and estuaries of Atlantic America in tropical latitudes.

Manioc (*Manihot esculenta*, yuca, cassava) A staple crop of lowland South America. Manioc is a high-yield plant whose tubers are rich in starch but deficient in protein, for which reason it must be supplemented by fish and game. There are two varieties: the "sweet" type whose tubers are eaten boiled or baked, and the "bitter" type which has poisonous juice. To extract this juice, the manioc is pulped and squeezed. The resultant mass can be either processed into flour, or toasted on a flat pottery disc (griddle) to make rounds of unleavened bread which can be stored.

Mano The upper, hand-held stone used (with a metate) for grinding maize (corn) and other hard seeds. See also **Metate**.

Mastodon An extinct Pleistocene animal resembling an elephant. The word literally means "breast-toothed," a reference to the conical protuberances on the molar teeth, which contrast with the flattened teeth of mammoths and other true elephants.

Maudslay, Alfred Percival (1850–1931) British scholar who made important photographs and casts of Maya architecture and inscriptions. The results of his explorations were published in 1889–1902 in a series entitled *Biologia Centrali-Americana, or, Contribution to the Knowledge of the Flora and Fauna of Mexico and Central America.* The texts which he transcribed formed the basis of early studies of Maya hieroglyphs.

Maya The past and present Indians of Guatemala, Belize, and the adjacent parts of Mexico, El Salvador and Honduras. By the early centuries AD they had created one of America's greatest civilizations which lasted (with changes and modifications) until the Spanish conquest.

Merchant God Ek Chuah was the Yucatec-Maya god of merchants and of cacao (cocoa). He is usually painted black, and depicted as a traveler with pack and staff.

Mesa An isolated tableland which falls away steeply on all sides.

Mesquite (*Prosopis juliflora*) A tree legume. The seeds are edible and the pods were sometimes chewed whole.

Metate The flat or trough-shaped lower stone on which maize (corn) and other hard seeds were ground. Used in conjunction with a mano. See also **Mano**.

Mica A mineral which splits into thin transparent plaques. In this form it was sometimes used in North America to make cutout ornaments. Ground mica, or micaceous rock, was sometimes added as a filler to pottery clay.

Microband A small band of two or three families leading a nomadic life as hunters and collectors of wild plants. See also **Macroband**.

Midden A heap or stratum of rubbish marking the site of a house, village or settlement.

Millingstone Stone used for grinding wild or cultivated seeds.

Mimbres ware Pottery made in the Mogollon area of the American Southwest between about 1000 and 1400 AD, and characterized by black-painted designs on a white background. Some designs are geometric, but the interiors of the finest bowls have stylized pictures of human beings, animals, insects and fish. See also **Mogollon**.

Mississippi culture pattern A cultural tradition, centered on the middle and lower Mississippi Valley but influencing most of the southeastern USA after about 1000 AD. The architecture and religious symbolism hint at contacts with Mexico.

Mitmaq The system by which the Incas moved entire populations and resettled them as colonists (*mitimaes*) elsewhere. In this way dissident groups were moved to places where they could do no harm, and were replaced by loyalists.

Mixtec A people, famous for their arts and crafts, who lived in the state of Oaxaca, Mexico. Their political and artistic influence was at its height after 900 AD.

Mochica The civilization of the coastal valleys of north Peru during most of the first millennium AD, best-known for its irrigation works, temple platforms and finely modeled and painted pottery.

Mochica design

Mogollon A cultural tradition centered on southern Arizona and New Mexico, and lasting through the whole of the Christian era. After about 1000 AD the Mogollon people began to build pueblos. See also **Pueblo**.

Molina, Cristobal de Took part in the conquest of Peru and, in about 1556, wrote an eyewitness account of his experiences.

Mummy In the Americas the term is used loosely for any well-preserved corpse, especially one elaborately prepared for burial. True embalming was not practiced, but the internal organs were sometimes removed and the body wrapped in shrouds, mantles or mats before interment.

Nahuatl The language of the Aztecs and of several other Mesoamerican peoples. Related languages, belonging to the Uto-Aztecan family, are spoken by tribes scattered from Panama to the northwestern USA.

Nazca (or Nasca) A valley on the south coast of Peru. From about 200 BC to 900 AD it was the center of a civilization which produced fine painted pottery and elaborate textiles.

Necropolis A cemetery or burial place.

Nelson, Nels C. A pioneer of stratigraphic excavation. Under the influence of Uhle and Kroeber he dug shell-mounds on the California coast, and later did important work in the American Southwest.

Nephrite A hard green stone, a variety of jade.

Neutron activation A method of analysis (and a peaceful spinoff from atomic physics) by which the composition of an object can be determined. The specimen is bombarded with neutrons, becomes weakly radioactive, and emits gamma rays. Analysis of the gamma ray spectrum shows which chemical elements are present, even in minute quantities.

Nodule A small lump of mineral; a piece of stone suitable for chipping into tools.

Obelisk A pillar or shaft of stone.

Obsidian A natural glass formed by volcanic activity. Its fracturing properties are similar to those of flint and, where available, it was the preferred material for chipped and flaked tools. When fresh, the edge is very sharp, but it soon becomes blunt with use. Obsidian of the quality suitable for tool-making is found in only a few places, and material from each source has a distinctive composition.

Olmec The name given to the people who created one of Mesoamerica's oldest civilizations in the Gulf Coast lowlands between 1150 and 400 BC. The Olmecs were famous for their sculpture and jade carving.

Paiute An Indian tribe of the arid region where the states of Arizona, Utah and Nevada meet. Their hunting and plant-gathering way

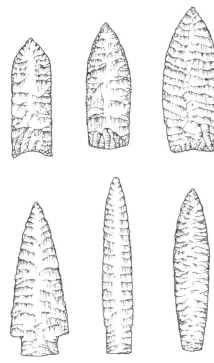

Plano Points

Plano points Unfluted lanceolate points (of many different shapes, but uniformly well made) used by hunting groups in North America from about 8000 to 4000 BC.

Platform pipe A smoking pipe in which the bowl (sometimes carved into the shape of an animal effigy) stands at the center of a platform-shaped base.

Plaza An open square or courtyard.

Pleistocene The geological period corresponding with the last, or Great, ice age. It began at least two million years ago and ended about 10,000 years ago with the final retreat of the ice sheets and the extinction of such animals as the mammoth and the American horse.

Pochote (*Ceiba parvifolia*) A tree of the ceiba or kapok family. The seeds and the bulbous storage roots are edible.

Pod corn A primitive variety of maize (corn), in which the individual kernels are enclosed and protected by floral bracts (i.e. chaff).

Pollen analysis The study of pollen grains preserved both in archaeological deposits and under natural conditions in peats, buried soils, etc. Pollen grains of different plants and trees have distinctive shapes, and the pollen content of the deposit is a reflection of the vegetation in the area at the time when the deposit was being formed. Besides reconstructing ancient landscapes, the pollen analyst can study the environmental changes produced by climatic fluctuations and the activities of man.

Polychrome Painted in many colors.

Popcorn A variety of maize (corn) whose kernels explode on heating.

Pot-boiler A stone which is heated and then dropped into the cooking vessel to bring the contents to the boil.

Pre-Columbian Belonging to the period before the European conquest of America.

Preform Points

of life shows many features of the prehistoric Desert culture. See also **Desert culture**.

Paleontology The science which is concerned with the study of fossils.

Paleolithic period The period during which tools were predominantly made of chipped stone, and when neither polished stone nor metals were in use. The Paleolithic begins with the emergence of early forms of man, and ends about 8000 BC with the close of the Pleistocene Ice Age. The Upper Paleolithic period begins around 40–38,000 BC with the advent of Homo sapiens and improved forms of tools.

Paracas A peninsula on the south coast of Peru which gave its name to a regional culture of the first millennium BC.

Pectoral An ornament worn on the chest, suspended from a cord around the neck.

Percussion flaking Technique of removing a flake from a block of stone by means of blows from a hammer of stone, wood or antler.

Pit-house House consisting of a shallow pit, with a superstructure of wood covered with turf, thatch or skins.

Pizarro, Francisco (1478–1541) Took part in Nuñez de Balboa's expedition which discovered the Pacific Ocean, but achieved greater fame as leader of the expedition which conquered the Inca Empire, entering Cuzco in 1533.

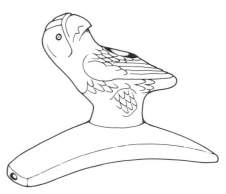

Platform Pipe

Preform An early stage in the manufacture of a stone tool, when the object has been roughed out by chipping but has not yet taken on its final shape.

Prehispanic Belonging to the period before the Spanish conquest of Latin America.

Prescott, William Hickling (1796–1859) American historian who was one of the first people to make serious use of early Spanish manuscripts and chronicles about the conquest and the native cultures of America. His two books on this subject, *The Conquest of Mexico* (1843) and *History of the Conquest of Peru* (1847) remain classics.

Pressure flaking Technique for shaping a chipped stone implement. Little spalls or flakes are removed by pressure from a fabricating tool, usually made of bone or antler. See also **Flake**.

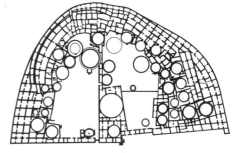

Pueblo Bonito, Ground Plan

Pueblo Village consisting of an agglomeration of living rooms and ceremonial structures, built close together and often arranged like an apartment house in several stories or terraces. Pueblos were constructed after about 700 AD in the American Southwest, especially in New Mexico and Arizona. Some of these pueblos (e.g. those of the Hopi and Zuñi Indians) are still occupied today. See also **Anasazi**, **Kiva**.

Puna The high grassland and plateau country of the Andes, noted for its herds of llamas and alpacas.

Putnam, Frederick Ward (1839–1915) One of the great professionalizers of archaeology, he helped to put the subject on a respectable academic footing. He was Professor of American Archaeology and Ethnography at Harvard from 1887 to 1909 and built up the Peabody Museum into a great research institute. He also helped to found the Field Museum of Natural History (Chicago), the Anthropology Department at Berkeley, and the Anthropological Department at the American Museum of Natural History. His field interests were early man and the mounds of the Ohio Valley.

Pyramid In the Americas, the word is loosely used to describe a tall, flat-topped mound or solid construction which usually supported a temple or other important building. Unlike Egyptian pyramids, most of the American examples are not tombs and contain no internal rooms.

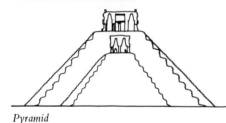

Pyramid

Quechua The language of the Incas and of Andean tribes related to them. It is still widely spoken from Ecuador to northern Argentina.

Quetzal A bird of the damp and cloudy mountains of Chiapas, Guatemala and Honduras. Its green tail feathers were prized in Mesoamerica for their decorative and symbolic value, and were an important article of commerce.

Quetzalcoatl The Nahuatl name for the Mexican god usually depicted as a Plumed Serpent. He was one of the gods who created mankind and the universe, was patron of arts and crafts, god of the wind and of the planet Venus. He was worshiped under many names, and his cult has a long history in Mexico.

Quetzalcoatl

Quinoa (*Chenopodium quinoa*) A food plant of Andean South America, in particular of regions over 3000 meters where corn will not grow well. It produces very many small seeds.

Quipu A device made with varicolored and knotted strings to assist in calculating and to transmit messages. Used by the ancient Peruvians.

Radiocarbon dating A method of obtaining a date for organic material by measuring its Carbon 14 (C14) content. Carbon 14, a radioactive isotope of carbon, is formed in the atmosphere and passes with normal carbon (C12) into all living organisms. When the organism dies, its C14 gradually breaks down at a known rate into C12. The longer the organism has been dead, the lower the percentage of C14 relative to C12. Wood, charcoal, skin, bone, shell etc. are all suitable for radiocarbon dating. The method works well for samples up to 70,000 years old.

Rancheria A small farming community in which the houses are widely spaced and surrounded by garden plots.

Retouch The trimming or retouching of a chipped stone tool to its final shape by removing small flakes (secondary flakes) after the preliminary work (the primary flaking) is complete. The word is also used for the traces (or scars) of flakes taken off at this stage.

Rio, Antonio del One of the early excavators at the Maya site of Palenque. His report, *Description of the Ruins of the Ancient City discovered near Palenque*, was published in 1822 and is the first illustrated description of Maya ruins.

Runoff That portion of rainfall which is not immediately absorbed into the ground, but runs off the surface and makes its way into streams.

Sahagun, Bernardino de (1499–1590) A Franciscan friar who went to Mexico only eight years after the Spanish conquest. His book, *General History of the Things of New Spain* (also known as the *Florentine Codex*) was originally written in Nahuatl and is the best single source of information on Aztec culture.

Sapa Inca Literally "Unique Inca"; one of the titles of the Inca ruler, an autocratic monarch who was considered a god.

Savanna Tropical grassland.

Scapula Shoulder blade.

Scraper A chipped stone tool with a semicircular, concave working edge, made on a blade, flake or core. Used in woodworking and for scraping hides.

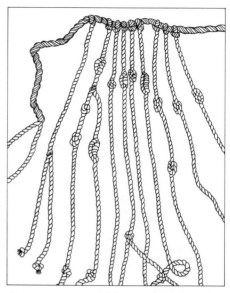

Quipu

Sediment A geological stratum formed of particles deposited under water on the bed of a sea, lake or river.

Seine net A fishing net designed to hang vertically in the water. The ends of the strip of netting are drawn together to trap the fish.

Serpentine A stone of dull green color, often used for ornamental purposes.

Serpent mound Large effigy mounds, in the shape of serpents, birds and animals are a feature of the Ohio and upper Mississippi valleys around 1000 AD. Some of these mounds contain burials.

Setaria (foxtail grass) A wild grass which grows in Mesoamerica and the southwestern USA. Its edible seeds were at one time an important item of food, and the plant was cultivated in parts of Mexico.

Sherd (potsherd) A broken fragment of ancient pottery.

Shifting cultivation (slash-and-burn farming, swidden, roza, long-fallow cultivation) All these terms refer to a system of cultivation in which garden plots are created by cutting down and burning sections of forest. These fields are then planted and harvested for a few years, until the soil begins to lose its fertility. At this point the plot is abandoned and allowed to revert to forest, while another field is prepared elsewhere. After a fallow period of several years, the original garden can be cleared and used once more.

Sierra Range of hills or mountains, used in a general sense for the highland regions of Spanish America.

Slash-and-burn cultivation See **Shifting cultivation**.

Spindle whorl Disc-shaped or globular weight with a central perforation. It is slipped into the lower end of a spindle, and gives added momentum to the rotation of the spindle in the process of twisting fibers into yarn.

Spokeshave A notched tool used for shaping and smoothing cylindrical objects such as spear or arrow hafts.

Spondylus (thorny oyster) A marine mollusc found in tropical Pacific waters as far south as the Gulf of Guayaquil, Ecuador. The shell was a popular material for figurines, beads and the like, and seems also to have had ritual or ceremonial significance in Peru.

Squier, Ephraim George (1821–1888) American newspaperman, diplomat and traveler in Latin America. His major archaeological books are *Ancient Monuments of the Mississippi Valley* (written with E. H. Davies and published in 1848), *Aboriginal Monuments of New York* (1849), and *Peru: Incidents of Travel and Exploration in the Land of the Incas* (1877). He also wrote on the topography, customs and antiquities of the Central American republics.

Steatite (or soapstone) A soft stone with a rather soapy feel, easily carved. It is quite soft when freshly mined, but hardens on exposure to air.

Stela An upright stone slab, often decorated with carvings and inscriptions. The erection of stelae was an important part of Maya religion, hence the phrase stela cult.

Stephens, John Lloyd (1805–1852) American lawyer, diplomat, traveler and archaeological explorer. He journeyed across Russia, visited Petra and the ancient cities of the Levant, and studied the Egyptian monuments along the Nile. He was already an accomplished travel writer when he met Frederick Catherwood, whose early travels and interests were so similar to his own. The two men teamed up to explore and describe Maya ruins in 1839–1842. After these expeditions, Stephens held various administrative and political appointments, and ended his career as a railway-builder in Panama. See also **Catherwood**.

Steppe Open grassland.

Stirrup spout A semicircular tubular spout set vertically on top of a closed vessel. The lower ends open into the body of the pot, and from the apex of the curve rises a single vertical spout. In side view the appearance resembles a stirrup.

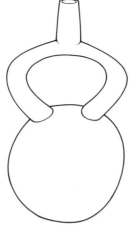

Stirrup Spout

Stone Age The period before the use of metals, when stone, wood and bone were the raw materials for tools.

Stratigraphy The recognition and description of superimposed archaeological or geological strata, and the study of the way in which they were formed. See also **Superposition**.

Stucco Lime plaster, used for covering walls and floors and for modeling in relief.

Superposition The principle which states that when one geological or archaeological stratum lies on top of another, and has undergone no disturbance, the upper one was formed later than the lower.

Sweet potato (*Ipomoea batatas*) A vine-like plant with edible, starchy tubers. In pre-European times it was cultivated in tropical regions from Mexico to South America. It probably originated in lowland South America.

Tang The narrow stem, or handle, of a spearpoint, arrowhead or knife.

Tello, Julio Cesar (1880–1947) With Uhle and Kroeber, was one of the founders of Andean archaeology. He excavated at Paracas, Chavin, Pachacamac, Ancon etc. and, as a native Peruvian, helped to organize the museums service and archaeological administration of his country.

Temple mound Flat-topped mound of clay or earth, which served as the platform for a temple.

Teosinte (*Zea mexicana*) A weedy grass, native to the dry subtropical zones of Mexico and Guatemala. The seeds are edible, and teosinte is possibly the wild ancestor of cultivated maize (corn).

Terracotta Baked or fired clay.

Tezcatlipoca Smoking Mirror, a Mexican creator god, represented in many different forms. He is often depicted with a mirror in place of his left foot, which was torn off by an earth monster. He was a god of the night and a sorcerer, closely associated with the forces of evil and destruction.

Tiahuanaco A city in the Titicaca Basin of Bolivia which became the capital of an empire embracing much of the south Andean region in 600–1000 AD.

Tlaloc Mexican Rain God ("He who makes things grow"), associated with mountains, floods, storms and lightning. Usually depicted with circles around his eyes and a fringed mask covering his mouth. Ruler over the paradise reserved for people who die by water (drowning, lightning, dropsy etc.).

Tlaloc

Toggle/toggled harpoon Spear with a detachable head used by ancient and modern Eskimos for hunting whales and seals. One end of a line is attached to the harpoon head; the other end is secured by the hunter. When the head of the weapon enters the flesh of the quarry and comes away from the foreshaft, a sharp tug on the line causes the head to turn sideways (like a toggle) so that it cannot be pulled out.

Toltec A people who held sway over much of north-central Mexico from the 10th to 12th centuries AD.

Toggled Harpoon

Tripsacum A wild grass, found from Texas to South America. It is a distant relative of maize or corn (with which it can be made to cross under laboratory conditions) but seems to have played no part in the evolution of cultivated maize.

Tuff A geological deposit of consolidated ash and dust ejected from a volcano.

Tundra Treeless Arctic plain; even during summer the subsoil may remain permanently frozen.

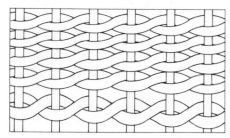

Twining

Twining A technique for weaving a textile or basket. The wefts are inserted in pairs, twining round each other between each successive warp. Because of this twisting, a twined textile cannot be woven on a loom.

Tzompantli Mexican word for the wooden rack on which the skulls of sacrificed victims were displayed. Human sacrifice was practised particularly by the Aztecs.

Uhle, Max (1856–1944) A pioneer of South American archaeology, Uhle was the first to apply the principles of stratigraphy and seriation to Peruvian materials. He discovered and excavated some of the main Peruvian sites, and established the sequence of cultures and pottery styles in several parts of the country. He also worked in Ecuador and Chile, and excavated a shell mound on San Francisco Bay.

Umiak Large open boat, holding 8 to 10 people, and made by stretching skins over a wooden frame. Used by the Eskimo for transportation and whale-hunting.

Uniformitarianism The principle which states that the geological processes which operate today are those which also operated in the past, producing the same effects at all times.

Usnu The raised platform on which the Inca ruler's throne was placed, and on which religious ceremonies were performed.

Woodland culture A cultural tradition, adapted to the wooded country of the eastern USA. The main characteristics of the Woodland tradition are: efficient farming, the construction of mounds and earthworks, and the use of pottery with cord-impressed or fabric-impressed surfaces. Within this tradition – which lasted from about 1000 BC until European advent – are many regional variants.

Xipe Totec Mexican god of springtime, seeding and planting. At ceremonies in his honor, a priest put on the flayed skin of a sacrificed man, which he wore until it rotted and fell to pieces. These rituals symbolized the renewal of the earth and the breaking through of fresh plant shoots in spring.

X ray fluorescence If a sample for chemical analysis is bombarded with X rays, it fluoresces. Spectrographic examination of this emission shows what chemical elements are present in the specimen.

Yachahuasi "House of Teaching," the school in the Inca capital at Cuzco where the sons of noblemen and of provincial officials were sent to be educated and taught Inca customs.

Zapotec The past (and present) Indian population inhabiting much of the State of Oaxaca, Mexico. Their major city was at Monte Alban. It is not certain when they first came to the Valley of Oaxaca, but by 300 AD a distinctively Zapotec culture can be recognized.

Zuñi Pueblo Indian tribe of northwest Arizona. See **Pueblo**.

Index